FOUR

GREEN HOUSES

AND A RED HOTEL

New strategies for creating wealth
through property

FOUR

GREEN HOUSES

AND A RED HOTEL

New strategies for creating wealth
through property

BIG SKY PUBLISHING
www.bigskypublishing.com.au

Pete Wargent

Big Sky Publishing Pty Ltd
PO Box 303, Newport, NSW 2106, Australia
Phone: 1300 364 611
Fax: (61 2) 9918 2396
Email: info@bigskypublishing.com.au
Web: www.bigskypublishing.com.au

Cover design and typesetting: Think Productions
Printed in China by Asia Pacific Offset Ltd.

National Library of Australia Cataloguing-in-Publication entry (pbk)
Author: Wargent, Peter, author.
Title: Four green houses, and a red hotel : new strategies for creating wealth through property
          / Pete Wargent.
ISBN: 9781922132383 (paperback)
Subjects: Investments--Australia--Popular works.
                Real estate investment--Australia--Popular works.
                Stocks--Australia--Popular works.
                Australia--Economic conditions--2001-
Dewey Number: 332.60994

National Library of Australia Cataloguing-in-Publication entry (ebook)
Author: Wargent, Peter, author.
Title: Four green houses, and a red hotel : new strategies for creating wealth through property
          / Pete Wargent.
ISBN: 9781922132390 (ebook)
Subjects: Investments--Australia--Popular works.
                Real estate investment--Australia--Popular works.
                Stocks--Australia--Popular works.
                Australia--Economic conditions--2001-
Dewey Number: 332.60994

To the traditional owners of Australia.

In loving memory of my one-time opening batting partner, talented cricketer and dear friend, David Randall (1985–2012), lost to cancer too young.

Thank you to my beautiful wife, Heather. Partly for her editing of the book, but mostly just for putting up with me.

The author will donate 10% of the proceeds of this book to the McGrath Foundation for breast cancer research and support.

Writing something new and different about personal investment, yet appropriate to our changing times, is a tough gig. But Pete Wargent, one of Australia's leading young financial commentators, has mastered this in his latest book. It contains an incredible wealth of real world insights from someone who has actually achieved what most readers will want to accomplish.

I have been investing for over 40 years and read almost every book written on property investment in Australia yet I still learned new concepts in this book. I recommend it for beginning investors to get a good grounding and for experienced investors to receive a fresh perspective.

Michael Yardney, bestselling author and voted Australia's leading property investment adviser.

It's hard to find a balanced voice that paints a common sense picture of our property markets. Peter is one such voice - his extensive expertise and experience in both finance and property is clearly evident as he takes us on a tour of Australia's real estate terrain imparting valuable lessons including holding for the long term and staying well diversified. I have no hesitation in recommending his book to anyone interested in real estate investment.

Catherine Cashmore, Real Estate Expert on The Circle (Channel Ten)

Contents

Introduction

My Aussie real estate tour de force

I am a property, finance and investment expert and author. But one thing used to trouble me a lot: can you call yourself an expert in real estate markets when you haven't actually seen them for yourself? I'm well aware that there are those who say that you can, and I'm equally sure that there are many who do. Indeed, some of our good friends in the US like to refer to themselves in a grandiose manner as 'global real estate experts' — apparently with no sense of irony.

These are often the same guys who have been predicting 50% to 85% meltdowns in prices for Australia's property markets for a long time now. As I write this, we are supposedly still waiting for that to happen. Meanwhile, smart counter-cyclical investors make their assessments of the best states in which to buy for future capital growth while sentiment is relatively low.

I understand the theory that you can do all of your research on every property market in Australia today simply by using the power of the internet. You can track sales prices, vacancy rates, auction clearance rates, rental yields and a whole host of other data. This is true to a point, but I do believe that if you haven't travelled to a region, then you may still lack a true understanding of some of the key factors and drivers of growth.

What you could miss via purely internet or press-based research might include the changing nature of an area's demographics, the rate at which construction is progressing or simply the less quantifiable feel of a suburb. Graffiti, youth problems, racism, levels of unreported crime or a high rate of homelessness are just a few of the things that rarely seem to show up on property reports.

I quit my full-time job at the age of 33 having successfully built a portfolio of shares, index funds and multiple investment properties, and was fortunate enough to be able travel the 'Big Lap' of Australia with my wife in our beloved Kombi van. We took a full 12 months to travel around as much of the country as we could, and we visited every significant real estate market in Australia.

We circumnavigated Australia on the Pacific Highway in an anti-clockwise direction (apparently benefiting from the assistance of a following wind by travelling that way around, though I never did quite work out if this was actually true or an old wives' tale). We travelled from Sydney to Sydney with a one-month trip around Tasmania, and visited all of the major towns and cities on the way. We visited and stayed in a great many of the smaller towns too.

This book will take you on a journey around the states of Australia and aims to provide detailed insight into the best property markets for investment as well as looking at some of the industries and businesses which we can invest in as shareholders.

A bit of history ...

These days I am self-employed and work as a consultant in the finance industry when interesting or exciting opportunities present themselves. The last projects I undertook were contracts reviewing the East Timor Government's investment funds and some work for the Central Bank in East Timor. I am also one of the founding Directors of a property buyers agency which helps others to achieve what they want in real estate.

So my background and expertise are in the realms of finance and investment, but what is slightly less well known is that I am also a historian. Back in my largely misspent youth I applied to study at Oxford University under the tutelage of one of the world's most famous historians, Niall Ferguson.

Niall is the author of some truly brilliant works which have inspired BBC television series, including *The Ascent of Money* and *The Cash Nexus* among others. Fortunately for him and for the university, Niall quite correctly ascertained upon interviewing me that not only was I then a rebellious individual of low motivation (replete with prerequisite long hair), I was also an opinionated little twit.

Following the inevitable rejection I instead studied back in the city of my birth at the University of Sheffield, where after three years I graduated with honours in a Bachelor of the Arts degree specialising in the economic and industrial history of my home city of Sheffield, a city that was once world famous for its steel and cutlery industries.

In part because of my background in history, and in part because 'those who fail to learn from history are doomed to repeat it', this book also takes a brief look at how Australia's property markets came to be and how they have developed over time.

I make my assessment of where the property markets might be headed and which are the states, cities and regions that might be worthy of consideration for investors and home-buyers today. I also look at the history and likely outlook for a number of Australia's listed companies and detail my own views on where the smart money is going to be headed in the share markets.

In my 2012 book *Get a Financial Grip* I discussed in some detail the choice of asset classes, and recognised that while investing exclusively in either property or shares can have the benefit of allowing you to become a specialist, over the long term a balanced portfolio of property, shares and cash is probably the best bet for most investors. On that basis, I will be discussing property and share investments throughout this book.

About this book

This book is a mine of information about how to and where to invest your money, and the mindset and strategies you can use to create wealth. Using my recent travels around Australia's real estate markets, I take a detailed look at the properties and the shares in businesses around Australia which you can invest in to grow wealth.

While I am a dedicated and long-time investor in shares and index funds, the foundations of my investment plan are built on **a portfolio of residential investment properties**. This book looks at the strategies that you can employ as an investor in property and shares in order to achieve your financial freedom.

I was able to quit my full-time job at a young age as I had used a buy-and-hold approach to investing in shares, diversified listed investment companies (LICs), index funds and investment properties over 15 years to secure my financial freedom. Now I help others to do the same.

This book is not an encyclopaedia of everything there is to know about personal finance. I've omitted peripheral issues or subjects that I covered in detail in my 2012 book *Get a Financial Grip* such as how to apply diversification and portfolio allocation to asset classes. This is a book about accumulating the best assets for achieving the target of financial freedom. For most investors this means investing in property and shares, which are the two principal growth asset classes. I discuss both asset classes in this book and the strategies which the average investor can use to become wealthy in today's uncertain climate. If you like, the book is both a 'where to' and a 'how to' guide.

In Part 1 I talk about what it means to have financial freedom, how to think like a wealthy person, use a combination of property and share investing to generate wealth, and get your finances in order so you know where you're going.

Part 2 is a whirlwind trip around Australia – where to buy and why. I give you some do's and don'ts of buying property, and discuss the future of the property market in Australia.

In Part 3 I discuss the ins and outs of Australian taxes in regards to investing, give you some tips on getting the most out of your super, and let you in on some share trading strategies, skills and secrets.

As a great fan of the game Monopoly I like to draw parallels between the board game and real life; you'll notice this icon throughout the book when I do this — it's just a bit of fun. Monopoly is an excellent reference point for how financial success is achieved in the real world. Over the years I've noticed the similarities between how the winners of Monopoly games operate and how successful investors work — with a strong emphasis on building assets to generate income rather than relying on a salary and spending most of it on rents, tax and other expenses.

When I was growing up, Monopoly was *the* board game in our family. Sure, we had other games and we certainly all loved our sports, but Monopoly was always the king of board games. Winning at Monopoly bestows the victor with a feeling of power and a position deserving of kudos, for you haven't just won a game, you have demonstrated your superiority in business, investment, finance — even life — over your fellow players.

Uncertain times

I note here that in some ways it is a little nonsensical that we even use the phrase 'uncertain climate'. The prevailing climate may have seemed relatively certain in 1929, 1987, 2002 and 2008–2009 and yet these periods all saw the genesis of sizeable stock market corrections — thus whether or not the climate seems certain to us now is something of a moot point, as we are so notoriously poor at identifying what is likely to happen in the short term.

The remedy is to make a viable investment plan for the long term involving accumulation of proven appreciating assets.

Right, I think we're all set, so let's hit the road ...

Part 1
Wealth Creation
Through Investment

1
BECOMING
AN INVESTMENT
MILLIONAIRE

1

Becoming a millionaire or multi-millionaire through investing is fundamentally very simple in Australia. When people look at property markets and share markets they tend to see risk. They worry that markets will go down in value and they will lose money. For this reason, they never invest meaningful amounts of money and they never become rich.

It is true that markets go up and markets go down. But the long term trend of property markets and share markets remains the same: they go up in value. Therefore, if you invest in a quality asset such as a well-located house or you buy shares in an outstanding profit-generating company, eventually you will become wealthy. Of course, this will take some time and a level of skill.

I said that the concept was simple, but it is not necessarily easy. To make the process of becoming wealthy through investing faster, you need to develop the skills to identify outstanding assets — properties and shares which will comfortably outperform the averages — and design a plan which is repeatable and will enable you to continue acquiring outstanding assets over and over again. Nothing in life worth having comes easily and therefore you will also need to ally yourself with some discipline and patience.

That's what this book is here to help you with. If you can commit to learning simple investment strategies, and apply discipline and patience to your knowledge, you will succeed over time and finish way ahead of the pack.

Your real goals

In order to become a successful investor, you first need to work out 'the why'. Why do you want to build wealth? It is sometimes said that if the *why* is strong enough then the *how* will take care of itself.

What this means is that you will give yourself the best chance of success if you first consider what your hopes and dreams are, for if you can visualise a truly inspiring goal then you will have taken the first step on the path to your success. Property and shares are not particularly exciting subjects in themselves. In fact, they can at times be pretty dull! What can be genuinely exciting, though, are the options that owning a great portfolio of investments can provide you and the opportunity to live the life that you dream of.

What would you be doing today if you could do anything?

In my case, I took 18 months away from Sydney to travel which gave me an awful lot of thinking time to consider what in life I felt was important to me. I came to realise that, for me, what I wanted was *experiences*. I lost a young friend to cancer and this forced me to think: if life can be so short, what do I really want to do with my time on this planet? I ended up deciding to move back to East Timor for some time, a country and people that I adore, and that is where I am as I write this book.

Each and every person is different, so your *why* will be different from mine. Perhaps you want to spend more time at home with your children. Perhaps you want to set up a charitable foundation or set out to climb Mount Kilimanjaro. The reasons will be personal to you. What successful investment can offer you is the opportunity to focus less on a salary and more on what is important to you. Wanting lots of money is not in itself a 'why' — instead you need to consider what you want to build wealth for.

Not all of your eggs should be in one basket

Investing in one asset class only could be a risky approach to personal finance. It is preferable to have a balance of assets. In this book, I also take a look at the share markets and which industries and companies might represent smart investments. I promote a strong argument in favour of continuing to buy into a diversified portfolio of industrial shares rather than trying to be too smart and consistently smash the index return through selection of individual stocks and clever market timing.

The good news for would-be investors is that this approach requires very little in the way of skill, rather a strong level of discipline and patience. By continuing to contribute to a diversified portfolio or fund of industrial stocks regularly, the effects of the highs and lows of the stock markets are smoothed, while the investor continues to benefit from the growing dividend income over time.

Capital growth holds the key to property wealth

It is certainly possible to save deposits for investment properties and to plough other savings into dividend-paying shares. However, the way in which it becomes possible to supercharge the growth of your portfolio is to invest in properties which appreciate quickly, so that you can draw out equity and acquire further investments using the equity created.

This book discusses how you can find the assets which will get you the growth needed in order to achieve this. I do not provide a blow-by-blow account of every step and procedure involved in buying properties and shares (Lord knows there are plenty of those books on the shelves already). Instead, I add value in the way in which I can do best: intelligent discussion of investment strategy in Australia for 2013 and beyond.

The rules in property investing have changed

In decades gone by, property investors had a relatively easy ride with respect to sourcing capital growth. In the 1970s and the 1980s Australia experienced periods of rampant inflation and saw the price of almost every property rise. After the float of the Australian dollar in 1983, in the 1990s, came increased competition in banking and a tremendous expansion in the use of credit for buying real estate, which again facilitated a huge boom in prices. Since the turn of the century we have had a prolonged period of lower interest rates and the cycle has moved on yet again with prices continuing to move upwards through the financial crisis.

Property is unlikely to have such a smooth ride in the future.

Times have changed and those who fail to move with the times run the risk of being badly burned by the use of leverage. In this book I detail the strategies that can be used to defend ourselves as property investors. First and foremost I believe that property needs to be seen as a minimum 20-year investment. If you go into property with a shorter timescale in mind, you might win but you also risk losing heavily due to the leverage involved. A longer time frame gives projected household incomes the opportunity to grow and compound, which should counter any possible deflation in prices if you invest wisely.

It is no longer always good enough to invest only in your own backyard — your home town or your home city. Property prices are relatively high in Australia today, so it is important for investors to invest counter-cyclically in the cities which are most likely to see the next round of capital growth. You need to be able to identify demographic and sociological trends and use them to your advantage. You may also need to consider properties which you can add value to in some way. In Part 2 of this book I take you on a tour around Australia and show you the best places to invest in property.

Winners have a proven method for success

Growing up in a family of five brothers, the environment was always very competitive between the lads as you might expect. In particular, the eldest three were of a reasonably close age and therefore we battled it out at every game and every sport imaginable. Memorably, my oldest brother won pretty much everything. I think that, in retrospect, he didn't play many games or sports in which I stood a good chance of winning (which basically meant cricket and, oddly enough, chess) but he was always keen to play at games he was likely to win — Monopoly and virtually everything else.

At Monopoly he was a master. No amount of teaming up against him could detract from his inevitable path to victory. He always seemed to have the uncanny knack of acquiring the best properties on the most valuable corners and rarely seemed to own a property without a neat row of green houses or a red hotel built squarely upon them. The cash just seemed to flow to him and each game was an inexorable progression to his vanquishing of every other player. In later life, I've seen similar traits in some people as investors — no matter what they do, money just seems to flow to them.

As dice are used in Monopoly, initially I felt that I must simply be unlucky. But luck alone could not explain why nobody could ever beat my brother at Monopoly. Over time, it became apparent that while there is some luck involved in the game, there is also a tremendous amount of skill in knowing which properties to buy, when to build houses for the most profitable outcome and how to engineer profitable deals with other players.

Acquire appreciating assets to generate wealth

So what is the point of the game? Well, the aim of Monopoly is to acquire assets to generate cash flow and passive income, and to end the game with multiple income streams flowing to you from other players who rent your properties. Although Monopoly was not originally designed with specifically this in mind, the way in which it so clearly mirrors reality is surely the key to its enduring success over many decades.

Playing Monopoly in real life

I sometimes hear people say that they would like to play Monopoly in real life. What does that actually mean? To me, that would indicate someone who has a desire to take their focus away from their salary and towards investing in a portfolio of assets which generates them passive income and wealth.

So you collect your salary each month. What are you going to do with it? In the simplest terms, you have two main choices: you can spend it on 'things' or you can invest it in assets with the aim of growing wealth in perpetuity. A major reason that most Australians never break free from the rat race is that they focus almost exclusively on increasing their salary but devote very little energy to building a portfolio of appreciating investments. In Chapter 3 I talk about how bringing in a wage isn't enough, and investing is the key to wealth.

Why don't more people invest successfully in property?

Why do so many investors get started in property investment but never go on to build a portfolio of any significant size? Here are four of the reasons:

Restricting reason 1 — Never planned to own a big portfolio

Firstly, some property investors never intended to build a big portfolio in the first place. While some investors start out with dreams of a big portfolio, there are plenty more who buy one investment property with the plan of retiring into it one day, and that constitutes their goal. Naturally, if this is the case then they are unlikely to own further properties.

Restricting reason 2 — Selling property

A second limiting factor for investors is a mistaken belief that when a property appreciates in value, in order to secure a profit the asset must be sold, instead of unlocking some of the equity via a line of credit. Selling the property might send the investor back to square one with no assets other than cash which has been eaten away by selling costs, agent fees and capital gains taxes. The best financial decision I have ever made is not selling any property I have ever bought, even when everyone seemed to be insisting that prices must soon plummet.

Restricting reason 3 — Peddlers of doom

There is now a mini-industry of commentators who see it as their job to predict that the property markets in Australia are due to collapse any day soon. It can be very unnerving for beginners who quickly begin to doubt their strategy.

Experienced investors know full well that property markets are cyclical and periodically do fall in value, but their time horizons are set so far beyond the current property cycle that they remain emotionally unaffected by the hype. Instead they take great comfort in knowing that while property values can and do fall, they also tend to increase significantly over the lifetime of an investor, which is a more appropriate time horizon for a successful investment strategy.

Restricting reason 4 — Wrong strategy

A fourth, and my final reason, is one which is becoming more common as inflation rates fall and that is that investors choose the wrong investment strategy. In particular, investors are prone to seeking out high spot yields but failing to select properties that will continue to grow in value and outperform inflation.

While it is possible to build a sizeable portfolio of assets through diligent saving, if you want to build a substantial multimillion dollar property portfolio then it is imperative that you find properties which appreciate strongly so that you can draw out some equity to re-invest in more properties in the next growth location. Investing in harmony with the property cycle of each state and undertaking renovations are two of the strategies that can supercharge your growth.

You might be surprised that it is possible for someone who started out with nothing and took a fairly normal career path to build a portfolio of investments that runs into the millions of dollars in value. Had you told the moron who was the 21-year-old me that I would now be in that position myself, I would have been extremely surprised, too. The good news is that it is not necessarily a complicated goal to achieve. However, what is needed is the right mindset, together with willpower and a level of discipline and patience.

A small number of properties can make a big difference to your wealth

I recently read a book entitled *Your Property Success with Renovation* by Jane Slack-Smith which, incidentally, is a fine read if you are interested in property renovations. In the book, the author produced some interesting figures from the Australian Bureau of Statistics, on the number of property investors in Australia and how many properties each of them owns:[1]

Figure 1.1 — Property investors in Australia

Properties owned	Investors in the 2009 financial year
1	1,195,856
2	294,158
3	88,296
4	32,011
5	13,329
6 or more	14,158
Total	1,637,808

As I write this paragraph, the population clock of Australia stands at 23,090,954 people.[2] It seems remarkable to me that in what is supposedly a property-mad nation, with the number of us owning an investment property being more than 1.6 million, fewer than 15,000 of us ever progresses to owning six or more investment properties.

However, please do not be drawn towards the myth that you need to own dozens or even hundreds of investment properties in order to build significant wealth from real estate. I found that over the last 15 years simply by focusing on continuing to acquire and then hold a portfolio of investment properties for the long term in the sweet spot of $500,000–$800,000 in value (i.e. within reasonable range of the median dwelling values for my home city of Sydney) I was able to reach my financial targets at a relatively young age without having to own scores of individual titles.

Your goals might be different from mine, but due to the leverage which can be employed in residential investment property and the benefits of compounding growth, I submit that for most investors, even just a handful of strongly performing properties can begin to make a substantial difference to the ability to grow wealth.

In fact, although the title of this book *Four Green Houses, and a Red Hotel* is obviously a nod towards the game of Monopoly, it does partly reveal what I believe to be the case when it comes to property investment. That is, for a significant number of average investors a portfolio of five properties — a realistic target — if backed up by a strong, income-producing share portfolio, could be enough to generate the wealth you need to live a comfortable retirement (and thus be taking the holidays and staying in the hotels that you desire).

Later in the book, I suggest that in some areas at least, apartments or units can today be superior investments to houses for some investors. But either way, it is certainly the case that due to the leverage that can be employed, a relatively small number of properties can make a great difference to your wealth when they are held over a period of years and decades.

In today's markets it is important to understand and use market cycles

One strategy which can work is for investors to acquire a small number of properties in a city that has experienced a long period of lacklustre or negative growth, and when these assets increase in value to reinvest some of the created equity in several more properties in another city slated for an upswing in prices.

While it may have been possible to achieve the goal of financial freedom through investing in only one city in days gone by — when growth was very strong and the rates of inflation were high — it is likely that today you would be better served to invest consecutively in two or more different cities that are at different stages of the property cycle. What is absolutely paramount to success in property is being able to invest in the right city, suburb and property type to get the capital growth which allows this strategy to work.

Chapter 1 Summary

- Consider your *why* — why do you want to invest? What are your ultimate goals in life? What would your ideal day be? Where? Who with? Doing what?
- The key to achieving financial freedom is continuing to acquire wealth-creating assets: it's that simple!
- The best asset classes for the average investor are usually residential investment property and profit-making, dividend-paying shares
- There will always — and I mean *always* — be people telling you that now is a bad time to invest
- Make a plan for the long term and execute it
- The best time horizon for holding a great asset is *forever*
- Take action and don't procrastinate!

2
AIMING FOR FINANCIAL FREEDOM

2

Set yourself up to win the money game

As an expert in personal finance, the most common thing I see in people today is that they tend to set themselves up for a life of financial misery as they chase impossible dreams. Those of us old enough and admit being born before 1980 remember that our parents never expected to have the latest gadgets as soon as they hit the stores.

Even those of us from middle class backgrounds fully expected to have black-and-white or second-hand televisions (or often no television) and were not at all surprised when our parents had to save in order to buy a new washing machine or refrigerator. Overseas trips simply weren't on the agenda for most of us either. In our family we drove to Wales every single year for a decade and camped in the rain for a week.

How the world has changed in 30 years! Consumerism has well and truly triumphed. Today, when Samsung or Apple releases a new product into the market we are unsurprised to see queues of many hundreds of eager customers stretching for more than half a mile down Sydney's George Street.

More than ever before, consumers want the latest technology and gadgets and they want them immediately. But it goes further than this. People today also want to travel regularly, to own a home in a prime location and drive brand new cars, and are destined to be disappointed when a lack of financial discipline is combined with unrealistic expectations.

The only way in which abundance will be achieved for most is to make sacrifices today for a wealthier tomorrow.

You will find that if you are able to take this simple but essential step, then you will end up winning twice over. Firstly, by spending less on depreciating consumer goods and more on investments you will ensure that your wealth grows and compounds for a more prosperous future. And secondly, you will find that when you have created a large portfolio of assets, the habit of thrift will have become so ingrained that you make wiser choices with your expenditure anyway.

My ultimate role models in this regard are my in-laws, who are farmers. There is something about farmers which means that they tend to make sensible and smart financial decisions. Agriculture is a tough industry in which to make a living these days. Perhaps it always has been. Consequently farmers naturally tend to develop a make-do-and-mend attitude and the concept of waste becomes total anathema. More than anything, farmers understand the concept of ensuring that tomorrow is prosperous by making sacrifices today.

Indeed, the analogy of farming is a very poignant one for investors — work hard, sow the seeds and feed the stock today, so that next season you will reap a productive crop and a healthy herd. By ingraining the discipline of spending less than you earn and investing the funds saved, the difference that can be made to your future prosperity can be staggering.

The goal of financial freedom

Fortunately, the real world doesn't have to be as brutal as Monopoly. We don't have to do 'better' than anyone else, we can seek out win-win situations and deals, and the only competition we are compelled to have is the competition with our own expectations.

That's not to say that some people don't think of the world in a hugely competitive way. Characters such as Donald Trump see the whole of life as one big money competition. Trump only sleeps for a few hours each night because he sees sleep as wasted time in the great race to be the richest human on the entire planet — he wants to be the wealthiest person in the world and believes that nothing is going to stop him.[1]

Strange though such an extreme goal may seem, it seems to work for Donald Trump because he loves the thrill of making deals and, crucially, he is passionate about what he does. I wouldn't advocate it as an approach to life for most of us as it will probably lead to unhappiness, for someone will always be getting richer faster than you. In fact, oil baron John D. Rockefeller may have been one of the very richest men in history, but even he was still said to be deeply unhappy until his later years when he belatedly discovered how to use his wealth to contribute and give back to society.

At the other end of the scale are those who see the world as one of scarcity: for every person who has achieved some success or wealth there must be less to go around for everyone else. Therefore the failure of others is seen to be good. This is not a healthy mindset either and is also unlikely to lead to a happy outcome. Successful people tend to view the world as one of abundance, where there is enough to go around for everyone.

Financial freedom could have many different definitions. The most important one is your own.

What is financial freedom? There could be any number of definitions. To some people it might mean being a multi-billionaire, or to others it could mean not having to work unless they choose to. To others still it might simply mean a passive income greater than expenses. When you visit other parts of the world you may realise that financial freedom for some simply means having one dollar in order to buy rice or vegetables for a day. It seems obvious to me that there is no one definition of such a phrase, and the only one that matters is the one that is relevant to you.

I know that when I started out investing my personal goal was simply to be able to take my focus away from chasing the impossible goal of an ever-increasing salary and instead focus on the goal of building a massive portfolio of assets and reducing my outgoings down to a reasonable level. More than anything else I just wanted to get myself off the dreaded corporate earn-and-spend treadmill.

The path to financial freedom involves spending less than you earn and investing the difference in appreciating assets.

The whole cycle just seemed so pointless to me. I would listen to people talking about how next year they would be earning this much or receiving a bonus of that much, and yet all that usually seemed to happen was that the tax man would swipe half of their income and the other half would get spent. It's a dangerous and potentially insidious trap. Often, all that people have to show for a few decades of work is a mountain of consumer debt and a super fund which is being bled dry by a fund manager.

Monopoly is born!

The idea for Monopoly was first conceived in 1903 by an American lady named Elizabeth Magie Phillips, a stenographer whose inventiveness manifested itself in the creation of the automatic carriage return for typewriters.[2] Strangely, given how the game is now viewed today as a representation of capitalism, the initial concept, which had the title *The Landlord's Game,* was designed to portray in a negative light the iniquity of concentrating land in the hands of private monopolies.[3] The game first appeared under the title *Monopoly* in 1935.

The board consisted of 40 squares, 28 of which were properties, including two utilities and four train stations, and the properties became increasingly expensive as players travelled around the board in a clockwise direction.[4] There was also a parking space, a jail and a *Go to Jail* square, but the *GO* square was instead known as *Mother Earth.*[5] There were also no *Chance* or *Community Chest* squares in the original game.[6]

Phillips believed that land should be taxed to punish landlords who grew monopolies and charged extortionate rents, so the game was less capitalist in its ideals than we might think from the game we play today. Her philosophy was strongly linked to ideas written in 1879 by Henry George whose work *Progress and Poverty* stated that the only worthy tax was a levy on landowners who charge higher rents.[7] After George's death, Phillips continued to carry his ideas forward through the board game.[8]

Although it is unclear whose idea it was, someone came up with the idea that the titles could be built upon or developed and by the mid-1920s the game Monopoly was born. The Monopoly game has been shipped out to all corners of the earth — from New Zealand, to India, Singapore and Saudi Arabia, and before the second World War, even France and Belgium sold the game.[9]

Initially, only the London edition of the game was available in Australia, but by 1985 an Australian edition was finally promoted. The basic layout of the board was very similar to that of the London edition with some subtle changes made. The Electric Company became Australia Post and the Water Works became Australia Telecom (the company we now know as Telstra).

The Australian version of Monopoly showed key streets from each of the eight capital cities, and one from Alice Springs. In 2007, in a bid to make the game seem more hip, Parker Brothers re-released the game as the Australian *Here and Now* Edition.

Which quarter are you in?

In one of his best-selling books, personal finance author Robert Kiyosaki introduced this neat little diagram:[10]

Figure 2.1 — The Game of Money

Age		Period
0–25		WARM UP
25–35		1st QUARTER
35–45		2nd QUARTER
	HALF-TIME	
45–55		3rd QUARTER
55–65		4th QUARTER
	OVERTIME	
	OUT OF TIME	

Source: *Who Took My Money?*, Robert T. Kiyosaki.

It is an interesting idea that Kiyosaki conceived. He suggests that until the age of 25, people are generally becoming educated and working out what to do for their careers. He then divides our working lives in to four quarters and challenges us to plan for when we will have achieved our financial goals. It's a brilliant concept because it questions the preconception that you must necessarily plough through your career to the traditional retirement age and then retire on whatever pension you have managed to accumulate. It doesn't have to be that way if you plan otherwise, he says.

Based upon Kiyosaki's table shown above, I am now at the end of the first quarter of the Game of Money. I suggest that life is very much like living a game of Monopoly in that the way to win the game is to accumulate assets that bring wealth back to us, rather than simply trying to win by going round and round in circles picking up only a salary that will be whittled away by tax, rents, building repairs, fines and whatever bad luck Chance throws at us. We also need to avoid making bad purchases that simply cost money: liabilities.

The good news is that once we have changed our mindset to a new way of thinking — accumulating **assets** that create wealth and not **liabilities** that drain wealth — our results become better and better (see more about this in Chapter 4). You can compound the growth of your investment portfolio.

To some extent, as long as you are prepared to learn the appropriate skills and set yourself a long-term plan, it doesn't necessarily matter whether you choose investment property or shares (or if you take my own preferred approach, investing in both) as your vehicle for creating wealth. The most important thing is that you decide to do *something*.

It is all too easy to spend every cent you earn and then some, but once you have decided to commit to investing this can have a great knock-on effect to your spending patterns, and indeed, to other areas of your life. You can be certain, though, that whichever investment path you choose to take somebody will be on hand to tell you that it is the wrong path.

> The most important thing is that you take some action rather than do nothing.

I have argued for many years that for most average investors, the best chance of achieving financial freedom is to invest in a portfolio of residential investment properties. It doesn't necessarily have to be a huge portfolio, though you may well wish to pursue that route as you progress further and learn the appropriate skills.

How the game of Monopoly is like real-life investing

In Monopoly, it can be an advantage to be the first player to start the game. In the real world, we all start from different places as well — some inherit wealth and others start with nothing. Some train for high-earning careers and others earn far less. Regardless of your starting position, however, in the real world your finishing position is entirely under your own control. The board has 28 title deed squares which players who land on them have the opportunity purchase. When a property is already owned and another player lands upon it, he or she must pay rent to the owner. If the owner has the funds available and he owns all the titles in a set of properties of the same colour, then he may build houses and perhaps a hotel upon those squares. The game of Monopoly mirrors successful real-life investment.

'But Warren Buffett doesn't invest in property...'

Dedicated share investors, of course, will always be quick to point out why property is not a good investment. Listed below are three of the more popular arguments you may hear.

Equities argument 1 — If property is so good, why don't the banks invest in it themselves?

Much of the major banks' core business is usury — or at least, lending! That is, banks lend money for interest income. Banks can lend their massive reserves of capital to borrowers for a relatively secure return and it is practical for them to do so. Banks do not exist to borrow money from other banks to invest in property. They exist to make billions and billions of dollars each year (and how!) with a relatively lower risk through their lending practices and other investments.

The Commonwealth Bank of Australia (CBA) generated a full-year profit after tax in 2012 of more than $7.1 billion, so they tend to do very nicely out of what they do. This profit figure was the highest net profit ever recorded by a non-mining company in Australia, so don't expect to see the banks changing their approach too radically any time soon.

Equities argument 2 — Why are companies taking property off their balance sheets?

This argument runs off at a slight tangent, because most average investors look towards residential property, whereas the property usually being referred to in the point above is commercial property.

In the past it was usual for companies to own their own land and buildings but this is not as common today, with more companies preferring to lease premises rather than own them. This is reflective of the high entry cost of owning commercial property and also a desire for companies to focus on their core business rather than dipping into property price speculation.

Equities argument 3 — If property is so good, why does Warren Buffett invest in shares?

The full answer to this question would be a very long one. The shorter answer is: the average investor is not Warren Buffett! Buffett and the team at Berkshire Hathaway are specialists in investing in equities. For such a company shares represent a low risk because they can buy shares in companies which pay them healthy income.

Having vast reserves of capital running into the scores of billions of dollars, Berkshire is also afforded the luxury of being able to sit back and wait for outstanding investment opportunities to come along at great prices, and therefore they attain great capital growth too.

I would tend to agree that if you have capital of a few million dollars in your bank account, the attraction of residential property as an investment is diminished. Instead, you could easily choose to invest in a diversified portfolio of equities that pays you a very healthy income and over time will generate capital growth for you too.

I am guessing, though, that you are reading this book because you do not have access to a few million dollars in cash. This is precisely why residential investment property becomes appealing for the average investor, as it presents you the opportunity to invest with millions of dollars that you may not otherwise have.

That's not to say that you can't invest exclusively in shares if you wish. But you can be certain that over the long haul you will not be able to compete with Buffett's returns. In its 2010 Letter to Shareholders, Berkshire Hathaway reported that it had generated a phenomenal 20.2% compounded annual return over the 46 years to 2010.[11]

Buffett is arguably the greatest equities investor of all time.

Can you achieve better returns than Buffett?

While a 20% compounding annual return represents a phenomenal achievement, even the mighty Berkshire Hathaway is unlikely to continue to achieve these returns in the future. Berkshire was able to achieve these returns partly because of its focussed approach to investment through holding massive stakes in only a few companies.

The pool of capital invested by the company is now so large that it is not possible to be invested in so few ventures and future returns will necessarily, therefore, be lower. Furthermore the 1970s and 1980s represented a period of higher inflation than we might expect to see in the future, so absolute returns are naturally likely to be lower for that reason too.

Figure 2.2 — Future returns for Buffett

Capital invested in equities	$75 billion
Total return on capital employed (ROCE)	$11.25 billion
ROCE %	**15%**

Now I'll admit that this is a gross and slightly ridiculous over-simplification of the likely performance of Berkshire Hathaway in the future, for the company does not only buy ordinary shares and hold them in the conventional manner. Berkshire will also use some leverage, it will engage in shorter-term arbitrage transactions and it will take positions in convertible stock, preference shares and fixed-income securities, for example.

But the figure for Return on Capital Employed (ROCE) may well prove to be pretty close to the mark over the long term. You can buy a single share in the Berkshire company and potentially attain similar returns if you have a spare $150,000, which is approximately how much one solitary share in the company now costs.

So how might we fare as individual investors if we tried to compete in equities? Truth be told, over the short term I have absolutely no idea, and nor does anyone else. Over the long haul a share investor in the past might have achieved returns somewhere in the region of 10% per annum depending upon the time period spanned and the investments selected, but as noted, inflation and therefore absolute percentage returns in the future are likely to be lower than was the case in the past. For the sake of argument, let's use the numbers below.

Figure 2.3 — Future returns for average shareholders

Capital invested	$100,000
Return from dividends	4%
Return from capital growth	4%
Total return on capital employed (ROCE)	$8,000
ROCE %	**8%**

If we were to maintain this approach over good period of time we will start to build some handy capital. Indeed, at a growth rate of 8%, due to the snowballing or compounding of wealth, over nine years we would very nearly have doubled our initial capital to $200,000.

The reason I believe average investors should consider residential investment property is that the leverage involved gives them the opportunity not only to compete with Buffett, but to *outperform* Buffett on a percentage ROCE basis. You may think that I have lost the plot in saying that, but let's look at some simple numbers. Let's assume that you learn the appropriate skills to invest in property at a long-term capital growth rate of 4% per annum, which is significantly lower than growth rates seen in the past, but might be a realistic goal for the future.

Figure 2.4 — Future returns for residential property investors

Capital invested	$100,000
Purchased investment property value	$500,000
Return from capital growth	4%
Total capital return on capital employed (ROCE)	$20,000
ROCE %	**20%**

So, am I really claiming here that your average investor might return an extraordinary 5% more on their capital than the legendary 'Sage of Omaha' Warren Buffett? The answer is: possibly yes, but with a caveat. By taking on board a *controlled level of risk* and employing leverage, being the use of the bank's money, we can accelerate our returns.

I should clarify here that in the early years of ownership the cash flow from a prime location investment property may be negative (particularly as interest rates will one day again run far higher than where they are now), but over the life of a long-term property investment rental income increases until the property is cash flow neutral and then eventually positive.

Now one might say that Buffett's returns are superior on a risk-adjusted basis, and that would indeed be true. Although Berkshire Hathaway does use leverage, it does not do so company-wide to anything like this level, its debt to equity ratio being only moderate. But the reality for average investors is that:

> If we want to become wealthy more quickly we have
> to expose ourselves to a controlled level of risk.

Well-run companies use a sensible level of serviceable debt to manage their liquidity, increase their returns and, ultimately, to increase their worth. As individuals we can do the same. If we take little or no risk on board, then we can expect our returns to be lower. For example, we would eventually become wealthy by paying money into a term deposit every month, but it might take us many decades as returns would be low and inflation would eat away at the capital.

Future returns on residential investment property

Of course, at this point shares-only investors would say that property prices won't continue to increase by 4% per annum over the long term. Short of constructing and then somehow successfully operating a time machine I can neither prove nor disprove whether this is the case.

But I do believe that while over the short term we can have no way of knowing the direction of property prices, over the long term the most useful proxy for residential property price growth is simply the growth in household incomes, the future trend of which presently looks likely to be somewhere near to 4% per annum. Naturally a skilled property investor is able to invest counter-cyclically in outstanding suburbs and property types, and is also able to use more advanced strategies including renovations which ensure outperformance of the market at large.

In fact, the further into the future we look, the more closely returns are likely to have mirrored the growth in household incomes. Short-term price movements are inherently uncertain, but if incomes continue to grow it is a near certainty that over the long term so will property prices.

Moreover, these figures refer to median price growth. While commentators love to talk about 'the property market' as if it a homogenous commodity, skilled property investors are attuned to the techniques that can generate them strong returns in all stages of the economic and property cycles. These will be discussed in more detail later in this book.

> Smart property investors will always aim to
> outperform the reported median price growth.

In the past very high inflation rates at times meant that to some extent it was possible to buy almost any property and be certain that within a few years it would have increased in terms of its market value. Whether or not the property value increased in line with inflation is a different matter. This trend gave many investors the mistaken impression that property is a one-way bet and led to some property writers becoming flippant in their assessments of likely growth:

- 'Property usually goes up by 10% per annum'
- 'Real estate will always cost more in the future'
- 'Well-located property always goes up'
- 'It is obvious that properties double in value every 7–10 years'
- 'You should never allow location to dictate a property purchase, only rental yield'

One unfortunate consequence of high inflation and easy growth was a tendency for some property writers and pundits to spend 80% or more of their time discussing current or spot rental yield and very little or no time discussing the most important factor in property investment, being the location and long-term demand for the property you are buying.

In property, as in all investments,
both supply and demand are vital.

While high inflation rates may have masked poor property investments in the past, there is absolutely no guarantee that they will do so in the future. In fact, there is a reasonably strong argument to suggest that we may be in for a prolonged period of low interest rates and perhaps relatively low inflation. Only time will tell.

I recently wrote an article on the subject of whether lower interest rates might represent a new normal or neutral position for the Reserve Bank. While I cannot see what is ahead with any certainty, it appears that interest rates are headed lower even without the impact of a global meltdown, and if an economic meltdown does happen then interest rates would quickly hit the bottom of the zero-bound range.

With property values in Australia relatively expensive as compared to many other countries it would be extremely foolish to buy property based around how much it rents for with a low regard to whether or not there will be an increasing demand for that type of property.

Other strategies for soft markets
— commercial property

Where prospects for capital growth from residential property are not great, investors may elect to turn to other alternatives for improving their returns. Just as shares give two-dimensional returns, investor returns in property come in two dimensions, being rental income and capital growth.

It is generally capital growth which creates wealth for property investors. Excess rental income is taxed as income whereas capital growth can grow and compound in a tax-deferred manner until such time as the investor is ready to sell. While it may be easier to become wealthy through capital growth at certain times investors may feel a preference for generating instant rental income to pay for living costs and this is where commercial property may have a role to play.

Commercial property can be riskier for the
average investor than residential property.

There are a number of reasons why I prefer residential property to commercial property. Firstly, residential property is generally easier to understand and finance for the average investor, partly because we have all had at least some experience of residential property, even if it is only by renting our place of residence. Commercial property often requires a higher deposit payment to purchase; in part because of its perceived volatility and level of risk. While rental yields can be very strong, vacancy periods can be longer and capital growth on commercial property may be questionable at times.

Of course, as always there are two sides to the capital growth story in commercial property. Yes, in times of recession you may find yourself with a property that lies vacant as small businesses fold and demand drops off. However, the flip side to this is that if you can time the market in commercial property then you can participate in the boom periods too.

Trends in commercial property can be very changeable.

There is another wrinkle here and that is in identifying the best locations in which to buy. For residential property, I have a good idea of where the highest demand for property will be in the future because I can follow demographic trends very closely. With commercial property I feel less able to carry out this analysis accurately.

Take the example of retail properties. What might be a trendy hotspot one season may become less fashionable in the next. If you feel that you understand the commercial market it might be something to get involved in, but as ever for me the question is: why would I introduce the risk of investing in something I understand less well? I can make very sound returns from residential property over the long term and certainly returns that are comfortably high enough to fulfil my own modest living requirements, so why would I take on the risk of venturing out into an asset class that I don't understand comprehensively?

Investors should always treat property as a business — and in commercial property this is particularly so. Overall, commercial property may be an appropriate asset class for experienced investors as they approach the cash flow phase of their investing lives, but commercial property requires a different skill set to investment in residential property. In my opinion, most average investors would be wise to focus on residential property and leave commercial property to the experts in that field.

Becoming a property millionaire

Why do I say that becoming a property millionaire is fundamentally very simple, but it isn't necessarily easy? If you buy a quality investment property worth $500,000 with a principle and interest loan which increases in value at an average 5% per annum, and you elect to pay down the mortgage, over the life of a 25-year investment you will have generated equity of nearly $1.7 million, although inflation will mean the figure will not have the purchasing power that it does today.

That might seem incredible, but it is the combination of leverage (borrowing) and the compounding growth which makes it possible — the equity gains snowball over time. Of course, most people want to become millionaires faster than this. If you are able to own two properties rather than one, this increases exposure to the market and allows equity to be created more quickly.

To become a property millionaire, you need three skills.

There are really only three skills you need to develop to become a millionaire through property. You need:

1. The knowledge to be able to select properties which will appreciate in value.

2. The discipline to spend less than you earn to invest in assets rather than spending all of your money on liabilities and treats.

3. Patience, for wealth is not created overnight.

The way in which great wealth is created is through reinvesting gains in further assets. Thus, experienced investors aim to find properties which grow strongly in value, draw out some of the equity which has been created (rather than selling the property) and invest it in further properties. While the property markets have soft periods and years where prices fall such as they did in 2011, over time the rapidly growing population and household incomes of the capital cities ensure that the trend in prices is upwards.

Gearing into shares

You can also leverage into shares and if you were to do this then naturally the potential return on capital employed (ROCE) for shares would also be higher. One way in which you can gear into shares is via the use of a margin loan (see Chapter 6). Alternatively you could trade contracts for difference (CFDs) or you could use derivatives such as options. I talk more about share trading skills and share investing in Part 3 of the book.

> Employed leverage for average investors is normally greatest in residential property.

Although the property versus shares debate is usually oversimplified with regards to the potential available leverage it is in fact entirely possible that a share investor might use as much leverage as a property investor (for example, you might take out a substantial margin loan to invest in a managed fund which is itself geared).

Overall though, it is fair to say that for the average investor, available leverage in residential property is greater and due to the asset class often being less volatile, usually more appropriate for leveraged investors too.

Chapter 2 Summary

- Convert your conventional income into income-producing and wealth-creating assets to make your money work harder for you

- To escape the corporate treadmill you must spend less than you earn

- Just as in the game of Monopoly, build a portfolio of assets to create more wealth

- To achieve greater returns investors use leverage to invest in appreciating assets

- Residential investment property usually offers the greatest leverage for most investors

- Commercial property can offer opportunities for investors when residential property is not performing strongly

- Commercial property requires a different skill set to investment in residential investment property — a skill set which most average investors do not have

---

- Skilled investors can use leverage in shares too — as always, when using leverage be prudent and only take on comfortably serviceable debt

- Property always seems expensive when you are buying it, but what is more important is how much the asset will be worth 20, 30 or 40 years into the future

3

BECOMING
AN INVESTOR
RATHER THAN A
WAGE EARNER

3

Why a good salary isn't good enough

As we move into adulthood, most of us by default end up in paid employment. Some more entrepreneurial types go on to build businesses and benefit from the more favourable tax laws, or perhaps gravitate towards self-employment. The rest must endeavour to increase their salary through hard graft and improvement of their qualifications and experience.

What you should aim to do is spend less than you earn and invest the residual amount in as smart a manner as possible. When your investments grow, you should then reinvest the profits. The theory is so very simple.

The step that is the undoing for most is spending less than they earn. Generally, individuals tend to devote a great deal of time to earning money, but devote very little consideration to controlling expenditure and even less time to how they can invest the funds that they are paid. What is the best thing to do with the pay that you have devoted so much of your time to earning? Spend it on things or invest it in assets which can return you wealth forever?

There are a number of reasons why a good salary does not necessarily lead to the creation of wealth. Firstly, the government quite rightly needs its share of the spoils in the form of tax which it uses to pay for amenities such as schools, roads, hospitals and infrastructure (I talk more about tax below and in Chapter 22). Secondly, if you don't invest your income somewhere safe then it tends to get spent very easily in this age of rampant consumerism. The days of a job for life also appear to be gone, so there are no guarantees that salary income will continue to increase throughout a working lifetime.

Why savings aren't enough

A common approach to personal finance is to attempt to hoard as much cash as possible before mortgages and other major monthly commitments have had the chance to build up. While saving money is a great start, and most definitely a strategy that is far preferable to wasting cash on unnecessary consumer goods, it does not tend to make for a great success over the long term. Saving some money as a cash buffer is definitely a smart thing to do, but at some point we need to consider investing in appreciating assets to begin to create wealth for us.

Cash in a bank account does pay some income in the form of interest, although due to the perceived safe nature of a bank account the interest rate tends to be a relatively low one. Cash does not deliver us capital growth in the same way that property or shares can. Over time cash tends to become devalued by inflation unless a good rate of interest is achieved. Another barrier to saving is that cash is usually accessible and liquid and therefore, sooner or later, an emergency comes along which results in the cash being spent (or we simply become bored of saving and decide to treat ourselves to a luxury such as a new car or an exotic overseas trip).

Do what you are passionate about!

Depending on your age you may already have a career mapped out for yourself, you may be deciding whether to change careers or you may be young and considering what to do for a career. One of the most valuable things that I have learned over the past few years is to try to make your vacation your vocation. That's a fancy what of saying: 'Do what you're passionate about'.

Now, I sense what you may be thinking. It could be something along the lines of: 'Well, I'd like to do what I am passionate about, but I like going to the beach and playing golf and that's not likely to pay the bills. Therefore I have to do what I am doing now which pays me a safe salary'. A fair and valid point and I fully understand that.

I used to have a reasonably high-paying job myself as a Financial Controller of one of the ASX-listed mining companies. I could have stayed working as a Chartered Accountant for another 35 years and worked my way up, one notch at a time … Group Financial Controller, Chief Financial Officer, perhaps one day even a Chief Executive Officer. So why didn't I? Honestly, the reason is that I couldn't see the point.

There is more to life than just work, work, work.

While parts of my paid employment were great fun and travelling to some of the mining tenements in south-east Asia was a great experience, other parts of my job bored the living daylights out of me. It was a drag to get out of bed every morning for another 12-hour day of meetings and number-crunching, and when I did finally escape work I would eat a takeaway, glug a couple of beers and be straight back to the office after six hours sleep.

What a waste of a life that would have been for me, doing something that did not inspire me. Could I have earned more if I'd stayed in full-time employment? Absolutely. I spent a couple of years travelling around Australia and then the rest of the world too, including a round-the-world cruise with Cunard — that cost me a fair few dollars as I'm sure you can imagine. I don't regret it for a moment, though; it was the best experience of my life to date.

So what I am saying is, sure, you don't have to quit your job and go and work three days a week as a volunteer lifeguard just because you like the beach. I realise that may lead to a level of financial distress. What I am suggesting is to try to think of a longer-term plan so that you can live the life you want to lead, not one that is dictated to you due to careless personal expenditure that requires long working hours to pay for it.

The *GO* square on the Monopoly board gives a major clue as to why saving our way to wealth does not tend to work. Can you spot the clue? If you noticed that the amount of the salary at $200 is incredibly low in today's terms, then you spotted the problem: inflation!

Figure 3.1 — Inflation over the long run

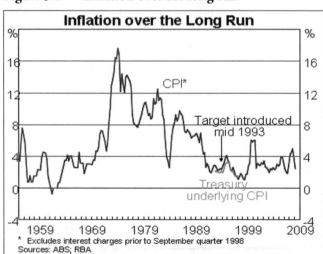

Source: Reserve Bank of Australia, www.rba.gov.au

While $200 may have been a reasonable representation of a typical salary in decades gone by, today even casual staff on a minimum wage would expect to earn a weekly wage that is well in excess of this. The graph above shows the reason for this, which is, that over many decades inflation has slowly but surely eaten away at the purchasing power of cash.

In fact, during decades of expansionary fiscal policy such as the 1970s and the 1980s, inflation was not even chipping away slowly — it was positively haemorrhaging the purchasing power of cash. Inflation is effectively a tax on those who are net savers, and also causes on-going headaches for retirees who are uncertain how to deal with the diminishing purchasing power of their capital.

The solution to the inflation problem is to invest capital in assets which appreciate and outperform the rate of inflation, which may include residential investment property. Shares represent another excellent asset class for growing wealth as they too can appreciate in addition to paying a healthy and tax-favoured income in the form of franked dividends.

The role of taxation

If you look at your monthly payslip, you will spot another problem with trying to become wealthy through a salary alone, and that is the chunk of your pay that is withheld at source in the form of PAYG or income tax. Shown in the table below are the individual tax rates for the 2013 tax year.

Figure 3.2 — Individual tax rates, 2013 tax year

Threshold ($)	Marginal tax rate (%)
18,001	19
37,001	32.5
80,001	37
180,001	45

Source: Australian Taxation Office, www.ato.gov.au

Suppose you saw a job advertised with a 'package of $110,000 per annum'. Sounds pretty reasonable, doesn't it? Upon closer inspection you may discover that around $20,000 of the package relates to a car allowance and the quoted figure is inclusive of superannuation contributions. The salary component is in fact closer to $80,000. Still, not too bad, you might think. Dusting off my calculator, here is how a salary of $80,000 is normally treated in the 2013 tax year:

Figure 3.3 — Example tax on an $80,000 salary in the 2013 tax year

	$
Gross Salary	80,000
Tax $0 — $18,000 component	-
19% Tax on $18,001–$37,000 component	(3,610)
32.5% tax on $37,001–$80,000 component	(13,975)
Medicare Levy	(1,200)
Total Tax	**(18,785)**
Net pay per annum	61,215
Net pay per month	**5,101**

The net pay of $61,215 per annum is significantly less than you might expect from an advertised package of $110,000 per annum, particularly when you consider that this equates to a little over $5,100 per month, or $1,175 per week. Australia is a relatively high-cost place to live today and it is easy to see how this level of income can be spent quickly.

You should therefore consider the methods available to reduce your tax bill, for which some avenues do exist (see Chapter 22 for more on how to legally reduce your tax). It also needs to be considered how a portfolio of assets can be built which generates wealth through compounding growth, allowing your assets to snowball in value. The problem with a salary is that it is linear. Every day you must wake up and head back to work to start earning afresh.

Why only superannuation is not enough

There are several flaws in the superannuation system. Fund managers tend not to significantly outperform the returns of the stock market index on a consistent basis and the effects of insurance premiums, taxes and the fees charged by your fund manager persistently chip away at your ability to grow a substantial nest egg (see Chapter 23 for more on superannuation).

A particular flaw is the staggering effect that a 1–2% fund management fee can have on your potential returns over a working lifetime. While in the early days the fees may not seem to impact your superannuation balance too significantly, over time the compounding growth which is *not* allowed to flourish can be phenomenal.

The average super balances at the retirement age for men and women are inadequate, and thus the majority Australians who live to retirement age claim some or all of the Age Pension allowance. The problem for those in the workforce today is that they could potentially live for several decades in retirement, and as inflation eats away at the purchasing power of a retiree's pension balance, a more significant final superannuation balance is likely to be needed to fund a prosperous lifestyle after departing the workforce.

> Most Australians do not retire comfortably
> on their accumulated superannuation funds.

That most Australians will end up drawing some or all of the Age Pension is not particularly surprising. Surveys have shown that a large percentage of the population believe that if they work through their adult lives to the pension age, then it should be the Australian Government's responsibility to take care of them in retirement.

The dollar value of the Age Pension you can draw, of course, depends on a whole host of circumstances including whether you are single or in a couple, the assets you have accumulated and other income you receive, and, indeed, the applicable year in which you begin to draw the allowance.

As an approximate guide, the most you are likely to see from an Age Pension is somewhere in the region of $385 per week including the supplement. This guideline figure should make it immediately apparent why you need a better plan for retirement than reliance on a government hand-out. If you live in a capital city you will be only too aware of how far such a figure does or doesn't take you today.

Cash windfalls

Countless studies have shown that when individuals in the real world receive a windfall of cash they tend to rid themselves of it in a remarkably short space of time. A common occurrence is for an inheritance — which may have taken a parent a lifetime of work to build up — to be passed into the hands of offspring, who then start weighing up all of the different ways in which they can spend the money...none of which involve socking money away into appreciating investments.

The best case tends to be that the recipient pays down a healthy chunk of their mortgage. The worst case is they decide to buy two new cars and a top-of-the-range plasma screen television, re-furnish the entire house, and book themselves on an extended holiday.

Why does this happen? The reason is that generally the working and middle classes tend to think differently to the wealthy when it comes to money. Most people consider that they earn money in order to spend it on 'things'. The wealthy understand that money can be invested to create more money. It is a subtle shift in mindset but the difference this makes to the financial affairs of those who practice the smarter approach is enormous.

Stop procrastinating about investing

Why do so few people get started in investing at a young age? Most of us know that investing some of our money for the future is a smart thing to do, and yet few commit to it with the discipline and commitment that investing deserves. There are a whole host of reasons why people procrastinate, and here are just five of them:

Procrastination cause 1 — I will invest later — I don't need to do it right now

Among many employees there is very much an attitude of living for today. This carefree attitude is often met with plaudits by a peer group, but we should question why people often prefer to see others spending their money rather than carefully putting some aside for the future. Could it be that if others are diligent it shines a light on our own frivolous attitude to spending money?

It's hard to be overly critical of people who earn money and then spend it all. I was young myself not so very long ago and I was busy doing exactly the same thing around the swanky bars and nightclubs of London.

The great thing about being young is that if you can start to save and invest, you have time on your side so you can begin to create outstanding results by allowing the power of compound growth to weave its magic. The earlier you start the better. It is true, however, that it is never too late to start making a significant difference to your financial future.

Procrastination cause 2 — I can't afford to invest

It's a common misconception that if we don't have tens of thousands of dollars squirrelled away then we do not have enough money to begin investing. We can get started out in share investment with a comparatively small level of funds, although we may be restricted in the number of stocks which we can hold. But even with a small amount you can buy into an index fund or even simply move funds from your bank account into a term deposit and your investing career is underway.

At the current stage of the property cycle it is likely that an investor would need a reasonable deposit in order to purchase a first property. This is not always the case and at certain stages of the property cycle banks can become open to the idea of lending 100% of a property's value.

Procrastination cause 3 — I'm doing pretty well

It is fairly typical for employees to believe that there is little need to invest as they are focussing on growing their income rather than their assets. While career progression is both admirable and smart, employees would be wise to remember that with a higher income comes higher taxes and often higher expenditure.

It is common for couples to begin cohabiting in their twenties at which point there can be two incomes in a household and few financial commitments. This relatively strong financial position tends to reinforce the feeling that investment for the future need not be a high priority as life seems to feel relatively easy. As couples grow older, they often buy a house and have children, and the financial commitments can grow significantly. Often the two incomes can become one income, or one of the partners may choose to work part-time.

> It's not always easy to find the money to invest ...
> so when you have it, ensure that you do it.

Suddenly there can be little or no spare cash left at the end of each month and investing for the future, while it might now seem like a sensible idea, can begin to feel impossible. At this stage, the couple may begin to wonder how they have so little to show for many years or even decades in the workforce.

The best time to start investing is always today because the longer we are in the game the more time compound growth has to work its magic. Investors who start young have a tremendous advantage over those who do not, although it is definitely never too late to start investing. It has been shown time and time again that you can make an enormous difference to your finances in a surprisingly short space of time if you show discipline and application towards the execution of a smart plan.

Procrastination cause 4 — I don't know what I'm doing

While it is certainly true that not knowing where to start can be a problem, this is most certainly not a reason to abandon the idea of getting started in investment. Information has been freely available to us for decades now in libraries, and in fact, in this day and age, information is even more available than it ever has been before.

Of course, the wider availability of information can prove to be a double-edged sword. There is certainly a vast amount out there on the internet, but you do need to be aware that free advice can often be worth exactly what you paid for it. The key, naturally, is to be careful who you listen to. In the world of investment it is always important to pay more heed to the viewpoints of those with a proven track record of success than those with no track record of investing at all.

Whatever your chosen path in investment, you can be absolutely certain that someone will be on hand to tell you that you are doing the wrong thing. But if that person has never invested in anything themselves, are they really the best-placed person to know?

Procrastination cause 5 — What if I lose my money?

The fear of failure or loss of capital when starting out is very real for most of us, and this is why for many, the only investment that is ever made is piling up cash in a bank account until an expenditure requirement comes around (and it surely will arrive) that results in the cash being spent.

Fortunately there are plenty of ways in which you can begin to invest with a very small risk of loss of capital. Once some confidence and capital has been built then you may begin to feel able to expose yourself to a controlled level of risk in order to secure higher returns. The best way to conquer the fear of loss of capital is to understand the risks, and therefore a commitment to ongoing education and learning is paramount.

> If your goals include an endless supply of expensive consumer goods, it is likely that achieving financial freedom will be unattainable.

Recognising the real assets in Monopoly and life

When I played Monopoly as a youngster, one of the most contentious parts of the entire operation was deciding which piece belonged to which player before the game proper had even begun. What was your favourite token? Did you like the car? Or perhaps you liked the dreadnought ship? While most of us argued long and hard over which player could be the motor car (which would inevitably power to victory, or so the theory went), my oldest brother, the Monopoly guru, rarely showed any emotion at all. He was totally disinterested in the arguments and usually ended up with a far less fashionable piece, such as the old boot, the Scottie dog or the hat. He knew that arguing over which piece he was allocated was a waste of energy as the pieces themselves did not impact the outcome of the game. It is far more important how we respond to the hand we are dealt rather than the hand itself, both in the game and in life.

Modelling successful mentors

I first read about the idea of modelling in a book by Anthony Robbins many years ago and I believe it is a truly great concept. The principle is that we should aim to identify a person or a dream-team of people who have achieved the goals that we want to achieve ourselves and model the strategies that have enabled them to reach their goals. It makes perfect sense if you think about it. Have I used this strategy myself at all? You bet I have! There are some fantastic coaches out there, we just have to identify them and learn from what they do.

Naturally, the modelling concept does have some limitations. It is not possible to know everything about another person and their thought processes, particularly if they are a stranger to you, but you should still be able to learn from others to determine which of their approaches have been successful and which have not.

By learning from the successes and the failures of others we should be able to take a shorter path to reaching our goals.

I can pinpoint exactly when my life took a turn for the better and that was the day I decide to switch off the television and start reading books and attending seminars detailing strategies for creating wealth. I had no idea when I started out that the subjects of finance and investment would become such passions of mine, but once I started reading and learning I simply never stopped. Even today, I commit to learning something new every single day. A never-ending commitment to education is one of my three pre-requisites for being a successful investor. The other two are: (1) taking action, and (2) making a commitment to learning from our mistakes (because we will surely make them).

Share and property investment clubs

Share investment clubs

One idea that you might be interested in when starting out in investing is that of share investment clubs. The concept received some bad press when a group in the US (the Beardstown Ladies) hit the headlines claiming to be consistently generating share market returns that would have placed them among the greatest share investors in history.[1] And perhaps they would have been, had their claims actually been accurate or substantiated.

No matter. The idea of a share investment club is to gang up together with a group of friends or like-minded people to begin to learn the basics of share investing using a pool of real money. It's a sensible idea, but you will find if you go down this route you will need a fairly exhaustive list of rules as to how much capital will be invested, what types of companies your club will invest in (and which companies might be excluded from selection on ethical grounds), what happens to the capital if someone wants to leave the club, and so on.

Finding like minds can be beneficial.

The advantage of a share investment club is that by investing together you can offer each other support and learn as you go as a group, the collective whole often having more sensible ideas than the individual. And you certainly don't need much capital in order to start a club, as books released on the subject have shown that the amounts invested can be just $50 per month per member.[2] This could also be a hidden trap though.

Joining a share investment club, contributing a small sum each month and learning the basics is a great starting point and it is commendable when people decide to take action — but joining a club alone will not secure your financial future. It will only be of use if you take what you have learned and apply it to your own finances with more substantial investments over the long term. As with many fields in life, there will be those who embrace their new interest and there will be those who lose interest and fall by the wayside. The challenge is to ensure that you are one of the former.

Property investment clubs

Property 'clubs' are often not clubs. Instead they are proprietary limited companies which exist to make profits. This doesn't mean that a property club cannot be a useful support network for you but as a potential investor you simply have to be aware of the potential risks.

One of the most annoying statements that can often be stated at property club sales meetings is the tired old phrase: 'Property goes up 10% per annum'. Really? How on earth can anyone possibly know what the future is going to bring with such certainty, particularly when it involves such an irrationally high rate of appreciation? I'll answer that for you: they can't. It is irresponsible of clubs to tell people who may not know any better what the future price of property is definitely going to be.

> Projected returns are fine,
> but only where they are substantiated.

Of course, we all have our own views and we can make an assessment of what we believe the future might bring, but that is completely different from making such a nonsensical blanket statement. For the record, with a target range of inflation in Australia of 2-3% it is my belief is that the average property price growth being as high as 10% per annum is extremely unlikely. Perhaps somewhere just under half of that figure might be a more reasonable guess over the long-term, being somewhere closer to the expected growth in household incomes. Of course, investors seek the outperforming property types and locations.

Property clubs might operate a system whereby you are invited to a free seminar which espouses the great potential benefits of property as an investment vehicle and then you will be offered properties to buy. The properties for sale are said to have been carefully researched on your behalf by the club, and for this they will take a commission from your payment for the property (although the commission will rather be sold as a discount from the developer). Property clubs can be a good option for some people should they find the process of investing themselves intimidating. Before getting involved, these are three of the key questions you should ask yourself:

Property club question 1 — Do you need the support?

Why join a property club at all? Well, the main reason for joining a club is for the support system that can be offered to you. You can meet and work with a system of people who have already been down the path that you are hoping to take. You must, however, to some extent be able to stand on your own two feet here.

Just as if you aren't sure whether you need a haircut the best person to ask is not a barber, a property club will probably always tell you that the only place in which you can build wealth is through real estate and the best time to buy is always now. Therefore, the most important thing to ensure is that you do your research and that you are never pressured into making a purchase or taking on debt which you are not 100% certain about.

Property club question 2 — Do you know that the club's research is genuine?

One of the selling points of a club is that they will, in theory at least, have carried out many hours of research into the best suburbs and best property types for investors. Therefore you do not have to carry out any research of your own, right? Unfortunately this is not the case. Frankly, if you buy any property at all without carrying out some of your own due diligence, then to some extent you deserve the results. You must always do your own research.

Property investment clubs often take their commission from developers, so there is an inherent risk that you are being sold properties for which no other willing buyers can be found. Here's a heads up — a property for which no buyers can be found is a terrible investment. Full stop!

Property club question 3 — What commissions will the club receive?

A common format is for a property investment club to receive a percentage of the property price as a commission and for the sales price to be non-negotiable. There is not necessarily anything wrong with this, but you do need to ensure that there is full disclosure of what commissions are being earned by the club and remember that you are foregoing an opportunity to negotiate a good deal on a property.

Remember too, that if a property is sold, for example, with a 6% commission that it take many years of your investment life for the property to increase in value sufficiently to cover that commission and transaction costs such as stamp duty. If the property is also negatively geared and costing you dollars each month, the time horizon to see positive returns could be even longer.

Summary on investment clubs

I'm not saying that you should not join an investment club. A club can offer you support and a network which you can leverage from. I am just saying if you do join a club go in with your eyes wide open. Clubs often exist to make profits by selling properties and receiving a sales commission, not only to make your life easier. If on the other hand you feel confident enough to invest in property without the support of a club then this may instead be the way to go.

Self-sabotage

Most of us do not have a wealthy mindset, which explains why most of us are not wealthy.

It is fairly well known that when many individuals receive an unexpected windfall of cash they tend to quickly find a way rid themselves of it and return to the financial position they were in before they received the windfall. This generally happens because most people have no context for investing the funds. Some will go on a shopping spree and quickly spend the money, others will undergo a slow but steady period of cash-burn, but the net result usually ends up being the same.

Another reason that this can eventuate is related to self-esteem. Without realising it most of us ascend to a level in life with which we feel comfortable and then plateau at that level. Thus, if we suddenly find ourselves in a position which we unconsciously believe is above our rightful station, we may begin to sabotage our success until we return to a position with which we are comfortable.

The good news is that once we become aware of the risks of self-sabotage we can devise a plan to mitigate the risks. This is why I feel that the best chance that most investors have of achieving wealth is a buy-and-hold approach to residential investment property and through building a diversified portfolio of industrial shares.

Seven steps on the path to wealth

There is a recognised path that we can all take towards a wealthier future. Just as the real 'secret' to losing weight is based upon eating less and moving more, the path to wealth involves spending less on consumable items, investing in appreciating assets and re-investing the gains. Rocket science it most certainly is not!

Note that here I am referring to becoming wealthy rather than being rich. Accumulating money for the sake of accumulating money is essentially a pointless exercise and is no sort of goal at all, and short-term riches are no use if they are immediately squandered. We all need to spend some time thinking of what we really want to achieve in life.

How do you want to live? What is the point of your existence? How are you going to make a worthwhile contribution? It is so easy for us to become totally self-absorbed in our own day-to-day problems and forget about how we can make a difference and live worthy lives. Here are the seven steps that must be taken to achieve the goal of wealth:

Wealth step 1 — Recognise your preconceptions about wealth

Do you have a preconception about what wealthy people 'are like'? I'd be willing to take a bet that, on a subconscious level at least, you do. We all tend to have some prejudices about different types of people whether we like to admit it to ourselves or not. It's the way the human brain works; we instinctively look to our past experiences to determine a view or perception of the present.

When I was growing up, there was an unspoken (perhaps sometimes even spoken) feeling that wealthy people are not to be trusted, and that perhaps there was something unethical about wealth. Probably the right thing to do would be study for a university degree and go into a respectable professional career rather than into becoming a businessman or pursuing non-professional employment. A huge number of ideas and preconceptions feed into our subconscious without us ever realising or becoming aware.

Mixed subconscious beliefs tend to lead to mixed results.

This is particularly so when it comes to the subjects of personal finances, investment and wealth creation. What other beliefs did you learn as a child? *Money doesn't grow on trees! We'll never be able to afford that!* While seemingly trivial our financial thermostat has been programmed into our subconscious without us ever having realised it. In order to change it, we must be mindful and aim to raise our self-esteem and what we believe ourselves to be worth.

Wealth step 2 — Add more value

You should always look to add more value in whatever you do. This is true when it comes to investment and is certainly true when we think of what we do for a living. Successful business owners provide products that improve the lives of others in some way. Investors who buy shares supply the capital for companies to grow. Property investors look to provide quality shelter and accommodation for renters in return for their rent payments.

In the field of employment, if you want to get paid more you need to think of ways in which you can make yourself more valuable to your employer. I believe that this concept is often ignored by employees, who expect to receive a pay rise each year regardless of whether they are providing more value to the company or business.

That is to say, employees often expect increased pay for tenure rather than for the level or 'value-add' of their performance. This is a dangerous attitude to take. If you are being paid a higher salary than the value you are adding to your employer, sooner or later it is likely that you will find yourself looking for a new job.

In some roles it is easy to see the correlation between our performance and our pay. A salesman, for example, is likely to be measured against a series of sales targets and thus, at any point in time, he is likely to have a fair idea of how he is performing against the expectations of his employer. In other roles, the correlation is less clear but the principles are the same. You should look to add as much value as you can to as many people as you can.

> If you can't think of ways in which you can
> add more value in your job ... think harder.

Here's an example: in my last full-time paid employment I was the Financial Controller of one of the listed mining companies. Finance departments are usually known for accounting, budgeting, forecasting, tax and compliance rather than for generating sales and cash for the business (in corporate terminology, accountants are therefore sometimes wittily referred to as 'fee burners, not fee earners'). In one sense then, it may be difficult to see how a Financial Controller can add more value to a mining company given that he or she is not directly responsible for mining and selling more copper and gold.

However, value can be added in other ways. If financial statements and records are kept in good order, a business should expect to save money through careful budgeting and control over expenses (much as in the same way an individual benefits from the same diligent approach).

Audit fees and consultancy fees should also be lower where the Financial Controller assumes responsibility for areas outside of his or her direct remit and ensures that the Annual Report and accounting records are presented in a clear and organised fashion. Diligent preparation of corporation tax returns, BAS statements and fringe benefits tax returns should ensure that the company does not pay more tax than it is due to.

Perhaps the answer for you is that you just need to be efficient and provide the same level of value as two employees. If you really want a pay rise, make yourself *invaluable* to your employer.

Wealth step 3 — Spend less than you earn

If you want to have money to invest, then you will need to spend less than you earn. Forgive me if this seems like an obvious point. It is a point that does need to be made, however, as it is at this point that many financial plans seem to falter. Most motivated Australians manage to find themselves a job or career and begin earning, which is no mean feat in today's competitive environment.

Most of us come unstuck by spending more than we earn.

Overspending is not necessarily always hard to understand. In the past three decades it has become more than acceptable to maintain constant credit card debt which attracts interest at horrifying rates. In decades gone by it was normal to save in order to make a purchase, which is no longer the case. Today it is far easier to pay for a purchase using one of several credit cards out of the hip pocket. As no cash changes hands it can tend to feel as though the transaction is less 'real', which is exactly how retailers and credit card providers want you to feel.

The problem is that access to credit is just so easy these days, even from a very young age. The banks very cleverly sign us up for bank accounts when we are in our teens, enticing with cinema tickets and goodness knows what else, before slowly but surely entrapping us with credit cards which teach us that using credit is an acceptable way to run our personal finances. Credit limits are easily increased and we are sucked into the trap of extortionate interest rates of up to 20% or more. Heaven forbid if we get caught in the bitter and unethical trap of payday loans and the like.

There is some better news, though. The great thing is that once we have made a conscious and informed decision to target financial freedom through investment an interesting shift starts to occur. Almost instantly you can begin to associate pain with frivolous and wasteful expenditure and pleasure with your new goal of setting some money aside each month for investment.

Wealth step 4 — Invest in assets that pay a wealth-producing rate of return

I'm not going to write a long section here about which assets produce wealth for investors over the long term. Instead, I'll just tell you. The greatest wealth is created from large business ownership, which is not the subject of this book. This book is here to tell you which assets to invest your income in, and the best two asset classes for growing your wealth over the long term. These are, in my opinion, residential investment property and equities (also known as shares) which are known as the 'growth asset classes'.

Sure, there are other asset classes too, including some which at various points in time can provide strong returns for a relatively low risk. In particular, there are a raft of hybrid assets and lending investments including government bonds, notes and bills, company debentures, convertible bonds and convertible notes. These assets are interest-bearing investments, and, as with any typical loan, at the end of its term you expect to get your money back.

Interest-bearing investments have often provided returns at a perceived lower risk than ownership assets such as property and shares. They might be secure because they provide the investor with a regular and predictable cash flow, and are less volatile than property and particularly shares might be.

At certain points in your life, this may be exactly what you are seeking, but if you want to create wealth for the long term then you need to look for assets that provide cash flow *and* appreciate in value too. Need some evidence? If an ancestor of yours had invested $1 in the stock market index in 1882, by 1997 it would have been worth around $500,000.[3] An equivalent $1 invested in an average bond portfolio would instead have been worth around $250.[4]

> ## Shares and property are two-dimensional assets which provide both income and growth over the long term.

The example cited above demonstrates that while income is certainly very important, if we want to generate wealth over the long term, it is important to invest in assets which provide income and can increase in value above the rate of inflation too. The way to do this is to spend less than we earn and to invest the difference in appreciating assets such as shares and residential investment property. While over the short term the values of these assets can fall or track sideways, over the long term the trend is very clearly an upwards one.

Wealth step 5 — Reinvest your profits

Investing in appreciating assets is a fantastic means of growing wealth, but the real key to becoming wealthy is actually to invest in appreciating assets and then to *re-invest the profits* into more appreciating assets. It is when this path is followed that massive wealth becomes possible through compounding growth, which is essentially a snowballing effect on your growing capital.

Wealth step 6 — Protect your wealth

The penultimate stage to attaining and retaining wealth is to protect the assets and the wealth that you have built. There are a number of different means of doing so. The first thing to ensure is that you limit your own means of and potential for self-sabotage. Psychologically, many do not feel worthy of wealth and therefore find ways to rid themselves of money very quickly after coming into some.

Observe how many lotto winners are stone broke within an incredibly short period of time after winning their fortunes. The same is often true of those who receive wealth from an inheritance. It can be spent very quickly on new cars and holidays until the wealth thermostat returns to the level which it was at before the windfall was received.

> ## It is wise for us to limit the potential we give ourselves to sabotage our progress.

This is one of the reasons that investment property is often the asset class which average investors see the most success in. Most of us feel that property is an asset class which, over time, is likely to increase in value and therefore we feel comfortable owning it for the long term without feeling the need to check values on a monthly, weekly or even daily basis. By retaining ownership of the asset for decades we allow the growth to compound, and by using leverage too, we create significant wealth.

If share investors are able to mentally switch off the stock market and hold on to a diversified portfolio of blue chip, dividend-paying industrial shares for the long haul they are likely to be very successful too. The problem for so many share investors is that they become spooked when values fall and sell their shareholdings at precisely the most inopportune moment, being the distressed-selling stage of the share market cycle, thus foiling their investment plans.

There are other important aspects to the protection of wealth too, such as owning assets in an appropriate structure as protection from lawsuits, and the use of insurance. Of course, insurance takes many different forms. Share investors use insurance in the form of automated sell-stops and sometimes through the use of derivatives such as put options. Property investors take out landlord insurance, contents insurance and sometimes elect to hold their properties in a trust structure as defence from lawsuits.

There are a whole host of other forms of insurance such as life insurance and car insurance. These are very broad subjects and space does not permit a full coverage of all aspects of legal structures, the tax implications thereof and all types of insurance. As such, these subjects are best discussed in detail with a financial planner if you are unsure.

Wealth step 7 — Contribute and give back

Every person who has experienced financial success has a level responsibility to give something back to the society that helped them achieved their wealth. This is not by any means the forum for preaching but I will just float a couple of ideas here. One idea which I practice myself is that of tithing — I give one tenth of my income from my writing and book sales to charity.

Of course, it is almost impossibly difficult to weigh up which charities are more worthy of donations than others, so my suggestion is simply to find a charity that has some meaning to you. I support a number of charities including the McGrath Foundation, which has a cause that is very important and meaningful to me.

Give and thou shalt receive.

If you fear that donating to charity could see your finances take a backward step, do remember that charitable donations can attract tax deductions. Besides, there is an argument to say that by tithing you may even become better off rather than worse. By giving away a portion of your income you are teaching your unconscious mind that you have more than enough wealth, which in turn may turn up your financial thermostat. It is true that we tend to achieve a level of wealth that is commensurate with our level of self-esteem, and charitable giving can surely only improve our self-worth.

Through giving back you will instantly begin to feel better about yourself. John D. Rockefeller, one of the wealthiest men in history, was also famous in equal parts both for his parsimony and miserable outlook. Late in his life after a health scare, Rockefeller discovered that for life to have meaning he needed to involve himself in forms of contribution and went on to be one of the greatest philanthropists the world has ever known. And he was a far happier person for it by all accounts.

Even if you do not presently have the funds to make charitable donations, you can still donate your time. There are charities all around the country who are crying out for volunteers, so even if you can only commit half a day per month, collectively we can begin to make a difference. During our travels my wife and I volunteered for BlazeAid and Conservation Australia. We loved it and met some fabulous people in Queensland and in the Northern Territory. Volunteer work can be another great example of a win-win deal.

Chapter 3 Summary

- Salaries are highly taxed in Australia which makes it very hard to build wealth from a salary alone

- In an inflationary economy, net savers tend to lose; winners invest in the assets which outperform inflation being shares and property

- The average superannuation balance even at the retirement age is woefully inadequate; you need to do more for your retirement than just paying super contributions

- If you want to win the game of investment, you need to learn the rules and educate yourself

- Investment clubs can offer you support, but please understand the full deal before you commit to parting with any hard-earned cash

- There is a proven and time-tested path to wealth — learn from the mistakes and successes of others and follow that path

- Spend less than you earn, invest in income-producing and appreciating assets and reinvest the profits

- Growth asset class values tend to boom, correct and then recover in cycles, but over time they tend to revert to the mean and cycles do not need to be feared.

4
YOUR PERSONAL
FINANCES

4

You need to know exactly where you are with your finances so that you can plan where you want to go. This is what accountants do with businesses. Accountants have two financial statements in particular which they use in order to assess the health of a business or individual, and these are the *income statement*, which sometimes known as a profit and loss account, and the *balance sheet.*

Some of the subjects covered in this short chapter I discussed in some detail in my 2012 book *Get a Financial Grip*, so I will keep this section brief.

An income statement is pretty simple, for it merely comprises what you earn and what you spend. This is what an income statement might look like for a typical employee, without any numbers added to keep it very simple:

Figure 4.1 — A typical income statement

Income Statement	
Income	**Expenditure**
Salary	Income tax
	Mortgage repayments or rent
	Car repayments
	Food
	Wine
	Other living costs
	Credit card repayments
	Personal or student loan repayments
	Holidays

The first thing that should strike you here is that there is only one form of income but many forms of expenditure. That's not unusual for most people; it's fairly typical to have a job and no other income of any significance except perhaps a little bank interest. It is also perfectly normal to have a range of expenses that suck up your income, for you do have to live after all. Can you spot the trap in this though? The trap is that when you earn more, the expenses tend to increase by an equivalent ratio too and thus there is never anything left over at the end of each month.

Take a run down the list of expenditure and you will see what I mean. You will know all too well that when employees earn more the government normally wants its share of the spoils and thus the income tax figure increases. If an employee gets a really healthy pay rise then it often follows that they want to live in a better house or apartment too, so the mortgage repayments or rent tend to go up. Fair enough. The trouble really starts when your mate is driving a flash new XR7 and you still have the ropey old Commodore that you bought at the age of 21. You had better upgrade the car too, just so you can compete with your successful friends.

To create wealth you **must** spend less than you earn.

It can seem to be an almost inescapable trap. Got a nice pay rise? Can't drink the goon wine any more, have to move up to the expensive Shiraz now, as that is more to your taste and level of sophistication. Get a 10% bonus? It wouldn't seem quite right to eat at *Hungry Jacks* now, better start having a few more restaurant meals out. It's what older people tend to do, so you can't really skimp on that. And it simply won't do to have a holiday up on the Gold Coast. Heck, you used to head to the Goldie for 'Schoolies Week'. It has be a trip to Hawaii now. You've worked hard, so you do deserve it…

It may sound as though I'm being facetious here, and perhaps I am a little, but the underlying message is absolutely a key message of this book. If every pay increase you receive is matched by a corresponding rise in expenditure, then you will be terminally trapped in the rat race of employment. If you think I am overstating the point, be assured that I know of people with gross salaries approaching seven figures who simply can't work out where their income all disappears to. It can be a very vicious trap indeed if you let it become one.

The approach of earning and spending up to the prescribed retirement age (which could well be 70 by the time you reach that age — *if* you reach that age) may be satisfactory for some people, but I suspect that it's a fair assumption that as you are reading this book you probably want your finances to be managed in a slicker fashion. Let's take a look at the other financial statement, the balance sheet:

Figure 4.2 — A typical individual's balance sheet

Balance Sheet	
Assets	**Liabilities**
House	Mortgage
Super fund	Car loans
Car	Credit card debts
	Other personal loans

A balance sheet effectively tells you how much you are worth in dollar terms. If you sold up everything you owned today and paid off all your debts, what cash would you have left? It's very much worth doing this exercise, just to work out what your starting point is. In fact, why not do it now?

Your net worth denotes — in dollar terms at least —
how much you are worth.

In the table above, I haven't included assets such as furniture, clothes, gardening equipment or golf clubs, although you may do so if you wish. The reason I haven't is that these are depreciating assets which tend to be worth much less than you have paid for them, and eventually they will be worth next to nothing. In fact, a car is a depreciating asset too, and if you own it for long enough it will probably be worth nothing more than scrap value.

If you are looking at your net worth and it doesn't amount to much, or the figure is negative, then don't panic. This is exactly what my book is designed to help you with. If I had bothered to do this exercise when I was 25, my result would have been poor. I didn't complete the exercise at that time, though, because I was too busy working 60 hours a week and spent most of the rest of the time playing cricket or in the pub.

It is not at all uncommon today for people to have more liabilities than they do assets even well into their middle age, meaning that their net worth is actually negative. A business which has net liabilities is sometimes said to be *insolvent*. However, be reassured that it does not matter at what point you are starting out from, only that you have made a decision to start improving your financial position and net worth from today going forward.

It doesn't necessarily matter where you are starting from...
what is important is actually starting.

So what is wrong with the balance sheet in the table in Figure 4.2 above? There is not necessarily anything wrong with it depending on what the related numbers were, but the problem for many of us is that there is only one appreciating asset to our name, being our house, and perhaps a small amount of money set aside in a superannuation scheme.

If the super contributions were not compulsory, a great many of us wouldn't bother contributing to that either. How do I know that? Well, in the UK pension contributions were not always compulsory and so a scary number of people simply contributed nothing towards their retirement until relatively late in their lives.

If they are able to continue working long enough for the 25 or 30 years required to pay off the mortgage, then this approach can pay a handsome dividend at the end of the process for the diligent worker. They will be left with a mortgage free property which they can live in unencumbered by debt.

However, unless that person knows how to unlock the equity in the property they will generally need to continue working in order to generate the income to live. This is a fairly standard approach to personal finance. As I say, there's not necessarily anything wrong with that, it is simply a slow but sure approach to building a nest egg, although the plan can be severely impacted by a redundancy, disability or divorce. If you want to build wealth more quickly than this you will need to expand your asset base, which will probably involve acquiring investment properties or equities...or both.

Controlling personal expenditure

You may consider the idea of controlling your expenditure to be a little dull, but if you are going to invest more money to create wealth, short of receiving a windfall, there are probably only two ways in which you are going to be able to do this. One is to earn more money, and the other is to spend less.

Of course, I could now take up a lot of time and space talking about every area of expenditure in our lives and how we might save money. I don't think that would be time and space well spent, as I trust you have the common sense to be able to work out how to spend less of your own money yourself! Naturally, working out some kind of budget or an acknowledgement of your major expenditures would be a useful starting point.

I have found that once you begin to understand that you are by no means compelled to work in a full-time job until you are 65 years of age or older — that you are free to choose your own path — you begin to view your personal finances in a different manner. Suddenly, your expenditure profile tends to improve itself naturally and you tend to waste less surplus cash on consumer goods and depreciating assets.

Your real wage

An excellent book called *Your Money or Your Life* by authors Joe Dominguez and Vicki Robin explains the importance of the subtle shift in mindset away from seeing money simply as something which we earn and spend. The book introduces two main premises.

The first is that we should calculate our real wage by subtracting taxes, the cost of work clothes and lunches paid for at work, and any costs of travelling to and from work. Also subtract your living costs such as what it costs you to live close to work — if you work in Sydney, for example, this expense might be far higher than if you live in, say, East Timor (as I do periodically as a self-employed contractor).

> Exactly where you choose to live affects
> your wealth significantly.

Divide this net salary figure by how much time you spend on your work. Include travel time to and from work and any time you spend getting ready for work or preparing in other ways. This can throw up a very scary figure per hour. I remember when I worked in professional practice that plenty of people worked 60–70 hours per week, wore very expensive suits and spent a small fortune on business lunches and other work-related expenditure. As higher rate taxpayers, their real wage per hour must have been awfully low compared to their own expectations.

The second premise of *Your Money or Your Life* is to calculate how much of your time something costs you. Suppose your real wage per hour after deducting taxes and costs of living comes in at $25 per hour (do the calculations properly and you may be surprised!). Now consider how many hours of work you will need to fulfil in order to pay for a holiday costing, say $5,000. Since we only live once and never get this time back, those 200 hours —assuming that you also have to sleep, that is around two full weeks of your life — have to be weighed against what we might be doing with that time instead.

> Reduce needless expenditure.

I have read some fascinating online resources where writers explain how they have systematically reduced all areas of their expenditure down to an absolute minimum, and are thus able to retire from the workforce in an incredibly short period of time. This approach of extreme thrift may not be for everyone but the principles are not entirely incorrect. You don't have to live on lentils and in extreme austerity, but if you want to achieve financial freedom then reasonably moderate living requirements are an important part of the equation.

Without having necessarily realised it at the time, this is essentially one of the strategies that my wife and I employed to super-charge our own wealth creation plan (minus the lentils). By working in countries with low tax rates and taking overseas contracts where our accommodation and daily expenses were paid for us, we not only increased our take home pay but massively reduced our expenditure. The contrast with a higher rate taxpayer toiling for 60 or 70 hours each week in a Sydney, New York or London job — and shelling out tens of thousands of dollars every year in rent and taxes before any other living expenses are even contemplated — is very stark.

Renting where you live

I will throw one idea into the mix here, and that is whether it might be smarter in some circumstances to rent your place of residence than buy one. This can help you to save money for investment purposes as it is generally cheaper to rent a place to live than it is to buy an equivalent property at most stages of the interest rate cycle. This is the case because rental yield percentages are often lower than mortgage rates, and because in a rented property the landlord often retains responsibility for any strata fees, repair costs and other holding costs of the property.

Renting where you live, while not for everyone, can sometimes free up more cash to invest in wealth-producing assets.

Admittedly, there are also downsides to renting property. One particular problem in recent times is that it is difficult to find long-term lets — landlords like to offer shorter-term leases so that they have the easy option to increase the rent annually or even every six months.

When you are renting there is every possibility that the landlord could sell the property and you might be asked to move out, and you often cannot make alterations to the décor without the landlord's express permission. These considerations may be of less concern to younger renters, but as you progress through life and becoming settled near good schools and facilities becomes paramount, you might find this to be more significant.

The upside to renting your place of residence is that it can offer you great flexibility, and instead of being encumbered with one large mortgage on your home which eats up 30%, 40% or even 50% of your after-tax income, instead you have a lower monthly commitment and can be freed to invest millions of dollars in investment properties, the mortgages of which are paid mostly by tenants and the taxman, rather than just by yourself. It's down to personal choice on this subject. Renting doesn't work for everyone but it has definitely worked for me and it is a strategy well worthy of consideration.

Accumulate assets, not liabilities

The central message of Robert Kiyosaki's huge best-selling book *Rich Dad Poor Dad* was: buy assets, not liabilities. So what does that actually mean? Kiyosaki's definition is that an asset is something which makes money flow to you, and a liability in his definition is something which drains money away from you. As a Chartered Accountant I might give you a slightly different and technically more accurate definition, but the basic idea is correct.

It's so simple, and yet it was seemingly a revolutionary concept for the majority of the population. When most of us get a pay rise, we tend to find ways to spend the money on things that will have no lasting value for us. A classic example is the good old automobile. A car is often defined as an asset because it is worth something: we could sell it and it would pay us money. The problem with a motor vehicle is that it is usually worth progressively less each year (it depreciates) and it costs us money in the form of insurance, repairs, tax and other running costs. So in this respect, it is definitely a liability.

What I recommend is not spending all of your surplus cash on consumer goods, cars, holidays and flash clothes which depreciate in value, and instead investing money in a range of assets which pay you money and are going to appreciate in value. The idea is so deceptively obvious, and yet it is also so effective. Below is an example of a balance sheet of an investor who has loaded their asset column with investments, but limited their liabilities to only mortgages for investment property.

Figure 4.3 — An investor's balance sheet

Balance Sheet	
Assets	**Liabilities**
Investment properties	Investment mortgages
Shares	
Bonds	
Term deposits	
Commodities	
Index funds, LICs and ETFs	
Superannuation fund	
Cash	

Investment property is a slightly more complex investment asset because it usually involves taking on some debt in the form of a mortgage, which means that you acquire both an asset and a liability. The reason an investor will do this is to use the bank's money to buy a far more valuable asset than the individual might be able to afford without assistance, allowing him or her to generate wealth through the property appreciating and, over the longer term, to generate income from the rent.

Kiyosaki would argue that you should only ever invest in property which is generating a positive cash flow from day one. In an ideal world we would definitely all do this, and it is incontrovertibly true that generating a negative cash flow cannot be a good thing. With interest rates in the US at near-zero levels for a number of years now and prices having crashed, it is very easy to find property in that country which generates a positive cash flow, but in spite of this, I wouldn't necessarily recommend venturing overseas for Australian investors.

Investing overseas introduces other risks including foreign exchange risk and sovereign risk.

In Australia, prime location property often generates a negative cash flow in the early years of ownership, although with interest rates having fallen from late 2011 and through 2013, interest rates are presently low enough that any negative cash flow need not be significant. There is a long-running debate as to whether investors should invest for growth or cash flow in Australia. The clear inference here is that you can only have one or the other, which is not necessarily true.

Simple mathematics dictates that it is capital growth which creates wealth. A few extra dollars in taxable rental income is handy, but it won't make you rich. But if you can find a property which booms in value, you are squarely on the track to financial freedom. Due to the inflationary nature of the Australian economy, if you invest in properties which are in high demand the rents tend to increase over time anyway, so my recommendation is always to pick the best investment property for growth that you can, while recognising that the rental yield plays an important role too.

Don't make the mistake of believing that future demand for a property is unimportant. It is the most important consideration.

In fact, with property values in Australia already relatively high in global terms, my opinion is that it would be incredibly foolish to base an investment decision on the current rental income of a property without due to regard to the future demand for that type of property. There are plenty of books on the shelves which will tell you that the location of a property isn't that important as long as the rent is good. I strongly disagree.

The four types of income

In a later book, Robert Kiyosaki explained that there are four types of income.[1] Kiyosaki lists these four categories or quadrants of income as being:

- **Employment** income
- **Self-employment** income
- **Business** income
- **Investment** income

Most adult Australians earn the first type of income, being **employment** income, and tend to sell their time to employers for money. Employment income has the benefit of being fairly consistent and reliable (provided, of course, that you don't lose your job) but has the major disadvantage of being heavily taxed. The tax rates now ramp up very quickly in the 2013 tax year, so you no longer need to be earning a particularly high income to find yourself in a marginal tax bracket which is pitched at around one third of your income.

The other downside to employment income is that it is linear. While employment income tends to be consistent and predictable, it is also reliant on us turning up to work each day, as if you stop turning up, generally speaking, you will stop being paid.

Income from **self-employment** is similar to employment income. Although there may be a little more flexibility around the tax deductibility of expenses, a self-employed person is still generally reliant on working each day to ensure that the money keeps rolling in. A **business** owner on the other hand, who has a team of people working for him or her, can continue to benefit from the business whether or not they are at work, which is a marvellous plus.

Businesses also operate in a more flexible tax environment whereby taxes are levied on the net profits after legitimate deductible expenses (as compared to employment income which usually has tax deducted at source before the employee sees the funds). While I am an expert in finance and investment and also an expert in how the mechanics of businesses work — group structures, preparing compliant financial statements, calculating business tax liabilities, and so on — the minutiae of how to build businesses is not my main area of expertise, although I am a Company Director myself.

Convert your income into income-producing, appreciating investments.

The **investment** quadrant is what Kiyosaki refers to as 'the playground of the rich'. Whether you intend to earn wealth through setting up and owning a business or through being paid as an employee, ultimately you should be looking to invest your capital to grow and compound your wealth. Investment income can often be tax-favoured. Dividends can come with franking credits attached, for example, and investment property in Australia benefits from negative gearing rules at present, to name but two advantages.

In Figure 4.1 we looked at a typical income statement, which has a salary income and an array of different expenses which tend to use up all of the income, and sometimes more. So what might an investor's income statement look like?

Figure 4.4 — An investor's income statement

Income Statement	
Income	Expenditure
Salary	Income Tax
Rent from tenants	Investment mortgage repayments
Part-time business income	Rent
Dividends from shares	Food, wine, other living costs
Interest from term deposits	Holidays
Interest from bonds	

This income statement still includes food, drink and other living costs — we all have to live, after all — but the smarter investor does not have masses of credit card debt and is not burdened with huge loans for consumer goods such as sports cars or boats. In the example above the investor has decided to rent his own home rather than take on a huge mortgage for a place of residence, but instead she has taken on multiple mortgages for investment properties.

She still earns a salary but having grown a portfolio of assets she also receives rent from her investment properties, dividends from shares and interest from other assets such as bonds and term deposits. In the example above the investor also has income from a part-time business which she might decide to turn into a full time business later.

> The trap that salaried employees can fall into is each pay rise being met by an equivalent increase in expenses ... the treadmill runs ever faster.

You will immediately notice the difference between this income statement in Figure 4.4 and that of the example shown in Figure 4.1. In the former example, there was only one stream of income — a salary — struggling to support a wide range of expenses. It may become seemingly impossible to escape from the rat wheel. In fact, it probably is impossible unless you can learn to spend less than you earn and invest the difference in a portfolio of appreciating assets. The remedy is to be mindful of where your money is being spent unwisely and take action accordingly.

Chapter 4 Summary

- Most individuals have one form of income — a salary — and many forms of expenditure

- The key trap to avoid is spending every pay rise on more 'things'

- Spend less than you earn and invest in assets which appreciate and generate income

- Avoid acquiring expensive depreciating assets such as cars and boats, or liabilities which will continue to cost you money and destroy your ability to create wealth and financial freedom

5
INVESTMENT
STRATEGY

5

Income-producing assets

As noted, to my mind, there are two simple ways to create wealth for the average investor. Firstly, to continue to buy into a diversified portfolio of industrial and financial shares, which tend to pay stronger dividends than their commodity stock counterparts. Hold for the long term and focus on the growing income stream rather than the day-to-day gyrations of the stock market.

The second method is to buy and hold income-producing real estate. While prime-location residential investment property that is highly leveraged can often generate a cash flow loss in the early years of ownership, over time inflation tends to increase the rental income and allow the property to become both income-producing and wealth-creating as the capital value of in-demand property increases over time. The ability to use the power of leverage or borrowing is the icing on the cake for investors.

Choosing stocks to trade or invest in

Before we move on to look at where and how to buy property, let's take a short look at share market investments because, despite what you may read elsewhere, a balanced portfolio is important.

How do you even decide which stocks to trade or invest in the first place? My suggestion would be to consider which industries you have some expertise in. What do you do for a living? What do you do for your leisure? Although you may feel that you have no expertise in any industry, in my experience people have more likelihood of success investing in the stock of companies which operate in industries that they know something about or take at least some level of interest in.

Once you have identified an industry which you might like to become involved in, focus on getting to know one or two of the companies within that industry inside out. This is where the power of focus can be used to your advantage to steal an edge over other investors and traders.

Many traders fail in their quest to become successful stock market traders and then move on to try their hands at currencies and derivative markets. My suggestion would be to save a lot of pain and not bother. If you have not mastered the art of trading stocks then you are unlikely to suddenly achieve miraculous success through a change of market or asset class. It is more likely to be the case that you need to work upon your temperament, money management skills and discipline. Also remember that commodities, derivatives or currencies do not pay dividends in the way that stocks do.

So if you are going to pick your own stocks, which industries do I recommend that you invest in or trade? The answer to that is simple: invest or trade in industries that you understand (those that are within your 'circle of competence'). If you have spent the past twenty years working in mining, it would seem rather illogical to then spend valuable hours learning about investing in companies that sell stationery.

What if you don't know about any industries? Firstly, question whether that is actually true. In Australia, we all spend money so by definition will interact with companies or businesses: think of food, drink, consumables, tourism, utility companies. We all tend to use them. Secondly, consider whether you can reach your goals simply by investing in a diversified portfolio of quality industrial stocks. Over time you will likely outperform the stock market at large and receive healthy dividends as companies use their technological, intellectual and services excellence to generate returns for you, the shareholder. Let's assess how some of the industries might appeal to investors:

Mining

We know that Buffett likes to invest in franchise-style companies. In this context a franchise company is one which provides a service that customers feel compelled to use, such as Gillette, the producers of razors. Buffett also likes 'toll-bridge' companies such as American Express which customers pay a fee or commission to each time they are compelled to use the product.

While Australia is a resources rich country and the mining giants can indeed generate huge profits, the industry as a whole tends to underperform on a market-wide basis. There are a number of reasons for this. Resources companies produce commodities and therefore cannot easily compete on sales prices or increase revenues charged as they please. Instead, they are largely reliant on digging vast quantities of ore and minerals out of the earth in order to generate large profits.

Resources companies also tend to need to re-invest capital in order to find, explore, evaluate and drill for new reserves, which impacts shareholder returns. While the resources companies attempt to smooth their returns through hedging their revenues forward, the returns are still to some extent cyclical depending on the strength of commodity prices. The good news is that over the next few years demand for commodities is likely to be strong due to the increasing demand from China and India, sometimes referred to as the 'Chindia boom'.

Over time, a portfolio of industrial shares is
likely to outperform a portfolio of resources shares.

Thus while investors very often attempt to outperform by picking out a few mining companies slated for good growth, it is actually simpler to outperform the index over the long term by picking a fund of industrial stocks. Where is the evidence to support this? As noted by Peter Thornhill in his excellent book *Motivated Money*, over the period 1979 to 2007, from a purely capital growth perspective the resources index increased by 12 times, as compared to 18.3 times for the industrials index (and 12.8 index for the All Ordinaries index).[1]

Shares are not only one-dimensional assets. They provide dividend returns as well as capital growth returns. As already implied, resources stocks generally pay weak dividends as they prefer to re-invest capital in search of new assets and resources. Thus, if dividends are included in returns over the same period, resources stocks return 27.6 times as compared to a massive 69.6 times for the industrials index (and 40.5 times for the All Ordinaries index).[2]

While these figures run to 2007 which is the period immediately preceding the global financial crisis and stock market meltdown, they do aptly demonstrate the point that over time a diversified portfolio of industrial stocks is very likely to outperform the stock market index, and will destroy the returns from an equivalent portfolio of resources stocks.

Financial services

Two decades ago, resources companies formerly made up around nearly three quarters of the Australian stock market by mining capitalisation — Australia's wealth was founded on minerals. But today only around one quarter of the market is resources-based.[3] This was partly as a result of huge growth in the financial services sector, which certainly presents some compelling opportunities for investors. Companies to consider include those who operate in insurance or the banks.

Health care

With the ageing population and increasing life-expectancy in Australia one industry which is certain to grow in size over the coming decades is health care. Just as with in investment in any industry, it pays to look for companies which look set to capitalise on the emerging trends. There are a number of dedicated health care companies on the stock exchange, some which specialise in a particular branch of medical treatment, others which offer a diversified range of services. The sector will grow over time, so the challenge is to identify the best-placed companies to capitalise on the opportunities which will inevitably present themselves.

Diversification through number of stocks held

I have met plenty of people who were so excited by the dividend yield of one of the major banks in particular that they were directing all of their spare cash into buying shares in that bank. While this approach is admirable for its commitment of focus there is one obvious potential flaw, being the total lack of diversification.

You will no doubt be familiar with the old adage: 'Don't put all of your eggs in one basket'. As it is possible to buy small parcels of shares it is possible to attain diversification by holding shares in more companies very easily. The table below show the tremendous diversification benefits of splitting your capital across a few companies instead of one.

Figure 5.1 — Diversification of a share portfolio

Number of stocks	% of portfolio in each stock
1	100.0
2	50.0
3	33.3
4	25.0
5	20.0
6	16.7
7	14.3
8	12.5
9	11.1
10	10.0
11	9.1

Number of stocks	% of portfolio in each stock
12	8.3
13	7.7
14	7.1
15	6.7
20	5.0
50	2.0
100	1.0

What the table in Figure 5.1 does show, however, is that to some extent there is a law of diminishing returns at work. While splitting your capital across three companies instead of one adds greatly to your diversification, adding a fiftieth and a fifty-first stock to your portfolio adds comparatively much less. Ultimately, if you are buying similar shares in the same stock market index then you should consider how else you can protect yourself, which might mean looking at other asset classes such as property or bonds.

Figure 5.2 — Tracking error

Number of Stocks	Tracking Error (%)
1	40
2	20
4	10
6	7
8	4
10	5
20	2
40	1

Source: *Online Investing on the Australian Share Market*, Roger Kinsky[4]

This table also demonstrates how a holding of very few stocks is likely to make your share portfolio far more volatile. If you hold just one stock, regardless of how the stock market performs you could do very well or very badly in any given year because your one stock may not track the index very closely at all. However, if you hold a portfolio of 40 of the major stocks, it is clear that your results are unlikely to diverge very far from the results of the market index overall.

Diversification through industries

One of the ways in which we can gain more diversification is to invest in a number of stocks that do not operate in the same industry as each other. You could, for example split your capital across the four major banks, but if the banking industry falls upon hard times due to adverse movements in interest rates, dwelling prices or mortgage defaults, then the diversification will have helped very little because all four of the major banks are likely to perform poorly in concert.

Instead, you might choose to invest in stocks from other industries which might perform strongly when the banks are doing it tough. As stocks in different industries can move in a non-correlated manner, spreading your investments across different industries can help in your diversification quest.

Diversification through asset classes

A problem with the approach above is that if there is a major stock market crash all stocks are likely to be punished, albeit some less than others. Those with a strong track record of generating healthy profits and paying strong dividends will be less volatile (known as having a low Beta stocks) than those which are speculative and fail to generate cash (known as high Beta).

There are a number of ways in which you can protect yourself from a stock market crash. One is to attempt to time the market and sell stocks when they become overvalued. While this is impossible to do perfectly, it is possible to buy when shares are cheap and sell when they become expensive through recognising the market cycles and when stocks are generally under- or over-valued. A modified approach for more experienced heads is rather than to sell stocks when they are expensive, is simply to *add more* holdings when stocks are perceived to be very cheap.

> Buy low, sell high ... or better still, buy low and never sell!

This involves a level of discipline and an ability to retain a level of funds in the bank so that you are able to capitalise when the right time arises, which is when market sentiment is despondent. This approach has the tremendous benefit of minimising transaction costs and capital gains taxes, but is very hard to do as most of us frequently have little or no spare capital. Therefore this approach is probably best suited to experienced and older investors.

The other alternative, and the one which I prefer myself, is to diversify through investing in different asset classes. I like to own multiple investment properties in more than one country in addition to Australian equities and UK equities, and this gives me diversification against adverse stock market movements.

Although it is possible to invest in other asset classes too such as bonds and other fixed interest investments, as I am at the end of the first quarter of Robert Kiyosaki's 'Game of Money' I prefer to stick predominantly with property and shares. Over a 30-year time horizon, I consider that any potential short-term market despondency is likely to have corrected.

Of course, when you start out in property ownership it is very hard to be diversified within that asset class as you generally start by simply owning one property. However, over time it becomes possible to diversify by owning different types of property in different cities and states.

Investing in funds

I often say that we should invest in industries which we understand or are within our circle of competence. Many budding investors do not truly understand many industries and have little inclination to learn about how to analyse individual companies — and often they don't have much spare time either.

The beautiful thing for investors is that this does not necessarily matter. We do not have to be Warren Buffett to reach our own financial goals. If we apply common sense to our investing then we are very likely outperform the stock market index over the longer term by investing in a diversified portfolio of dividend-paying industrial shares.

Exchange traded funds (ETFs) and listed investment companies (LICs)

The advent of exchange traded funds (ETFs) and listed investment companies (LICs) has made investing in funds and diversified holdings an easily accessible option for investors. ETFs are simply investment funds that are traded on the stock exchange much like stocks, and an LIC is exactly what is says on the tin — it's an investment company which is listed on the securities exchange. ETFs are one of the fastest growing products in

Australia with several billion dollars under management. Here is a brief summary of the pros and cons of ETFs:

Figure 5.3 — Advantages and disadvantages of ETFs

For	Against
Easy to trade	Specialist ETFs may be illiquid; may not always be easy to find a buyer/seller
Real time pricing	Bid/ask spread may be wide for illiquid ETFs
No minimum investment amount	Brokerage costs each time you trade
Cheaper than managed funds...	...but still there are fees
More tax efficient (less turnover, can choose when to incur capital gains)...	
Share market ETFs pay dividends with franking credits	

Index funds

An index fund will simply tend to track the index you have chosen to invest in. Thus you cannot materially outperform or underperform the index you have chosen to invest in, you will simply match it. I have a UK FTSE index fund that was set up with monthly contributions back in 1997 and we continue to pay a monthly contribution even today more than 16 years later. Do you think I sit glued to the screen staring at the FTSE index each morning hoping for it to go up? Of course not, the idea is absurd! But let's stop to consider this for a second.

If you are buying shares with a view to selling them next year, you clearly want them to go up in value. But what is your strategy next year? To sell and then buy more shares? In which case you probably want the share market to keep rising again. Can you see why it is difficult to build a coherent share market strategy? If you are a net buyer of shares over the next few years you actually want share prices to go down rather than up, so that your cash will buy more shares. This is precisely why steadily buying into index funds can represent such an easy strategy.

> Index funds offer a simple and efficient method
> of investing in a diversified share portfolio.

One of the neat effects of an investment strategy of continuing to buy units regularly is the application of what is sometimes called *dollar cost averaging*. Essentially what this means is that if you contribute the same dollar figure to the fund each month, when the index is low you purchase more units and when the index is high you purchase fewer units.

Some authors, including Robert Kiyosaki have tried to slate the concept of dollar cost averaging instead noting how he invests in real estate because it gives him control. After the subprime crisis and the US property crash the idea of having some diversification and continuing to drop amounts in the share market at regular intervals — to spread the entry cost — suddenly seems like a very good idea.

Dollar cost averaging into a diversified portfolio or LIC gives great peace of mind as you do not have to worry greatly about timing the market. Provided you have chosen an index with a long term upward trend (as I have suggested elsewhere, the industrials index shows great long term returns) then over time you will do very nicely indeed, without paying a fund manager to create transaction costs in trying to outperform the index. All you have to do is have the diligence to keep contributing and the right mindset of watching the ever growing dividend income stream instead of obsessively focussing in share prices. I consider this strategy a little further in Chapter 25.

Reversion to the mean

You may have heard the phrase *reversion to the mean*, but what does it refer to? Mean reversion is a mathematical concept which notes that while the prevailing price of an asset is sometimes overvalued and sometimes undervalued, over time it will tend to revert towards a long-term average. The idea is often used by traders in the stock markets so that when a share price is considered to be below its long-term average or intrinsic value then it is deemed to be a 'buy' and if it is above its long-term average it is marked down as a 'sell'.

Figure 5.4 — Reserve Bank Dwelling Prices to Income chart

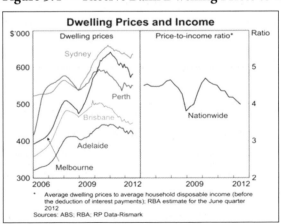

Source: Reserve Bank of Australia, www.rba.gov.au

If you buy when prices are attractive then theory says that eventually the price is likely to revert to the average valuation or above and we will profit. The concept can easily be applied to other asset classes include including exchange rates, commodities or real estate.

The flaw in mean reversion for stock prices

There is one fatal flaw in the mean reversion concept for the behaviour of share prices. If you stop to think about it, you might be able to work out what it is. The flaw is that the mathematics takes no account of the legal status of a company which is able to file for bankruptcy. In simple terms, if a company becomes insolvent, a stock price can hit zero and stay there forever, and it will never return to an average price. While property prices can both rise and fall sharply as we have seen in the United States, they will never hit zero as the land will always retain value, particularly if it is prime location land which is in continual high demand.

Long-term trends

If we look at the long-term trend of market prices we can begin to make some useful observations. Firstly, we can note that the trend for both stocks and property is an upwards one. Secondly, while at times prices become speculatively high or demoralizingly low, prices do tend to revert somewhere close to an average over time. We can also see that while market crashes seem devastating when they are occurring (2008–2009 still currently looks extremely painful in the rear-view mirror), experienced investors wisely consider that 'this too shall pass'.

Observe the bursting of the technology stock bubble from 2000 to 2002, which now appears to be of less consequence. The sheer terror of the 1987 Black Monday crash as automated computer trades unravelled now resembles an insignificant, almost laughable minor blip in the upwards-trending chart. Seasoned investors sometimes delete sections of price charts and ask beginners to consider what would happen to their investing psyche if they were able to switch off the market noise for long periods. This is something which property investors are usually better able to do than share investors due to the historic lack of a daily quoted market price.

Figure 5.5 — Dow Jones history chart

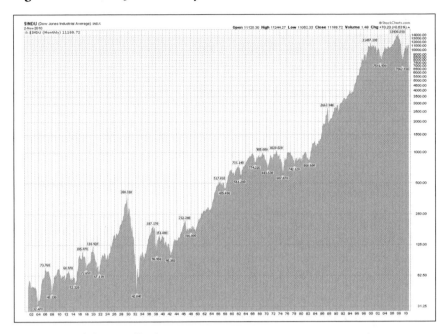

Source: www.stockcharts.com/freecharts

History shows us that while prices can certainly crash sharply, the crashes often follow a period of irrational exuberance. The huge stock market crashes of 1929 (Dow Jones falling from 380 to 200) and 1987 (the Dow again falling by approximately 500 points to around 1750), for example, were both immediately preceded by irrational appreciation in market valuations. Despite market corrections continuing to occur in cycles, the Dow index today sits far higher at above 15,000 points, having more than doubled in value since its last nadir in 2009.

Speed limits on asset values

While prices can at various times steam far ahead of intrinsic values, market prices ultimately do have a speed limit. Periodically dwelling price-to-income ratios in real estate markets may become very high indeed (Hong Kong being a prime contemporary example) but with property prices sensitive to interest rates, there does come a critical point where properties cease to be affordable.

The natural speed limit for real estate prices is ultimately the ability of owners to service mortgage repayments.

In this context, the easing of property values and the slicing of the cash interest rate from 4.75% to a record low of just 2.75% in Australia in May 2013 delivered a welcome affordability dividend. Of course, it is very difficult to calculate an intrinsic value for residential property, because values (perhaps one should say *prices*) tend to be driven as much around what property is worth to emotion-driven homeowners as much as they are by imputed rents or yields for investors.

What we can observe from price history charts and from falling interest rates is that affordability is better than it has been, and in some cities affordability of certain property types has improved fairly significantly since the relevant preceding boom period.

The natural speed limit for stock prices is ultimately governed by the ability of companies to generate cash. The technology stock bubble showed that market prices can become hugely irrational for a period of time, but eventually a company must start to generate cash to justify its valuation (the rational valuation of a company is the sum of its future cash-generating ability adjusted for risk and discounted back to today's value). The companies which never generated any cash or profits during and after the technology stock boom in time became valued at somewhere close to $nil. No cash-generating ability ultimately equals nil value.

Three lessons of mean reversion

There are three lessons that we need to take away from the concept of reversion to the mean:

Mean reversion lesson 1 — It can be hugely beneficial to attempt to time our entry to the market

In property, this means you should look to invest in cities which are due to experience a boom in population and real growth in household incomes. This will allow values to increase in the future by increasing the speed limit for prices. You should also look to cities which have not recently experienced booming values. In the share markets, this means you should look to buy when stocks are trading at price-earnings ratios that are significantly below their long-term average.

Mean reversion lesson 2 — Stock prices do not always revert to the mean

You should not risk all of your investment capital in a handful of company stocks — some diversification is preferable, whether it is through investing in a more diversified portfolio of stocks or into other asset classes such as investment property, or fixed interest investments such as bonds. Companies can fail and become insolvent so some diversification is desirable.

Mean reversion lesson 3 — Timing the market perfectly is impossible

History and experience shows us that is actually impossible to consistently time the market perfectly, but if we also allow ourselves *time in the market,* growth asset classes tend to be forgiving of imperfect timing. You should aim to time your entry to a market as far as is possible but accept that you are unlikely to the get the timing precisely right and therefore unnecessary procrastination should be avoided.

The yield trap

People often tell me they have found a great investment because of its high yield or income. I will now explode a few myths about why yield can be a very misleading and often a dreadful indicator of the quality of an investment. We need to understand the dimensions of yield and growth and how they interact with each other. This is beautifully illustrated by Peter Thornhill in his share investment book *Motivated Money.*[5]

Back in 1980, he notes, term deposits were paying around 10% interest, so on the face of it were far more attractive investments than, for example, a portfolio of industrial shares, which were yielding only around half of this percentage.[6] High yielding (and supposedly low risk) investments tend to be attractive to retirees who seek certainty of income. There is a hidden trap, however, and it is this: a high yield is not the same thing as a high income.

High yield does not mean high income

A yield is simply a spot figure calculated at a point in time. Income of $100 on an investment of $1000 gives a yield of 10%, which is superficially attractive. Income, however, is different to yield, income being the actual dollar figure that the investment pays you over time.

Suppose a retiree invested $100,000 in term deposits in 1980 due to the perceived safety of receiving income of $10,000 in the first year seeming more attractive than the lower dividend yield of supposedly riskier shares.

By 1993, however, an initial $100,000 portfolio of industrial index shares, whilst still paying a seemingly weaker dividend yield of around 5%, was paying income of closer to $20,000, and by 2006 a huge dividend income of around $75,000 on a portfolio value of a massive $1.75 million.[7] What happens to the capital value, purchasing power and income of a $100,000 term deposit over that time? Oh dear. So much for the high yield!

Investing solely in high yielding investments upon retirement such as term deposits might only be a good investment if you plan on dying quickly. What we actually want, rather than high yield, is a high income over time. The percentage yields on shares over the long term tends to fluctuate with prevailing sentiment and prices, so yields do become comparatively higher when share prices crash and lower when prices boom. Thus a stock market meltdown is a great time to buy both for yield and future capital growth.

The yield trap in property

There is much talk of the benefits of investing in properties which generate a high yield. We do need to note, however, that high yields tend to exist where capital growth has been restricted due to uninspiring levels of demand for some reason. Very similar principles apply to property as they do to shares.

When prices are high, yields tend to be lower (and vice versa), but over a longer time horizon we might expect rental yields to revert close to a mean or average, and therefore what we actually want is properties which experience great capital growth. The rental income will generally follow over time.

Counter-cyclical property investors get great yields anyway

If you elect to invest counter-cyclically in property when sentiment is low, you can attain excellent yields even on prime location property — just as share investors who invest after a crash get great dividend yields on blue chip shares.

This is particularly the case for apartments being a dwelling type which tend to generate higher yields than houses. The chart in Figure 5.4 illustrates the phenomenal increase in dwelling prices in Melbourne experienced since 2007 as compared to other capital cities. Depending upon which provider you source the data from, the average gross rental yields you might expect to see on apartments range from a mediocre 4.5% for Melbourne to somewhere around 5.5% for Sydney, and higher still for Brisbane.[8]

In other words, by electing to invest in property which has recently experienced sharply rising rents but not capital growth, just like share investors, counter-cyclical property investors expect to receive both future capital growth and a solid yield too. Smart investors look for rental yields above the quoted average and manufacture higher yields by adding value to properties through cosmetic renovation.

Thus if average properties in prestige suburbs can attain 5.5% yields we should question how much value there may be in seeking out yields of 6–7% if this involves investing in an area which over the long term will not experience as great a level of demand. Apartments in the inner suburbs of Sydney, for example, will over the coming decades experience a phenomenal increase in demand due to the planned huge population growth, while construction remains inadequate and costly.

What can growth do for us as investors? Being an Anglo-Aussie who also invests in a portfolio of UK properties I frequently refer back to what is happening in England for clues, as some of the property markets there are more developed. While many property owners in the UK regions who bought in the period after 2007 are holders of property with negative equity, prices in London continue to surge to comfortably the highest levels they have ever seen.

Ask people who bought a house back in the 1980s and 1990s in Britain how they've fared and they say that they have done well. Why? This is because the property is worth more in dollar terms than they paid for it. But have they really done well? Most likely they have no idea because they may have few other investments and no worthwhile benchmark against which to measure performance. Typically, house prices moved upwards through the inflationary 1980s and yet further as credit growth expanded in the 1990s, but have tailed off in most areas outside London over the last half decade.

I know of people, though, including some Aussies, who many years ago bought only one or two properties in prestige areas of London such as Mayfair and the West End postcode of W1, who now have little interest in paid employment because the price of their properties has increased so substantially.

As you might expect, whilst yields remain relatively low on a spot figure percentage of property price, their rental income is staggering. A three-bedroom flat in Mayfair today tends to rent for somewhere between £125,000 and £350,000 per annum ($200,000-$500,000). So much for those lower yields! Expect to see similar trends unfolding in the premium suburbs of Australia.

Properties in prime-location suburbs of the major capital cities over time can be massive outperformers both in terms of rental income and capital growth.

Lower yields, maybe, but far, far higher income. Understand this fundamental difference and you can be a winner too.

Property market corrections

Through 2011 and the first half of 2012 we saw a level of correction in most of Australia's property markets, as anxious owners were keen to realise their gains and new buyers became unwilling to enter the market at the peak of the cycle. Residential property market corrections often react differently to share market downturns, as a high proportion of dwellings are held by owner-occupiers rather than solely investors, which is in stark contrast to the dynamic of equity markets.

Legendary fund manager, philosopher and philanthropist George Soros observed that 'only once in a blue moon' does a short circuit in credit markets act as the trigger to a genuine free-fall. Instead property markets often have prolonged flat periods of moderately easing prices as household incomes have an opportunity to catch up and the property market takes a well-earned breather.

The good news for property owners is that the falls through 2011 and early 2012 were both moderate and monotonous, and further they seem to have stabilised somewhat over a period of time. In most areas moderate growth has returned. While excitable journalists and vested interests will continually report that property prices 'could fall by as much as 10% to 20% over the next two years!' investors simply need to be aware that property is a long-term game with an unpredictable near-term outlook.

The long-term view is important

All market corrections should be viewed in a wider context. The Dow Jones, by way of an example, roared back up to all-time highs of well above 15,000 points, more than doubling in only a few short years after the global financial crisis. Whether or not the recovery remains so strong I don't yet know, but the example shows that sentiment does not remain at a nadir forever.

Crashes can be also be corrections — depending on your timeframe

As noted, looking at the 'horror' stock market crash of 1987 (with all of its sensationalist headlines and crashing markets losing nearly a half of their value very quickly) in the rear-view mirror, the crash looks like little more than a blip in the chart. In the year to September 1987 the All Ordinaries index increased in value by a spectacular 100% up to a peak of 2106. Then, from late September 1987 the index fell by precisely 50% from 2106 to 1151 in less than two months.

There are two things to note here. Firstly, that if we remove 12 months from the chart, the crash is nowhere to be seen: the market is simply where it was before the irrational exuberance began. Secondly, even after the global financial crisis brought the market tumbling down again, at the time of writing the All Ordinaries index (XAO) today sits back around 5000 points — a world away from the values seen in 1987.

Understand the arithmetic

In the 1987 example above we have doubled one to get two, and then we have halved two to make one. It is very simple mathematics, so it should be a correspondingly simple paradigm shift to change your mindset from a short-term to a long-term horizon. Instead of worrying about the next six months or year, try to visualise where the market will be 30 or 40 years from now and invest accordingly. Will you want to have acquired more assets or sat on the side-lines and procrastinated?

The property markets need a shot of confidence

While it seems logical that property prices should rise no faster than household incomes, what instead tends to happen is that prices stagnate or drift lower for a period of time, before appreciating sharply. Markets are not rational, and they never have been because they are affected by human emotions — and humans are not rational beings.

What property markets need for strong capital growth to return is a shot of confidence. This may take some time to come, but we know that markets are cyclical and come it will. Interest rates look as though they may yet fall further at this juncture. Low rates will gradually lure investors back into the market. Of course, to out-perform we should always seek markets, suburbs and property types that look set to boom on a counter-cyclical basis.

Investing as you approach retirement

I have already discussed a little which asset classes you should consider investing in, my belief being that property and shares are the two asset classes which give the average investor the best chance of achieving financial freedom over time. There is an additional consideration here though, and that is whether it makes sense to switch focus toward income assets rather than growth assets as you approach the retirement age.

The traditional investment approach suggested that we should buy our own property as a place of residence and then split our remaining assets between shares and bonds dependent upon our age. As we get older, the theory suggested, we should move more of our wealth in to 'less risky' assets such as bonds. The logic in such an approach is fairly obvious. In 2008 and 2009, it was very distressing to witness employees of close to the retirement age watching their superannuation balances smashed downwards by the global financial crisis due to the ensuing crash in stock valuations.

Figure 5.6 — Traditional portfolio balancing

Age	% in shares	% in bonds
20	80	20
25	75	25
30	70	30
35	65	35
40	60	40
45	55	45
50	50	50
55	45	55
60	40	60
65	35	65

The table above suggests that we should subtract our age from the number 100 and invest this percentage of our assets in shares, the balance to be allocated to bond investments. There are problems with this approach too, though, which I will now explain. Firstly, the approach takes no account of the fact that we are all different and have different cash flow requirements and goals. The difficulty with bonds as an investment is that they are not a financial instrument designed to facilitate capital growth.

Bonds tend to generate a healthy and regular cash flow, but they are not normally assets which are acquired for their growth potential. As such, in an inflationary capitalist economy, assets such as property and shares which appreciate over time are like to create greater wealth.

There are two dimensions to consider when assessing returns from assets, being income and growth. Bonds provide regular income but rarely capital growth. Over time, shares can provide you with both. The concept of moving the bulk of our wealth into income assets as we approach the retirement age does have some benefits; however there is also a potential flaw in this strategy.

Bonds tend to provide consistent income but no growth.

Suppose we retire at the age of 60 and invest heavily in bonds at this point. The flaw here is that in this day and age it is entirely possible that we might live for another 40 years after we leave the workforce. This is not as far-fetched as it may once have sounded. Even if within my own very limited circle of acquaintances I know of people who have lived well beyond the age of 100 so it is entirely possibly that it could happen.

The effect of inflation on a portfolio of fixed income investments over that kind of time period is potentially devastating and therefore it is worth considering whether we might be better to remain invested in a diversified portfolio of shares and focus on the growing dividend stream (which should outperform inflation over time) rather than only the day-to-day gyrations of the share prices.

While prime location in property in Australia often generates a negative cash flow in the early years of ownership, as rental income increases with inflation, properties become cash flow positive. Therefore, just as with shares, properties which are held for the long term can offer both dimensions of rental income and capital growth.

Chapter 5 Summary

- Market valuations tend to revert to a mean or average over time, but individual companies can and do fail (therefore some level of diversification in stocks is vital)

- Yield can be an extremely poor indicator of the future performance of an investment

- The markets of growth asset classes move in cycles, thus you should aim to buy when prices and sentiment are low

- Averaging into a low cost LIC that is focussed on industrial stocks can be an excellent low-risk approach to building wealth over the long term — focus on and enjoy the dividend stream rather than always watching share prices

- Over the long term, moderate inflation seems likely to prevail

- Interest rates appear likely to be remain low for some time at the time of writing

6
THE ROLE OF
THE BANK

6

The development of Australian banking

The first bank to be established in Australia was the Bank of New South Wales in 1817 followed not too long after by the Bank of Australasia in 1835 which later became the ANZ bank we know today. Originally the central bank function was performed by the Commonwealth Bank of Australia but this function was assumed by the Reserve Bank of Australia (RBA) in 1960.

The RBA is a very important institution and one which property investors in particular need to be aware of, for the Reserve Bank sets the monetary policy in a bid to control inflation between its targeted range of 2–3% and to maintain price stability. Although the bank does have other tools within its armoury, its prime means of affecting inflation and price stability is the setting of the cash interest rate which in turn affects the rate at which lending institutions set mortgage rates.

With most investors in Australia opting for variable rate mortgages rather than fixed rate equivalents, the housing market is particularly sensitive to interest rate movements in this country, and therefore property investors are wise to have an awareness of the policies of the central bank.

There are presently only four major banks in Australia.

Today, there are four main pillars in the world of Australian banking which, in order of market capitalisation and with their stock market codes are: Commonwealth Bank of Australia (CBA), Westpac Banking Corporation (WBC), ANZ Bank (ANZ) and National Australia Bank (NAB).

The Australian Government currently believes the four pillars approach to banking is in the best interests of the economy and of the nation and therefore is unlikely to allow further mergers to take place between these major banking institutions. The banking industry is now regulated by two institutions in particular, being APRA and ASIC. The roles and powers of each are frequently debated, but, fortunately for the reader, this book is not the forum for that debate. Interestingly, there is much talk of Macquarie Bank becoming a fifth major player in the sector.

The Reserve Bank of Australia (RBA)

The central bank in Australia is the Reserve Bank of Australia (RBA). The role of the RBA is to conduct appropriate monetary policy and has the remit of promoting the stability of the currency of Australia, the maintenance of full employment, and the economic prosperity and welfare of the people of Australia.

History has shown that there is some level of correlation between the movement of the Reserve Bank's interest rates and the confidence in property markets. This is expected because a high proportion of leveraged property owners have mortgages with variable rates, and it therefore follows that property markets are highly sensitive to cash rate movements.

For this reason, it makes sense for property investors to understand thoroughly how the monetary policy operates. You can read more about the monetary policy and the musings of the Reserve Bank on the RBA website www.rba. gov.au — in particular, take a look at the Press Releases section of the website. I also post about monetary policy, inflation and interest rates and how they interact regularly on my free daily blog at http://petewargent.blogspot.com.

While it is tempting to think that prices in the property market naturally find their own level, trends are inextricably linked to the interest rate and monetary policies of the RBA. For this reason it pays to take heed of what the Governor and Board of the RBA say about the housing market and the outlook for the economy in general.

As speeches delivered by Reserve Bank officials have a tendency to belie the agenda of those who deliver them, we can glean insights into motives and likely future actions. In 2012, possibly for the first time, the RBA introduced dwelling price to income ratio charts to support its Statements on Monetary Policy.[1] One such chart can be seen in Figure 6.1 below and shows dwelling prices to be around four times disposable household income before interest deductions, which is far cry from 8 or 9 times that is sometimes claimed.[2]

The RBA also went to great lengths to show that while Australian property is by no means cheap as compared to other developed nations (difficult though such a comparison is to draw up), nor is it outrageously expensive.

The Banker

In the game of Monopoly the bank assumes the role of looking after the title deeds for the properties on the board and maintains the float of currency for the game. The bank collects taxes, fines and interest and it also pays out salaries. Titles may also be mortgaged at various points in the game and can be bought back by paying a premium to the bank of 10% of the mortgaged value.

The role of banker is allocated to one of players, ideally the one who is the best auctioneer. It is important that the player selected as banker keeps his or her own funds separate from those of the bank and that no 'accidental' mistakes are made in this respect! Unlike in the real world, the bank in Monopoly can never go broke. If it runs out of money the bank can write an IOU to any player on an ordinary piece of paper.

Figure 6.1 — Dwelling prices of developed countries

Source: Reserve Bank of Australia, www.rba.gov.au

What is clear to me from the rhetoric of the Reserve Bank is that while it does not desire dwelling prices to inflate unsustainably, it also does not want prices to fall sharply, instead preferring to promote a period of moderate or no growth while household incomes steadily improve over time. The figures they provide are surely intended to support their argument against a housing bubble existing. Here's the RBA Governor Glenn Stevens in his own words:[3]

'Australian dwelling prices, relative to income, are in the pack of comparable countries. In this comparison, the United States seems the outlier. We should never say a crash couldn't happen here ... but it has to be said that the housing market bubble, if that's what it is, seems to be taking quite a long time to pop — if that's what it is going to do. The ingredients we would look for as signalling an imminent crash seem less in evidence now than five years ago'.

Investing in banks

Buying shares in Australian banks has traditionally been seen as a solid investment in this country, and this can be seen in the strong market capitalisation of each of the major banks. This reflects that the banks have consistently generated billions in profits, and unlike in the US and the UK, we have not seen major financial institutions collapse through the global financial crisis.

There are two dimensions to consider when buying shares and their likely returns. Firstly, there is the dividend yield, being the element of the taxed net profits that are distributed by the corporation to the shareholder, and treated as income for the shareholder. The second dimension is capital growth which is determined by the future direction of the share price. As we will see, Australian banks, while not trading at particularly high price-earnings ratios, are actually among the most expensive in the world when considered on a share price to book value basis.

Of course, the market capitalisation, being the number of ordinary shares on issue multiplied by the prevailing share price (essentially the stock market's valuation of the companies) varies on a day-to-day basis depending on the movement of the share prices, but the market caps of the major banks in Australia are sitting between $50 billion and $90 billion at the time of writing. These corporations are genuine behemoths.

The relatively expensive valuation of the banks as compared to global counterparts raises an interesting question: are we better to invest in the shares of Australian banks right now, or would we be smarter to instead use the cheap capital on offer to us (with interest rates so low, banks are offering mortgages at very attractive rates) to invest in property?

Figure 6.2 — Banks' Price-to-book-value Ratios

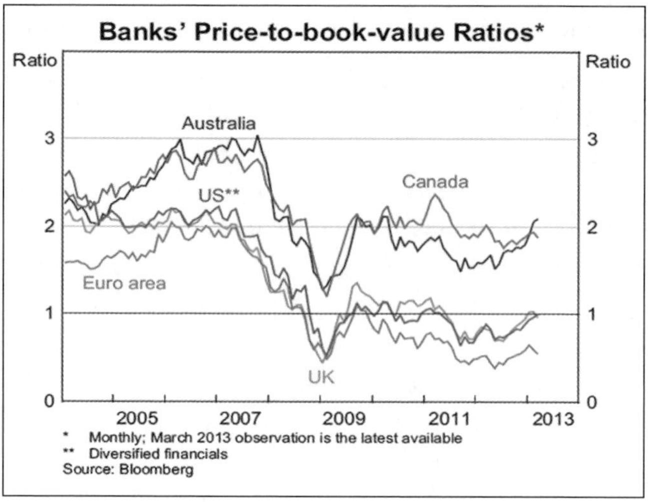

Source: Reserve Bank of Australia, www.rba.gov.au

The chart in Figure 6.2 above shows how Australia's banks are valued compared to elsewhere in the world. Bank stocks in Europe are relatively cheap reflecting some major corporate collapses during the financial crisis and a lack of confidence in the banking system in general. Faith in Australian banks is presently much higher. One of the main reasons that the major banks have endured as such a popular investment for individuals is their vast profits and the very attractive dividend payments.

Figure 6.3 — Australian major banks — dividend yields 2012

Bank	Stock code	Dividend yield 2012
Commonwealth Bank	CBA	5.6%
Westpac	WBC	6.7%
ANZ Bank	ANZ	6.0%
NAB	NAB	6.9%

The table in Figure 6.3 shows the strength of the dividend payments from Australia's major banks as at August 2012. Naturally dividend yields vary over time depending on the dividends announced and paid, and the market capitalisation of the banks. The important point to note here is that the banking sector as a whole as at August 2012 yields high dividends on average as compared to a market average yield of 5.3%. This means that the banks are good investments for those with a focus of receiving a solid income from their shares, which is a strong strategy in uncertain times.[4]

Of course, there is a second dimension to consider when balancing returns on bank shares, being the potential for capital growth. As noted in Figure 6.2, the price-to-book valuations (i.e. the value of share prices as compared to the value of net assets on the company balance sheets) of the banks are presently fairly high as compared to elsewhere in the world. Therefore, it might be reasonable to suggest that although dividends will continue to be healthy from the banks, the immediate outlook and prospects for capital growth are less clear, particularly after stock valuations experienced very significant run-up from June 2012 through to the middle of 2013.

One matter which should be taken into consideration when considering the banks is the implicit guarantee which the major banks receive from the government, which ensures that should one of the major banks become insolvent it will be bailed out, ultimately by the taxpayers.

This fact in itself can lead to the major banks becoming bigger for they become able to wield huge borrowing power as counter-parties are comforted by the guarantees and are more inclined to take on risk in the knowledge that their downsides are protected. Indeed, aiming to become larger actually reinforces that the institution becomes too big to fail!

> The major banks receive an implicit guarantee
> from the government.

Those with a passing interest in economic history will know that Karl Marx and Joseph Schumpeter spoke of 'creative destruction' or 'Schumpeter's gale' in a capitalist economy. The term was later twisted a little by free-market economists who argued that just as species need to adapt and thrive through survival of the fittest, so it should be for companies in a capitalist system.

Well, it is not so today. In 2008, Kevin Rudd's government announced a ban on short-selling, ostensibly to shore up the wider stock market, but there was more than a little suspicion around at the time that the measure was taken in support of Macquarie Bank's ailing fortunes. This suggested that the implicit guarantee might run even wider than the four major banks. Recent times in the US have shown that government guarantees need not even be restricted to financial institutions, with the bailout of the failed company, General Motors.

At the time of writing, the major banks have sustained a sharp run-up in prices through to the middle of 2013 and maintained PE ratios of around 15 (for more information on PE ratios refer to Chapter 26), so it might be argued that on an earnings basis and given the strength of the dividend payments the banks only offer reasonable value for the long term.[5] It is probably the case that the strength of the Australian dollar in recent times has discouraged investors from overseas in the Australian stock market, and therefore stock market valuations have not recovered from the financial crisis of 2008-2010 anywhere near as quickly as those in the US, for example, although they went on a very good run from the second half of 2012.

Mortgages

Mortgages are a key component of successful property investment.

In the world of property investing the banks often represent a lifeline. Only a relatively low percentage of people today would be able to buy property at all were it not for the banks putting up a significant portion of the capital.

Choose a lender

When taking out a mortgage there are a number of key decisions to be made. Firstly, you must choose a lender. As noted, there are four major banks in Australia and these institutions presently carve up around 80% of the new mortgage loan market in this country.

However, you are by no means compelled to take out a mortgage with any of the main banks — you can look elsewhere to other lenders who at times may offer lower interest rates. When choosing a lender it makes sense to check the credit rating of the bank in question. Although credit ratings have at times proved to be of little or no use, such as in the US during the financial crisis, they should at least offer some guideline as to the creditworthiness of the institution in question.

Choose a lending product

The second major decision is to choose the lending product which will determine the interest rate we pay on the loan and whether the loan is a principal and interest loan or an interest only loan. This can be an intimidating process if you have not undertaken it before and therefore engaging a mortgage broker could well be a smart move. Mortgage brokers may not charge you fees directly instead earning commissions from the lenders, but you should be aware of what commissions a broker stands to earn so that he or she does not push you towards an inappropriate loan product.

A principal and interest loan is usually taken out for purchases of a principal place of residence (PPOR) as owner occupiers normally want to get a mortgage paid off. If you are living in a PPOR then the interest repayments on the mortgage will not attract a tax deduction and therefore the mortgage may be seen as 'bad debt' — that is, debt to be paid down as quickly as possible.

Partly due to the tax treatment, interest only loans tend to suit property investors more than homeowners.

A property investor might, on the other hand, decide to take out an interest only loan which has the strong benefit of significantly lower monthly repayments. Naturally the downside to this is that the loan does not get paid off. Of course, it is down to personal choice when it comes to choosing the type of loan you want, but in general interest only loans are useful to property investors because they are easier to service than principal and interest loans.

If a property investor intends to refinance a mortgage when a property has increased in value in order to buy more properties then an interest only loan makes sense, for there is something curiously circular about paying down a mortgage only to redraw it again. If interest rates become very high then you may feel that paying down a mortgage represents a smarter move than investing your capital elsewhere, in which case there are interest only loan products that allow the investor to pay down lump sum amounts off the principal.

The concept of the interest only loan scares some people, as they worry whether they will ever own the property outright. It entails a paradigm shift but the way smart investors look at interest only loans is to consider what the property might be worth at the end of loan period. Consider the example of my wife's first house which was originally bought for £72,000 in 1997 — even after only 15 years of the mortgage term the property is worth around four times the purchase price, and consequently the mortgage balance now feels immaterial, although it clearly was not so at the time of purchase.

Choose a fixed or variable rate

The third decision to make is whether to take out a fixed rate mortgage or a variable rate mortgage — or even a combination of both which is the each way bet. As the name suggests the rate you will be charged on a variable rate mortgage varies depending on the prevailing interest rates at the time.

A fixed rate you can lock in for a set period of time, which gives you more certainty over the repayment amounts. In the normal course of circumstances the fixed rate you can lock in could be a little higher than the prevailing variable rate. At various points in time, though, fixed rates may become cheaper than variable rates when the yield curve is inverted (which is a fancy way of saying that the market estimates that the Reserve Bank is likely to reduce interest rates in the near future).

> Fixing rates brings certainty, but sometimes at a cost.

It is very difficult to second guess what will happen to interest rates as they are affected by a vast number of factors including inflation, the strength of the economy and GDP growth, retail sales, unemployment and the strength of the currency, to name but a few.

Therefore, some may consider it to be a mug's game to try to outsmart the banks when it comes to forecasting what will happen to interest rates. In general, I prefer to roll with the punches and accept the variable rates that are on offer. At times, when the economy is struggling a little, interest rates may run lower and therefore our repayments become cheap. At other times, the economy and inflation may be stronger and therefore interest rates will be increased to cool sentiment and inflation, and our repayments will then become higher. The compensating good news for property investors is that sometimes the higher interest rates will be reflective of a preceding period of dwelling price growth.

However, as I have multiple mortgages on investment properties, having all variable rate mortgages would leave me a little exposed if interest rates went very high, and for this reason I do also have some fixed rates too. There are three important criteria for when you should consider fixing a loan, which are:

- Banks are competing for mortgage business on interest rates

- Fixed rates are available below the variable rate

- Interest rates are forecast to fall

As a rule of thumb you should not fix for more than three years as this reduces the risk of interest rates plummeting and you being left fully exposed to a higher fixed rate. A safer approach is to fix only 50% of your mortgage balance.

Mortgage insurance

When you take out a mortgage from a bank but you have a deposit which is lower than 20% of the property value you may be charged Lender's Mortgage Insurance (LMI), though some banks may waiver the LMI if you can stump up a 15% deposit.

Do not be deceived by the name — the insurance is on behalf of the lender to compensate for you being a riskier customer (due to you not having a 20% deposit) and does not benefit you as the property purchaser at all. You may be able to capitalise the LMI into the mortgage balance and as such may not have to pay it immediately in cash, however this obviously increases your mortgage balance — and therefore this strategy reduces your equity and increases your interest payments.

Deposits

The deposit you need to buy a property varies depending on the prevailing risk appetite of the lenders. As I write this it may be possible in Australia to buy a property with a 5% or a 10% deposit. Over in the UK the banks still remain relatively risk averse following the collapse of Northern Rock, and are often insisting on higher deposits (which has removed many buyers from the market). In headier days 100% mortgages may again become available in Australia and therefore it may be possible to buy property with no deposit at all, though where this is the case expect the LMI to be steep, perhaps as much as $20,000 in the case of a $500,000 property.

Margin loans

Investors have the option to buy shares in the banks. Conversely investors can also use the bank's capital to help buy more shares in the form of a margin loan, which is another form of investment lending. Share prices tend to be more volatile than property prices and for this reason share investment is perceived to be riskier than property investment (this is not necessarily the case — moreover, it depends on the skills and strategies of the investor).

Consequently, you can expect margin loans to charge interest that is higher than the equivalent interest rate for a mortgage on a residential property. Products vary depending on the lender, the prevailing cash interest rates and economic climate, but currently at the time of writing you might expect to pay somewhere close to 10% interest on a margin loan, though perhaps a little lower.

So are margin loans a good thing? Well, I am not going to say that you shouldn't use margin loans because I use them myself and therefore I would be hypocritical! However, I am a little ambivalent as to their value for the average investor. Bear in mind that although the negative gearing rules which provide tax benefits to some of those who borrow to invest are handy, if you take out a margin loan to buy shares you still must consider how you are going to generate a return high enough to beat the loan interest charge.

> Using a moderate level of debt to invest in the share markets may be not a bad thing.

One analogy that might be used is that even the most successful cash-generating companies and investors use a moderate level of debt in order to magnify their returns and therefore as an individual we might elect to do the same. The key word here is *moderate*. Using margin loans extensively and beyond our means is a bad idea and can lead to substantial loss. Due to the inherently volatile nature of share prices, if the market takes a downward turn a lender is likely to issue you with a margin call which could result in you having to sell shares at the most inopportune moment. This is how investors in shares can end up taking a painful capital loss.

A curious characteristic of margin loans is that they can be ramped up sharply by using newly acquired shares to acquire further shares. So if, for example, you buy shares in BHP Billiton (BHP) using a margin loan, the new BHP shares you own can be used as collateral to take out a further loan. The risk inherent in this strategy is that if the market tanks, then you may be forced to sell shares at unattractive prices in order to meet the forthcoming margin call.

If margin loans are used moderately, they can help to magnify returns. You should be looking to invest in companies that pay healthy dividend income as this will to some extent offset the pain of the margin loan interest. Then, if you have avoided buying into shares when they are too expensive we should over time see share prices move in an upward trend. The margin loan allows the investor to hold more shares than he or she would otherwise have been able to do and thus increases returns.

CFDs

Contracts for difference (CFDs) are discussed in Chapter 24, but are briefly mentioned here as they represent another form of leverage for investing. Due to the very high leverage that is employed using CFDs and the high level of interest charged, CFDs are generally only appropriate for trading rather than investing. Most average investors would be wise to steer well clear of CFDs until they have mastered the basics of trading.

Lines of credit

I am often asked to explain what a line of credit actually is. In life, we tend to understand matters when we can compare them to other matters with which we are familiar, and in this context I liken a line of credit to a credit card.

A little like a credit card, a line of credit does not necessarily give you a huge injection of funds (as a personal loan might). Instead, you draw upon a line of credit when you need it to pay for something which you cannot afford to pay for today. Thus you only begin to pay interest on the amount used. While credit cards tend to charge a high rate of interest, lines of credit charge much lower interest rates and therefore can sometimes be appropriate tools for drawing upon for investment purposes. Naturally if you use a line of credit for living costs rather than for investment, any interest charged thereupon will not attract a tax deduction.

Credit card debt

Many years ago now I came across the below idea, but I have now forgotten where I read it, so I hereby would like to apologise to the author of the finance or investment book which I have borrowed this concept from:

Author: Do you want to hear about a sure-fire investment I can recommend to you?
Friend: A sure-fire investment? You bet! Tell me more ...

Author: Well, it's a guaranteed winner, a gilt-edged investment that will return you a certain 20%+ per annum, with absolutely no risk of loss.
Friend: I'm on it. Just tell me where to invest!

Author: OK, here it is, so listen up close. Are you ready for this hot tip? Pay off your credit card.

OK, so the conversation transcribed above might be a little silly but the principle of it is absolutely correct. I know of people who have $20,000 sitting idle in a low-interest savings account but a near-permanent $20,000 in credit card debt attracting 20% or more per annum in interest charges. I understand why psychologically people prefer to do this, but from a purely financial point of view it makes no sense whatsoever.

Earlier in the book I referenced the idea of compound growth and how over time compounding interest can begin to build us serious wealth. Unfortunately compounding also works in reverse. For example, if we stuff cash under our mattress, it will become worth comparatively less each year as inflation takes its toll. Similarly, if we leave credit cards in an overdrawn position the interest charges mount up and compounding interest begins to work against us rather than for us.

As property investors we are cognisant that price inflation can represent a transfer of wealth from the lender to the borrower. Theoretically, you could say that the same applies to credit card debt as to mortgage debt. However, banks recognise this and charge giant premiums for debts held on credit card, even if the initial teaser rate is low. Start with your most expensive bad debt and resolve to pay it down relentlessly!

It is very rare that I feel moved to make predictions that are too specific for the potential to end up with egg on one's face can be great. However, I am going to stick my neck out on this subject. Through 2012 a number of articles surfaced which suggested that Australians have fallen out of love with debt and that Australia is in for a sustained period of deleveraging.[6]

The theory is that Australians have become sensible and going forward are likely to eschew credit card debt in a new general spirit of thrift? Not in the universe I'm living in, they won't be! Briefly, here are my three reasons for predicting that over the coming decades credit card debt will escalate to levels of misuse we cannot even contemplate today.

Credit card abuse, reason 1 — Trusting my instincts

As an inhabitant of Sydney CBD, over the second half of 2012 I began to witness the return of consumers to the shopping malls (if indeed they ever went away), particularly when Apple and Samsung released new products and queues could be seen stretching for hundreds of metres. I feel that rising retail trade figures will eventually begin to back me up here. I suspect that here has been mistaken an episode (short-lived uncertainty leading to prudence) for a trend.

Credit card abuse, reason 2 — Short memories

People today have short memories and become fatigued very easily. If my instincts are correct, Australians are already growing weary of saving and are moving back towards rampant consumerism again.

Credit card abuse, reason 3 — Human nature

As humans, we tend to let matters run to crisis or epidemic levels before considering that we might need to address problems. Do I need to list some examples? Rainforests, carbon emissions and global warming, over-population, sub-prime debt, the Cold War and nuclear weaponry … the potential list is almost endless.

I believe that something similar will also happen with credit card debt. We have 'normalised' credit cards. It is now apparently OK to run our finances in permanent consumer debt. Even teenagers can be furnished with multiple plastic cards these days. A new era of thrift and sensible personal finance? I don't think so — and although it's increasingly rare to hear anyone use this phrase these days: 'Sorry, I'm just not buying it.'

Chapter 6 Summary

- The Reserve Bank's monetary policy with regards to interest rates plays a key role in affecting the confidence and direction of the housing market

- Buying shares in the banks can generate strong dividends; the outlook for capital growth in the near-term is less clear

- The major banks have great exposure to residential property — although they receive an implicit guarantee from the government, consider diversification

- Pay off your credit cards and other bad debts as soon as possible for a guaranteed return

- Sensible and moderate use of margin loans can help to magnify returns for share investors

- Mortgages on properties are intended to run for decades — take some time to ensure that you get the right loan product for you

- CFDs are dangerous products in the hands of the inexperienced and are better left to experienced traders

- A line of credit can be used to borrow against the increased value of a property, but moderation is again paramount

7
MANAGING
RISK

7

As your wealth increases, your appetite for risk tends to decrease. While peers, friends or family may be inclined to say that any success you may have can be attributed to luck, it is the case that the more you commit to learning, the luckier you appear to become.

> If you don't take a chance, you don't stand a chance.

Chance cards

There are 16 Chance cards in a game of Monopoly and, as the name implies, the outcome from picking a card is inherently uncertain. Most of the cards — 10 of them — dictate that a player moves to another square. Thus a Chance card earlier in the game is likely to be a good thing as it may give the player an opportunity to purchase a vacant title.

Chance does have a role to play, but by making a commitment to always improve and to learn from mistakes, applying discipline and patience, the role of chance can certainly be diminished. In life, it is usually more important how you respond to events than what actually happens to you.

Eliminating the ten major property investment risks

While chance will always have a role to play in investment, experienced investors are able to manage the risks. There a number of risks to be managed in investment. Below, I look at ten of them in turn and specifically how they might apply to Australian property investors.

Investment risk 1 — Market risk (or systematic risk)

Market risk may affect all investments of an asset class in a similar manner, such as in the event of a market-wide price crash, and as such is a risk that cannot easily be mitigated through diversification. While buying properties in different states might diversify market risk to a partial extent, if the wider property market crashes diversification is unlikely to assuage systematic risk successfully.

Property investors should additionally consider investing in other asset classes which tend to move in a non-correlated manner to real estate. Property investors can also focus upon a longer investment time horizon which allows correcting markets greater opportunity to recover.

Investment risk 2 — Liquidity risk

Equates to the possibility that an investor may be unable to buy or sell an investment when desired (or in sufficient quantities) due to limited opportunities. Illiquidity is a salient risk in real estate. It is difficult to sell a property quickly should the need arise, which is not the case for large cap stocks or government bonds. Liquidity risk in Australian property is best mitigated through investing in landlocked capital city suburbs with eminent demand and constrained supply.

Investment risk 3 — Specific risk (unsystematic or business risk)

Equities investors and fund managers talk much of specific or business risk, being the measure of risk associated with a particular stock or security. Also known as unsystematic risk, this typically refers to the risk associated with a specific issuer of a security. Businesses in the same industry may have similar types of business risk. The issuer of a stock or a bond may become insolvent or lack ability to pay the interest or principal in the case of bonds.

Specific risk in property investment is somewhat different, and rather relates to the risk of acquiring a loss-making property or one which delivers sub-optimal returns giving rise to opportunity cost. Specific risk can be mitigated through diversification, although this can represent a challenging proposition in property as dwellings tend to be expensive.

A frequently invoked strategy of property investors is to acquire different types of property in different states. Careful, detailed due diligence and research of any property purchase also tends to reduce (if not eliminate) specific risk.

Investment risk 4 — Interest rate risk

Interest rate risk normally refers to the possibility that a fixed-rate debt instrument will decline in value as a result of a rise in interest rates. Where an investor buys a security offering a fixed rate of return, they introduce an exposure to interest rate risk, examples thereof including bonds and preference shares (preferred stocks).

In Australian investment property, the interest rate risk instead lies in variable rate mortgages as the cost of capital can materially increase when the Reserve Bank ratchets up the cash rate. The risk can be mitigated through the use of fixed rate mortgages and prudent cash flow management.

Investment risk 5 — Foreign exchange risk (or currency risk)

Foreign exchange risk arises from a movement in the price of one currency against another. When the Australian dollar appreciates the value of foreign-held investments declines. Conversely, if the dollar weakens the value of foreign investments effectively increase.

Presently the strong Australian dollar attracts investors to overseas investments, in particular to US real estate. Is this a good strategy? Perhaps, as our dollar may eventually depreciate and some US property markets have corrected. But is there a foreign exchange risk in investing overseas? Absolutely, for exchange rates are inherently unpredictable. Few commentators in 2008 opined that the Aussie dollar could ever be worth 110 US cents, and yet it indeed became so.

Currency risk tends to be greater for shorter term overseas investments, which have insufficient time to revert to a mean valuation in the same manner as longer term equivalent ventures.

Investment risk 6 — Sovereign risk (or social/political/legislative risk)

Sovereign risk is associated with the possibility of unfavourable government action or social upheaval resulting in investment loss. Governments retain the power to amend laws affecting investments, and rulings which result in an adverse investment outcome are representative of legislative risk. One frequently highlighted legislation risk in Australian property investment is the possible phasing out of the negative gearing tax rules.

Investing in developing or unstable countries variously offers opportunities for substantial returns but, reflecting the risk-return trade-off principles (of the CAPM model) may bring a heightened associated sovereign risk.

Investment risk 7 — Credit risk

In investment, credit risk normally refers to the possibility that a bond issuer becomes unable to service expected interest rate payments or a principal repayment. Typically, the higher the credit risk is, the higher the interest rate on the bond.

In property investment credit risk often lies in the investor rather than the lender, although there is of course a possibility that lending institutions can become insolvent as was seen in the US during the subprime crisis of 2007-2009. Property investors should retain a liquid buffer in order to mitigate the risk of mortgage default.

Investment risk 8 — Call risk

Call risk also usually refers to bond issues and the possibility that a debt security will be 'called' prior to maturity. In bonds, call risk prevails when interest rates fall, as companies redeem bond issues with higher coupons and replace them on the bond market with lower interest rate issues to save cash.

Can call risk impact Australian property investors? Yes, but conversely when interest rates run higher. Investors with high exposure to adverse interest rate movements may cyclically be considered risky by mortgage providers. Investors in Australian commercial property have periodically been known to be subjected to the real estate equivalent of a margin call, being forced to reduce debt exposure through the redemption of assets.

Investment risk 9 — Reinvestment risk

Reinvestment risk usually refers to the risk that future coupons from a fixed-interest investment will not be reinvested at the interest rate prevailing when it was initially purchased, which is more likely when interest rates are declining. Zero coupon bonds are the only fixed-income instrument to eliminate reinvestment risk due to having no interim coupon payments. The most straightforward way for property investors to avert reinvestment risk is simple: never sell.

Investment risk 10 — Inflation risk

Also known as purchasing power risk, the possibility that the value of an asset or income stream will be eroded as inflation diminishes the value of a currency. The risk is the potential for future inflation to cause the purchasing power of cash inflows from an investment to decline.

Inflation risk is best countered through investing in appreciating assets, such as real estate, dividend paying stocks or convertible bonds, each of which has a growth component allowing them to outperform inflation over the long term. The good news for property investors is that favourably-located Australian real estate has long been recognised as a tremendously effective inflation hedge over time.

Speculating versus investing

What is the difference between speculating and investing? It is never entirely clear for it depends on our definitions. Benjamin Graham took some time and space in his book *The Intelligent Investor* to define what he believed to be a worthy definition of investment.[1] Graham believed that there should be some level of certainty around the return of the investor's capital and a worthwhile percentage return to compensate for having made the investment.

Dedicated share investors would say that if they are focusing on the dividend or income stream and holding for the long term they are definitely investors, while anyone who is focussing exclusively on share price action is clearly a speculator. The time horizon must surely have a role to play in the respective definitions. If you are entering a trade for a time period shorter than a few years then it is likely that speculation is the order of the day as you are relying on asset prices moving in your favour.

Indeed, some would go further than this and say that any transaction where you are reliant upon selling for more than you bought for is price speculation (as would be the case if, for example, you were buying antiques, vintage cars or gold) and should be known as participating in the greater fool theory. That is to say that hopefully one day a greater fool than you will come along and pay you more for the asset than you paid yourself.

> Investors tend to focus more on income and speculators more on capital growth.

Under this definition, therefore, property investment might instead generally be termed as property speculation. In fact, when property markets are increasing in price investors are labelled with all manner of derogatory terms: 'rent seekers', 'evil specufestors', 'debt-funded suckers' and much worse. So be it. Property ownership has been a part of the world for millennia and no modern capitalist system would operate in the same way without it. Investors take comfort in the fact that over the long term property prices do increase. More than this, over the long term property becomes an income asset too as rents increase, thus providing two dimensional returns (income and growth) in a similar manner to shares.

Indeed, the only reason why property does not provide income and growth immediately after purchase is because investors tend to borrow substantially in order to purchase. If you buy a property for cash, it pays you rent and delivers growth, just as for shares. But it is the very fact that property investors do use leverage and hold for the long term for compounding growth which means that they usually finish at the head of the pack.

Returns should be measured on a risk-adjusted basis.

When you see in magazines which asset classes are deemed to produce the highest returns, you may see global bonds at the top of the list, then international equities, then Australian equities and Australian property, before the fixed interest investments and cash. What these charts can sometimes overlook is that firstly, the returns are not adjusted for risk — global bonds have sometimes been returning high yields precisely because of the perceived risk of default which the average investor is ill-equipped to assess.

Secondly, while property may have returned less in percentage terms it has tended to be a less volatile and less risky asset class, and due to the leverage that homeowners and investors employ, they tend to finish far ahead of most average share investors over the long term. Of course, I have played this argument out with shares-only investors many times. I invest in shares myself but still I believe that for the average investor, the best chance of achieving financial freedom before the retirement age is to invest counter-cyclically in residential investment property — and hold on to your investments!

For the average investor, the best chance of achieving financial freedom is to invest counter-cyclically in residential investment property for the long term.

Share investors will claim to the bitter end that equities are the only productive asset class, the only asset class that adds real value and the only asset class that truly offers income and growth. They prefer to overlook that stock market crashes can be incredibly painful for investors, and while investors know that theoretically they might elect to hold on as prices will return to growth over the long term, the reality is that many bail at the worst possible moment, being the market's nadir. It is great in theory to focus on only dividends and operating results, but in practice watching your portfolio halve in value is felt by any investor, regardless of experience.

When I point out that my wife and I own property bought more than a decade-and-a-half ago that has provided not only huge capital growth and generates and enormous positive cash flow, the pro-equities response is: 'Well, prices are going to crash soon so enjoy it while it lasts'. This is ironic, really, as they were also saying that before the global financial crisis and prices did indeed crash — but it was those of shares rather than property which tanked in Australia! Thus it was those employing the buy, hold and focus on the income stream approach who saw their net worth absolutely crucified by around 50%.

From my perspective, over the long term both property and shares represent fabulous asset classes, but if you are in property for the long run, the power of leverage will see this asset class generate the higher returns. While property may seem expensive when you are buying it, the reality is that decades into the future the mortgage held against the property can seem relatively trivial as property values continue to forge ahead driven by household income growth.

Generational attitudes to risk and investing (and what we can learn from them)

'Everyone thinks of changing the world, but no-one thinks of changing himself.' — Leo Tolstoy

It's an interesting quote. If you stop to think about it, the world is going to change whether we like it or not. It always has done, and it always will. The key question is whether we can learn from the changes of the past to make for a better future.

Wartime generation

The wartime generation lived through times of great uncertainty and high inflation. People tended to be family-focussed and had many admirable attitudes. Folk showed spirit in the face of adversity, did not air their dirty washing in public, they had a make-do-and-mend attitude and frowned upon the idea of instant gratification.

Most tended to live within their means and frugality was the order of the day. They believed in the old adage: 'Neither a borrower nor a lender be'. The wartime generation were confident in themselves but mistrusting of authority. People 'knew their place' and in times of such instability, were perhaps unlikely to invest for the uncertain future.

Baby Boomers

The Baby Boomers are known as society's bottleneck — there are just so many of them aiming for the same place! The Boomers tended to want prestigious job titles and the corner office. The idea of a job-for-life was still pervasive and switching careers was far less common. The Baby Boomers were also known for having more freedom. They were sometimes hedonistic and, some of them at least, had great social skills. But there was also a live-for-today attitude. Baby Boomers had seen parents and friends die in wars. People became less afraid of debt.

As a toddler back in England in 1982, I can remember the adverts for *Access* credit cards becoming ubiquitous — 'your flexible friend!' — I was too young to understand what it all meant, but they certainly seemed to be friendly little characters, didn't they? Rampant consumerism boomed and reigned supreme. Car loans became perfectly normal too. After all, why should you save for something when you can have it today?

Governments, by and large, have taken a similar viewpoint, taking on huge debt to pay for wars, pensions and social security. The Welfare State is generally regarded to have emerged at the end of World War II in 1945, to reflect the findings of Beveridge's 1942 report in the UK which idealised security from cradle to the grave.

The Baby Boomers were inexperienced and largely uneducated as investors. Some bought shares as part of government privatisations of utility companies (in the UK, this meant British Gas and British Telecom) in the 1980s, but most investors had portfolios that comprised of their house, shares in one or two privatised floats and nothing else. It was all about the pension.

Generation X

Today the pension system has radically changed. With people living longer, the generous defined benefit pension schemes are largely a thing of the past for Generation X. Today, we have defined contribution or accumulation funds. What this means is that it is up to us whether our pension balance is healthy enough at the date of retirement, and not our employers.

What else has changed? Well, today women can do it all too. Women can be the top business people and the best investors if they so wish. Half of the human race need no longer hit upon a glass ceiling in their careers, though some would certainly argue that women have had to strive for greater excellence to achieve the same goals as men.

Generation X-ers want more freedom and often the freedom from being controlled by a boss. Many of us had distant parents and are often unsure as to whether to have children ourselves. What Generation X-ers definitely need to learn is that superannuation funds and the Age Pension are unlikely in themselves to provide for a wealthy retirement. We need to take control of our own destiny.

The Census of 2011 showed that we are also less likely to identify with any one religion than those of decades gone by, although we are not necessarily any less spiritual. Charitable giving is still seen to be a worthy endeavour, though, interestingly, perhaps a little less so in Australia than elsewhere (I believe that this is changing as we mature as a country).

Generation Y and the Millennials

Generation Y and the Millennials — those entering the workforce today — are far more technically savvy than any generation has ever been before. The younger generations often have great self-belief and little fear. Information flows fast, people become famous and infamous overnight (and they often want to be), and people can change jobs even faster.

Millennials have the spending power (of their own and their parents' money!) to shape the future of world economies. There are more of them than there were Generation X-ers, and they are the largest generation of young people since the Baby Boomers.

Seven lessons that we can we learn from these shifts are:

- We need to **take control**; relying on the pension or our super fund will not be good enough

- Today we can **'better ourselves'**, and the route to doing so is education

- We should learn to live within our means and embrace **delayed gratification**

- A sense of community and **charitable giving or tithing** is a good thing

- Carefully managed, serviceable **debt for investment** is not to be feared — indeed it can be greatly beneficial to the smart investor

- The world is a smaller place and a **more fluid place** (for example, we can invest in overseas shares and emerging markets for diversification, or we can easily invest in investment properties in another state that is slated for capital growth)

- Freedom of access to the internet, libraries and bookstores, if well used, can **educate** us and provide the tools for us all to invest safely and successfully

Life was no easier for earlier generations

It seems to be commonplace for people of today to complain that property prices are outlandishly high as compared to decades gone by. In dollar terms, this is unequivocally true. However, it is worth considering whether taking an attitude that life was far easier for generations before us, is to some extent both unhelpful and misguided.

Although property prices may have been cheaper in earlier decades, other dynamics existed which meant that life was by no means far easier for the Baby Boomer generation and those who preceded them. Of course, house price to income ratios were lower in the 1980s than they are today, as banks were far less inclined in decades gone by to lend more than three times an annual income for a property.

However, a number of factors have conspired to fuel the growth in dwelling prices. Incomes have grown strongly and there are a far more dual-income households today than was the case in the 1980s. In fact, females make up a significantly higher percentage of the workforce than was the case just a few decades ago (around 60% in 2011 as compared to just 46% in 1978).[2] And further, interest rates are significantly lower today than they were in the more inflationary 1970s and 1980s. Lower interest rates led to a material but not totally irrational increase in household debt as repayments became more serviceable.

There are a number of observations to make here. One is that it is unfortunately more difficult to save a deposit today than in earlier decades, simply because house prices are higher, though at various stages of the property cycle sometimes no deposit may be required by financiers. However, although it seems to be very fashionable to talk of how it is impossible to get on to the property ladder today, I would suggest that it is incorrect to believe that your parents' generation invariably had life much easier than you did. For one thing, they had unpredictable and volatile higher interest rates (and thus high repayments) to deal with.

Saving a deposit today can be very difficult.

In fact, a useful exercise would perhaps be to ask people who are 30 years older than you are if life and mortgage payments were always easy for them in their earlier years and note their responses! I would be interested to hear some of the replies.

I also believe that it is very important to take note of the language that we feed to our brains. If we say that something is impossible then unconsciously we are unlikely to commit to achieving the goal as we do not believe we will achieve it — then failure becomes all but guaranteed. If getting on the property ladder seems difficult, we may need to be more creative by perhaps buying jointly with another party, using a parent as guarantor for the loan or investing in a cheaper suburb or state which is within our range.

Of course, those who are bearish on house prices will point out that this is inappropriate and we should not fuel ever-increasing property prices. Ultimately, you have two choices here. One is to sit and wait for property in Australia to become cheap in spite of the population increasing by significantly more than 350,000 people with each passing year, as inflation and household income growth continue to push the capacity to service household debt higher.

The other option is to find a way to start investing and securing your financial future. While nobody can say for certain what will happen to property values over the next one, two or five years, we can be absolutely certain that in thirty years' time property values and rents will be far higher in dollar terms than they are today. As a property investor that is exactly what you should be focussing on, rather than short-term scaremongering.

By acquiring proven quality assets and holding on them indefinitely we limit the opportunities we allow ourselves to make rash or sub-optimal investment decisions. This approach is at the other end of the risk spectrum from the high-frequency share trader whose emotions can run high and has the potential to make materially damaging investment decisions on a daily or even hourly basis.

Chapter 7 Summary

- While chance does play a part in investment, by building a sound plan for the long term we can reduce the impact of luck dramatically

- The route to financial success is through education and action

- We should all have the discipline to live within our means

- There are risks in all investment asset classes but these can be mitigated through education and understanding of the risks

- The pension system has changed, it is now for us to take control of our own financial future; relying on your employer, your fund manager or the Government is not good enough

8
KEEPING IT
LEGAL

8

Play by the rules

One more very short but important Chapter before we dive into how and where to invest in property.

When it comes to wealth creation and investing we should always play by the rules and not be tempted to bend them. It is too easy to create wealth legally over the long term so why bother taking risks and shortcuts? I have known people who fiddle their tax returns by a few hundred dollars here and there in order to take shortcuts, but from my perspective it simply is not worth it. It also seems to be the case that those who start out taking short-cuts find that due to reinforcement of their behaviour (i.e. not being caught or investigated) they may be inclined to take greater risks later.

Go to Gaol!

In the board game of Monopoly you can be sent to gaol purely through bad luck, by landing on a wrong square. If you do so, you will be directed to go directly to gaol, and you are not to pass the *GO* square or collect $200 salary. You can also be sent to gaol for rolling three consecutive doubles with the dice. Due to these factors, the *Gaol* square is the busiest on the Monopoly board. Gaol is a hefty punishment in the early part of the game, for your fellow players will continue to collect properties and move further ahead in the game as they travel around the board, while you must sit helplessly in the cell.

In Australia, we have all heard of the bad boys who decided that they would not play by the rules and who ended up paying for their crimes in various ways, such as Christopher Skase, Rodney Adler or Rene Rivkin. Successful investors do not feel compelled to bend the rules. The one area where it seems that people on occasion do feel the need to take short-cuts is with their tax returns. I suspect this is because with certain types of expenditure there is a bit of a grey area as to what constitutes a genuine deductible expense.

There is no point in taking shortcuts — better to know
the rules of the game and play by them fairly.

It is illegal to underestimate your tax liabilities, it is unethical and the small amount of tax that you might save is in no way worth the risk of the possible consequences. It is far too easy to build assets and income sensibly and securely for the long term, so why bother bending the rules?

Insider trading

It is a phrase you might hear often in the press, but what actually is insider trading? Insider trading is defined as the illegal practice of trading on the stock exchange to your own advantage through having access to confidential information. Insider trading is illegal and the penalties if you are caught can be extremely severe, so therefore it shouldn't happen much, right? Do me a favour! Whatever anyone may tell you, insider trading is happening in our stock market every trading day, without fail.

You can be prosecuted for insider trading if the prosecution can prove that:

- You possess information on a stock (or other financial instrument) that could have a material effect on it

- You are aware or should be aware that this information is not generally available

- You then trade the stock or tell someone else about the information in the knowledge that they will then trade.

We should all be aware that insider trading is illegal, so how might it happen?

- You work for a company and buy shares or advise others in the knowledge of a forthcoming project, opportunity or other news (I've seen this happen more times than I can relate)

- You work as an accountant or lawyer and hear of opportunities for a company (or that a company has a major problem such as debt restructuring)

- Somebody working within a company tells you inside information to which you should not be privy, the information not being publicly available.

Does insider trading happen much?

You bet it does! It is my opinion that insider trading is absolutely rife in Australia. If you ever play with stocks down at the small cap end of the market you will see seemingly inexplicable stock price movements which miraculously seem to precede market sensitive news. Of course, it is often incredibly difficult to prove insider trading or wrong-doing, and it is also often a fine line between, for example, a broker trying to gain an edge by asking a company for information and trading on market-sensitive inside information illegally.

It may not be always completely clear to you whether you are acting within the law. A good rule of thumb is that if you are ever in doubt, steer clear from trading stocks where you have information that may not be generally available or disclosed to the stock market.

Hedonistic behaviour

This small section of the book may of little or no relevance to you, so do feel free to skip it if you wish. I feel that if these two paragraphs help one person to steer themselves away from the trap that I fell into than they will have been a worthwhile inclusion. In countries such as Australia and the UK we have a culture which often actively encourages binge drinking, smoking, gambling and at times the taking of illegal drugs too.

As alcohol, tobacco and punting are all legal there is sometimes a tendency to see them as less damaging addictions than those which are banned by the law, yet often they can have as dramatic an adverse effect on the quality of people's lives.

The best investors are controlled individuals!

This is relevant to investment because it is very commonly the case that those who drink to excess regularly, gamble or frequently abuse other substances have shambolic personal finances – the link can be surprisingly direct. Be mindful!

Ethics in investing

Whichever asset class you choose to invest in, you must do so in harmony with your ethics. If you invest in shares, consider whether there are certain industries which you will not invest in. Nobody can make this decision for you, for it is a personal one. As a property investor I won't ever let a property that I would not be prepared to live in myself. I know that others don't agree with me on this, but I believe in karma. I also believe that whichever field you are operating in the way to create value for yourself is first to add value for others. Give and thou shalt receive!

Successful people tend to operate consistently in harmony with their own ethics and values.

Tenants tend to respond well to being treated well. I've never had a significant vacancy or malicious damage in any of the properties I've ever owned, and hopefully I never will. Sure I could have saved myself a few bob over the years by spending a little less on repairs and maintenance, but cutting corners in that regards is just not the way I play it. I always say yes to any sensible request for repairs and in exchange tenants have always paid their rent on time without exception. That is what is known as a win-win deal.

Regarding ethics in equities, I prefer to invest in ethical index funds. I am also considering whether to stop investing in mining companies going forward as I don't believe it is a terribly ethical industry — it is an admittedly difficult dilemma though as I hold shares in mining companies that are cash-generating machines.

An ethical index fund generally will avoid investing in companies that are involved in, for example, munitions, alcohol or gambling and the results can diverge somewhat from the wider index (companies which operate in industries such as gambling are often protected from new entrants but must also comply with tough legislation). You have to make your own decisions on such matters.

An ethical index fund may not perform at exactly the same rate as the XJO index (in many instances they have performed better but this will not always be the case, especially as 'unethical' industries are often heavily regulated and thus protected from new competitors), but we all have our own rules and codes of conduct. Ultimately, it is up to you to decide.

OK, that's enough theory. Let's now crack on with how exactly and where to invest your capital!

Chapter 8 Summary

- Learn the rules, the taxes and the law — in particular consider reading Michael Yardney's *What Every Property Investor needs to know about Finance, Tax and the Law*

- Play by the rules — do not be tempted to take shortcuts

- It is too easy to build wealth legitimately to make bending the law worthwhile

- You will need to consider your ethics when you invest and work out what is a comfortable strategy for you

Part 2
Investing in Property in Australia

9
PROPERTY INVESTING FOR GROWTH AND CASH FLOW

9

Capital growth and rental returns

What are we really trying to achieve by investing in property? I will assume here that most people invest to make money rather than for the pleasure of being a property owner or landlord. There are two different ways in which we can create wealth through property. Firstly, we can receive money from rent, and secondly the property value can increase. Skilled investors can improve both the rental returns and the property value through renovation.

Pay the Rent!

In Monopoly, individual titles generate a small amount of rent each time the relevant square is landed upon by another player. If all of the titles in a set are owned then the rent can be doubled, or in the case of the stations, increased three-fold. Should the owner of the set then decide to build green houses or ultimately a red hotel on the titles of the set, then the rents can be moved up very sharply indeed. The game often ends where an unfortunate, impecunious player lands upon a title developed with a hotel and is unable to pay the rent as it falls due.

Returns on investment property come in two dimensions:
capital growth (price appreciation) and yield (rental income).

I will discuss here in a little detail the different approaches that are used by investors — those who target capital growth and those who focus on yield in the hope that capital growth will be delivered someday too. Of course, what a smart investor aims for is both capital growth and a strong cash flow.

A handy tool for investors: The rule of 72

The rule of 72 is a handy way of calculating how quickly (or slowly) an asset may double in value given a particular growth rate. The way it works is to divide the number 72 by the expected annual growth rate percentage of the asset. Thus if an asset increases in value by 7.2% per annum then it will take 10 years to double in value (72/7.2 = 10 years). If a stronger growth rate of 9% per annum can be achieved then the asset will double in value in only 8 years (72/9 = 8 years).

Property returns from cash flow

The first element of the return from property is the cash flow. You might often see this measured as a percentage yield, being the annual rent divided by the property value. So a property that is worth $500,000 and generates $25,000 in rent per annum is said to have a 5% gross yield. This helps to assess whether a property is likely to cost us money each year as we can compare the rental yield to the interest rate that we are paying on the mortgage. While property generates rental income, there are expenses and holding costs to pay such as the mortgage repayments, strata fees, repairs costs and property management fees. Where overall income is greater than overall expenses after tax, the property is said to have a positive cash flow.

There has been a long-running debate as to the merits of investing for a positive cash flow or for capital growth. Positive cash flow investors long insisted that a property with even a $5 a week negative cash flow must be spurned and that negative gearing must never be accepted, dedicated capital growth investors (although I do own plenty of positive cash flow properties, if pushed I'd align myself to the capital growth camp, for it is growth that creates wealth) argue that a moderately negative cash flow in the early years of an investment can be acceptable — as rental income is likely to increase over time with inflation.

It is sometimes the case in Australia that the capital growth and the yield of a property can have an inverse relationship — one being strong and the other not — though this is by no means always the case.

> Combine a standard rental income
> with long-term poor growth and you the result
> is higher yields. Combine a normal rental income with
> long-term great growth and the result is ... lower yields!

While nobody could argue against the fact that it would be preferable to have both a positive cash flow and great capital growth, those of us who own property purchased in the 1990s or before were left to question: yes, but what happens to that positive cash flow when interest rates are ratcheted up again? Unless you have fixed your mortgage rate the positive cash flow may become a negative one.

There are usually quite a number of holding costs associated with owning a property such as property management and re-letting fees, unforeseen repairs and the cost of any vacancy periods. Therefore, depending on the size of the deposit paid on the property, whether the mortgage is an interest only product or principal-and-interest loan, the level of depreciation allowances and a number of other factors, the rental yield percentage would probably need to be somewhere close to a couple of per cent higher than the mortgage rate in order for an investment property to be breaking even on an annual basis.

Most average investors do not go into residential property solely with a goal of making big profits from cash flow. If income is your primary goal you may have picked the wrong asset class in residential property and should at least consider whether you might direct more of your attention towards commercial property, shares (which pay dividends) or possibly bonds, which pay a regular and predictable cash flow in the form of interest payments. Property investors should look for properties which will secure them great capital growth over the long term. Strong cash flows will normally eventually follow but later in the life of a long-term investment.

While it is the capital growth which ensures that property is a great investment over the long term, we do not want to acquire assets which will cost us significantly each year in terms of cash flow, and therefore will want to ensure that we pick a property with a reasonable rental yield. We may also opt to pay a larger deposit which minimises the mortgage payments, use interest only loans and undertake some renovation work in order to improve the rental income. In capital cities, apartments or units often generate stronger yields than houses.

In the table in Figure 9.1 below is a numerical example of a property with a strong rental yield of 7%. The capital growth is relatively moderate at 4% per annum. Take a look at what happens to the value of the property and the rental income as the years pass.

Figure 9.1 — Property with a strong cash flow

Year	Property value @ 4% growth p.a. ($)	Rental income @7% yield ($)
0	500,000	35,000
1	520,000	36,400
2	540,800	37,856
3	562,432	39,370
4	584,929	40,945
5	608,326	42,583
6	632,660	44,286
7	657,966	46,058
8	684,285	47,900
9	711,656	49,816
10	740,122	51,809
11	767,727	53,881
12	800,516	56,036
13	832,537	58,278
14	865,838	60,609
15	900,472	63,033
16	936,491	65,554
17	973,950	68,177
18	1,012,908	70,904
19	1,053,425	73,740
20	**1,095,962**	**76,689**

By using the rule of 72, we can calculate that a property takes 18 years to double in value at 4% compounding capital growth (72/4 = 18) and indeed the table above does show that the property has doubled in market value after 18 years to a price of more than $1 million. The rental income increases over time too, so a property with a 7% yield will be generating a very healthy cash flow for the investor over the long term.

Budding property investors often ask me how high a yield is needed in order to generate a positive cash flow. There is no absolute answer to that question, for it depends upon so many factors. These include the quantum of available depreciation allowances, the percentage deposit you intend to pay, whether your proposed mortgage is interest only or involves repayment of the principal (and whether the mortgage rate is fixed or variable), the level of holding costs which can vary such as repairs, strata fees and vacancies, and yet more variables. So when people calculate that a proposed property investment will generate $5.75 a week positive cash flow, I tend to be healthily skeptical as to the misleadingly precise nature of the calculations.

What we can say is that given that mortgage lenders tend to set their loan rates somewhere higher than the Reserve Bank's cash rate (in order to make the loan worth their while a bank must lend at a reasonable premium to the prevailing risk free rate) and due to the other holding costs associated with investment property, the gross yield often must be very strong to generate a positive cash flow in Australia.

Positive cash flow property — a short history

Around the turn of the century Robert Kiyosaki self-published what would slowly but surely become his best-selling finance book *Rich Dad Poor Dad,* and in this book he discussed how real estate investments should generate a positive cash flow. Ideally, they always would too. The trouble was that in Australia, interest rates back in the 1990s were high enough and rental yields low enough that a positive cash flow was not the default outcome for most investment properties. Interest rates fell through the 1990s from the nosebleed level of 17% at the start of the decade to far more moderate levels as the millennium year approached.

After the turn of the century, global stock markets tanked as the technology stock bubble burst and interest rates remained fairly low for a sustained period of time in response to the worsened outlook. The Reserve Bank retained a cash rate of a historically very low 4-5% which meant that positive cash flow was indeed a possibility on certain types of property such as tourism property, managed apartments and those located in rural areas or cheap regional centres.

From around that time and beyond, therefore, Australian bookstores were filled with a series of books on the subject of investing for a positive cash flow which argued that we should never allow the location of a property to affect the overall investment decision and that the quest for capital growth as the most important factor in a property investment was 'a myth'.

Investors need to update their investment
strategies when economic conditions change.

126

While investing for a positive cash flow was a workable strategy in 2002, interest rates naturally tend to move in cycles and as the stock market and confidence in the economy filtered back, rates were gradually moved up again. By 2008, the cash interest rate had moved all the way back up to above 7%.

If the cash rate is at this kind of level you generally have to find a property with an extremely strong rental yield in order to generate a positive cash flow unless you are putting down a huge deposit or manufacturing the yield in some other way (such as solving existing vacancy problems, undertaking a major renovation or perhaps subdividing a property).

The response from those flying the flag for positive cash flow property was that, in spite of all that had been said before about the supposed perils of negative gearing, a moderately negative cash flow was acceptable in the early years of ownership, and that we should also aim for growth. Sound familiar? It certainly should, because that is what those of us who negatively gear some of our properties had always argued too. Perhaps we weren't so very different after all?

To some extent then, you might argue that the cash flow versus capital growth argument is not so much a matter of principle as one of degree. What property investors must weigh up is how important a strong yield is to us. In 2013, apartments even in inner Sydney suburbs are generating average yields of around 5.5% (and through undertaking cosmetic renovations, yields can begin be moved somewhere higher than this) so I personally don't feel the need to venture too far away from the city's inner- and middle-ring suburbs. For others, rental income is an investment lifeline and they will consider more remote areas.

Capital growth creates wealth; rental yield is important too.

The trap to avoid is incorrectly thinking that cash flow is the only important part of an investment, for if you invest in property that is in low demand in a country as expensive as Australia now is, you might risk seeing the price of your property plummet. And while some may argue that this does not matter if you are holding for the long term, my experience is that it does matter. Time and again I've seen investors hold on to an investment (be it in shares or property) which is falling in value only to eventually crack and sell it at the most inopportune moment, that of course being the bottom of the market.

There is a twist in the tail here, and that is that interest rates were again dropped to record low levels during and following the global financial crisis, a meltdown which was sparked by the subprime crisis in the United States. By the middle of 2013 the cash rate had fallen to a new low of just 2.75% in Australia and the yield curve remained inverted as the mining construction boom approached its inevitable peak (suggesting that further rate cuts may yet follow), so positive cash flow property is well and truly back on the agenda, and not only for those investing in distant or outer suburbs. While the future is, of course, inherently uncertain, the wrinkle may be that we now see a prolonged period of lower interest rates.

With European and other governments groaning under a mass of barely sustainable debt and the Federal Reserve in the US vowing to leave interest rates at near-zero levels for some time yet, interest rate hikes seem to be off the table, for a while at least. Certainly in the US and the UK policy-makers will be fearful of choking the green shoots of recovery growth with too many successive or sudden interest rate rises.

Property returns from capital growth

The other dimension of property returns is that of capital growth or appreciation. As a general rule wealth is more easily created over the long term through capital wealth rather than cash flow. This is partly simple mathematics, and partly due to the tax system. It's very hard to generate any wealth through rental yield, even if you can find a property which does pay you a few extra dollars each week. But if you can find a property which doubles in value then you are well on the way to generating wealth through investment property.

Figure 9.2 — Property with strong capital growth

Year	Property value @ 7% growth p.a. ($)	Rental income @4% yield ($)
0	500,000	20,000
1	535,000	21,400
2	572,450	22,898
3	612,522	24,501
4	655,398	26,216
5	701,276	28,051
6	750,365	30,015
7	802,891	32,116
8	759,093	34,364

Year	Property value @ 7% growth p.a. ($)	Rental income @4% yield ($)
9	919,230	36,769
10	983,576	39,343
11	1,052,426	42,097
12	1,126,096	45,044
13	1,204,293	48,197
14	1,289,267	51,571
15	1,379,516	55,181
16	1,476,082	59,043
17	1,579,408	63,176
18	1,689,966	67,599
19	1,808,264	72,331
20	**1,934,842**	**77,394**

Again using the rule of 72, it can be seen that a property which grows in value at 7% per annum compounding capital growth doubles in value in a fraction over 10 years (72/7 = 10.28 years). The implications of this for the property investor are huge. This shows that it to create wealth it is absolutely vital to target the highest capital growth areas and suburbs you can find.

The difference between 4% and 7% capital growth may not on the face of it sound too significant but over a period of decades the difference a higher capital growth rate can make to your wealth is phenomenal. You will also notice in the second example that while the rental income is initially far lower, over time the income from the more in-demand property increases too, so that over the long term the property with the strongest capital growth is easily the best performer.

Wrapping up on capital growth and cash flow

Naturally I note that these are totally unrealistic examples in one sense, for property price growth and rental yields are extremely unlikely to move in such a linear fashion. Australian property cycles often seem to take around eight years to play out, and within that eight years prices are likely to spend some time falling and further time flat, before seeing an upward jump in values. Similarly, rents tend to move less smoothly than is implied by the tables above — often rental growth precedes a period of capital growth rather than the two variables moving in lockstep.

Even today it is still often debated which of the two is more important, cash flow or growth? The answer is not straightforward as it depends upon your own circumstances. If you find that funds are tight for you then cash flow will naturally take on a greater importance. However, what is definitely the case is that it is capital growth which creates greater wealth. While higher yields might be tempting and indeed welcome in the short term, regardless of where you decide to invest in property, you must look to obtain capital growth.

In the numerical examples above, while the cash flow property in the first example shows a stronger yield initially, by year 20 the second property is worth nearly double that of the first — and it has a stronger rental income too.

> It is more difficult to generate wealth through
> cash flow than capital growth.

It is possible to source properties which generate more rental income than expenses, particularly while interest rates are low. However, something my wife and I have found is that when you hold a property for more than 15 years the cash flow can become very strong, more than doubling the mortgage repayments or even more in some cases. Note that the income will start to attract tax (much like a salary income) unless you have other deductions which can be offset against it.

Compounding growth

The tables above also demonstrate the power of compound growth at work. Notice how where a consistent growth rate is achieved by an asset, the actual dollar value it increases by becomes larger with each passing year. In the example of the property showing a 7% per annum capital growth, in year 1 the asset increases in value from $500,000 to $535,000, which is an increase of $35,000. Further down the track, the property increases in price in year 20 from $1,808,264 to $1,934,842 — this is a far greater increase in dollar terms of $126,578, although the percentage increase remains unchanged at 7%.

This illustrates why property and shares can both be such effective asset classes for investors with a long term time horizon. If you can choose assets that increase in value in an inflationary economy and attain an acceptable rate of return in excess of the inflation rate, your wealth can continue to snowball or compound in perpetuity. The assets that tend to outperform inflation can include property in locations that are in very high demand and shares in outstanding companies which can continue to grow their return on equity (ROE) and earnings per share (EPS).

Negative cash flow and premium property

In the real world of investing, premium property can generate a woeful cash flow with rental yields slipping lower as a percentage of the property's value as you move towards the premium sector of the market.

Thus, for the average investor it is usually wise to focus on properties closer to the median value of the market which generate stronger yields and are also within reach of a greater number of potential property buyers, leading to a higher demand. If you do need to sell a property, it is far easier to shift a property that is within the price range of 80% of likely buyers in that suburb than one which may only be of interest to a handful of buyers at the top of the market.

Premium properties are often owned by the super-wealthy for whom monthly cash flow is less of a concern. It is sometimes overlooked that owners of property at this end of the market may be cash buyers who do not have significant mortgage debt and therefore the monthly cash flow is of less concern to them. Premium apartments can have enormous strata fees. This is another reason for most average investors to steer clear.

Minimising a negative cash flow in property

There are several steps that can be taken in order to reduce a negative cash flow. Firstly, and most obviously, this can be facilitated through selecting property types which generate a stronger yield in the first place, which often means investing in apartments rather than houses. If you do opt to invest in an apartment it is imperative that you select one with moderate strata fees and one with an adequate sinking fund to cover likely future repairs costs. Ignore this at your own risk.

Too often investors buy what seems to be a great value apartment only to discover that the sinking fund is empty and a levy must be raised for repairs and maintenance to common areas, which accounts for the cheap purchase price. Another way in which cash flow losses can be minimised is to invest in properties which have high depreciation allowances as these can be shown as deductions on your tax return and can reduce your tax bill significantly under the currently existing negative gearing rules in Australia.

Consider all applicable cash flows when investing in property.

New properties often have very appealing depreciation allowances, but it should be remembered that this can be because items that are new do indeed tend to depreciate in value. It may therefore often be preferable to buy a property which is fairly new rather than buying property off the plan which can entail some risk. Another way in which depreciation allowances can be high is on properties which have been recently renovated.

Use a surveyor to help you ascertain the value of depreciation allowances. It is theoretically possible to estimate them yourself but I would definitely advise against this as your estimates will almost certainly be inaccurate and the tax office will not look at all favourably upon such errors. The cost of using a surveyor is not prohibitive (perhaps around $500 plus GST) and surveyor fees should attract a tax deduction in themselves. Over time the depreciation allowances will more than pay for the fees too, and indeed and many surveyors offer a guarantee to this effect.

It is also important to consider how you will finance a property. I have a mixture of principal and interest loans (which gradually pay down the debt) and interest only loans where the principal stays fixed. Naturally an investment property which is financed with an interest only loan has a stronger annual cash flow than one for which the principal is being repaid. If you are planning to invest in multiple investment properties the debt is more comfortably serviced using interest only loans rather than principal and interest products.

The best of both worlds: Sourcing yield and growth

As I have alluded to, in days gone by, it was both common and convenient for commentators to carve up properties in to two types. There were the capital growth properties, normally located close to the cities, would not yield great rents, but should in theory achieve great capital growth. Then, there were the remote outer-suburb or regional properties which supposedly showed lacklustre growth but the percentage rental returns were higher (in part, again theoretically, because the capital value of the property did not increase very much).

Of course, this is an oversimplification, and yet there is some truth in the concept. Higher rental yields are sometimes achieved due to property having shown low growth, and lower rental yields may be reflective of a property having grown in the past. No matter. It is the future we are interested in. In my 2012 book *Get a Financial Grip*, I discussed the types of properties I invest in and why I think that they are the best types of property for me.

I like 100 square metre, two bedroom units in the major capital cities in land-locked suburbs where vacancy rates are very low and supply is not meeting growing demand. One bedroom units can be fine investments too, but two bedroom units often offer a better dynamic for investors, partly due to the fact that two occupants might have a greater purchasing power than one, and partly because two bedroom units can accommodate either a couple or two friends, siblings or work colleagues, thus appealing to a broader demographic. I look at units in lifestyle suburbs near to the major capital cities with good transport links and where the demand is exceptionally high.

> Find property types that will be in the highest
> demand in the future.

Of course, I appreciate that what is best for me is not necessarily ideal for everyone. In some more affordable cities and suburbs houses make for better investments due to them being in higher demand in those cities and being restricted in supply. We all have different risk appetites and different goals. Some people want or need higher rental returns, some are only interested in capital growth and some target a combination of both. It depends on your income, age, goals and outlook.

What I will say again though is this: whatever your preferred strategy in property may be, whether it is buying apartments, houses, renovating to sell or another strategy, with property already expensive in Australia you simply must choose property for which you know there is a continually high and growing demand. Ignore this rule at your peril! Some years ago, I was reading stories of 'investors' buying properties in towns that they had never heard of because they had found a property that on paper may have generated a positive cash flow. Of all the possible approaches you can take to wealth creation this is probably one of the worst strategies I have heard of. Please don't follow that path.

Invest through two property cycles for wealth

To create significant wealth through property investment, you generally need to remain fully invested through two property cycles. The most effective strategy is often to acquire a small number of properties in anticipation of the valuations of these properties increasing.

When these properties have appreciated, you might draw down a line of credit — effectively borrowing against the increased value of your dwellings — in order to acquire further investment properties in another location where you expect to see capital growth. When the newly-acquired investments later experience a boom in value you should have accumulated a significant pool of equity.

While there is an awful lot of information out there about all the various methods and techniques you might use to invest in property (A-REITS, major renovations, flipping, vendor financing, property options and many more) the truth is that in investment as in life, the most effective ideas are often the simplest. Simply continuing to owning prime-location investment properties many not sound very exciting as a strategy, but the results which this strategy can produce can be very exciting indeed.

Owning quality property for the long-term is the simplest and often the most effective wealth creation strategy there is.

For my wife and me it was precisely this approach of investing through two property cycles that allowed us to generate such a significant pool of equity at a young age. We refinanced a property which had boomed in value to invest in numerous other properties while continuing to save deposits and invest in shares. When our new portfolio of properties went through a boom period too we suddenly had a very large portfolio of assets and the income we earned from our salaries then seemed to be relatively insignificant.

It sounds so easy, and in principle it is. The minutiae of property investment can often seem complex, but the biggest battle is often the battle with our self. We need to maintain discipline and demonstrate patience, we need to have the fortitude to continue when others are continually telling us that the markets are about to crash (I have heard this every single year for more than 15 years now) and we need to limit our own potential to self-sabotage and destroy what we have achieved.

Chapter 9 Summary

- Property wealth is more easily created through capital growth rather than rental income

- It was fashionable for a time to say that location in property investment is less important than the rental income — this is definitely not true

- It is vital to select properties for which there is a continuous strong demand

- Interest rates are presently low so negative cash flow even on prime-location property need only be minimal or even neutral

- Smart investors look for properties which provide great capital growth and a strong rental yield

10

THE $4 TRILLION QUESTION:

What is the Future of Australian Property Markets?

10

Price history of Australian property

Australia has been a country with a high rate of home ownership for more than half a century, the rate of ownership increasing to above 50% by 1947, to 63% in 1954, and all the way up to 70% by 1961 — as compared to, say, under 50% for the UK at that time.[1] The trend of a high rate of ownership has continued right through until today, when a similar level of ownership prevails. The importance of this cannot be overstated, for it is precisely this desire to own our own home that has driven property prices ever higher in Australia.

> Property markets, unlike the equity markets,
> do not represent a pure investment asset class.

After the float of the dollar in 1983, foreign banks entered the lending market and created more aggressive competition.[2] As banks chased new business, this led to something of a relaxation in lending standards, an array of new products and an excessive expansion of credit.[3] Price rises were also fuelled by a growing population, favourable tax laws for investors and a great increase in the number of two-income households.

Consequently, much of Australia's property today is relatively expensive in global terms. While many of the world's real estate markets such as the USA, Ireland and Spain took a veritable battering during the global financial crisis and in the period thereafter, in Australia we saw interest rates fall sharply and a spike in property price growth. Melbourne property values continued to grow sharply through 2010 too, the median price appreciating massively by more than a third over an 18 month period.

During 2011, however, property values in most major Australian cities took a breather, and some continued to fall in value moderately in the first half of 2012. The dropping of the cash interest rate from 4.75% in November 2011 to a half-century low of only 2.75% through to the middle of 2013 seemed to stem the tide. It remains to be seen whether or not the year 2013 will be remembered as a significant upturn in the cycle.

Figure 10.1 — Dwelling price growth history by city

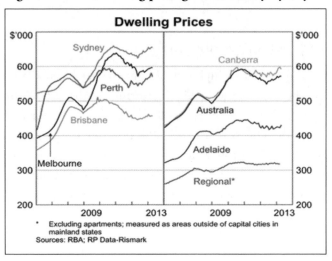

Source: Reserve Bank of Australia, www.rba.gov.au

The graph above reflects dwelling prices in the period from 2006 until 2013 and is one which will be referred to on several occasions throughout this book. The graph shows how some cities such as Perth and more recently Melbourne have seen tremendous spikes in dwelling price growth. Sydney, on the other hand has seen relatively moderate growth since its last major boom period through to the early part of 2004.

Sydney and Brisbane have underperformed in recent years.

While historically Sydney's dwelling prices were far higher than those of every other city in Australia, this is no longer the case. This may imply that Sydney is due to outperform the other capital cities. Brisbane too has seen little or no capital growth for more than half a decade and is now the cheapest capital city on the mainland in which to buy a house.

The future trends for Australian property

There is a tendency for property investors to read only the news which supports their view that property prices must only ever run higher, as though real estate is some kind of a magical risk-free asset class. Come on, get real! The greatest risk in the field of investment often comes when people start believing that an investment is a sure thing or a no-lose scenario, for this is precisely how bubbles are created. Then you start to hear things like:

- 'Property obviously doubles in value every 7–10 years'
- 'Stocks have reached a new, permanently high plateau'
- 'It is different in Australia because…'
- 'Property prices go up by 10% per annum'
- 'It's different this time'

If there truly was an asset class for which you could use massive leverage and be certain that 'prices obviously double every 7–10 years' then every investor and every business in Australia would board the bandwagon. Nobody would ever rent commercial premises and go into business — we could simply all borrow to invest in property and forget about working ever again. Naturally, there are no free lunches and it's not quite that simple.

Few subjects in the world of finance generate as much lively and emotion-fuelled debate as the topic of what is going to happen to residential property prices in the future, and this is especially true in Australia. How can we separate the useful from the absurd, the sublime from the ridiculous, the spruiking from the doom-purveying?

The very first thing we can do is resolve to appreciate that investing in property is a long-term game. If you are buying a property with the intention of selling it within a short timescale, the odds of any great success are immediately diminished, particularly because of the level of transaction costs which buying and selling property attracts, and partly because of the uncertainty surrounding what will happen to prices in the immediate future. You might time the market extremely well, but you also might not.

> Property is usually best treated as a
> long-term investment, which is why you tend to
> 'make more from property when you're asleep'.

People are generally very poor at making predictions. You don't need to take my word for that - you can simply check the finance magazines at the library from the period immediately preceding the financial crisis. My word, don't people love to make predictions? And my word, people are bad at them! The financial press is absolutely stuffed to bursting with tips of hot stocks, hot suburbs and hot super funds. The problem is that the supposedly hot investments often turn out to be tepid or lukewarm at best, and sometimes they prove to be downright freezing.

Back in 2012 I attended the Sydney Home Buyers Show at Darling Harbour, where I watched *Property Observer's* Jonathan Chancellor give an excellent talk on the subject of hot-spotting. He pulled together a list of five '100 Hot Suburbs' press articles from 2011 and of the 21 suburbs nominated in all five articles, he determined how many of them had shown growth.

The answer was two. And one of these had just been hit by the news that mining companies were planning to start building their own employee accommodation thus possibly increasing supply. That should tell you most of what you need to know about how easy it is to time a property market with that level of accuracy and timing.

That said, one of the correctly nominated suburbs was Gladstone, a suburb that many had picked as a no-brainer for capital growth as I noted in my book *Get a Financial Grip,* which did prove to be the case. The take-home message is to look at long-term fundamentals rather than suburbs that are seemingly moderately under-priced today. A seasoned investor wants to see strong population growth, an undersupply of available dwellings, little or no land available for release and genuinely strong real wages growth.

> The average growth of household incomes could be the most rational proxy for future property price growth.

The property markets will continue to be cyclical as they are driven by the human emotions of fear and greed. However, over the course of future cycles I believe that the average growth rate in property prices will be lower than in cycles past. This is partly due to lower inflation levels and much to do with the growth of credit being extremely unlikely to continue to expand at the dizzying rate seen through the 1990s.

Instead, I believe the most rational proxy for future property price growth is the growth in household incomes, which over the course of future property cycles might be in the region of 4% per annum. The challenge for property investors is to seek out the cities, suburbs and property types which outperform the median rate of growth significantly. Note that while these figures might a useful proxy for growth rates over the long term, over the short term there are no guarantees that property prices will not fall. This is why a long term outlook is essential.

Does this mean that property can be a wonderful investment? Over the long term, yes absolutely. Think back to the numbers we considered in Figure 9.2 in Chapter 9. It is the leverage that is available to investors in residential investment property which means that over time they can become millionaires. Naturally this introduces some risk into your portfolio but this can be countered through investing for a longer time horizon.

Population growth

The importance of population growth to the future of Australia's property markets also cannot be overstated. It is the projected population growth for this country and the urbanised nature of the property markets which lead me to be confident in the upward trend in certain types and locations of supply-constrained properties over the longer term.

Figure 10.2 — Projected population growth of Australia

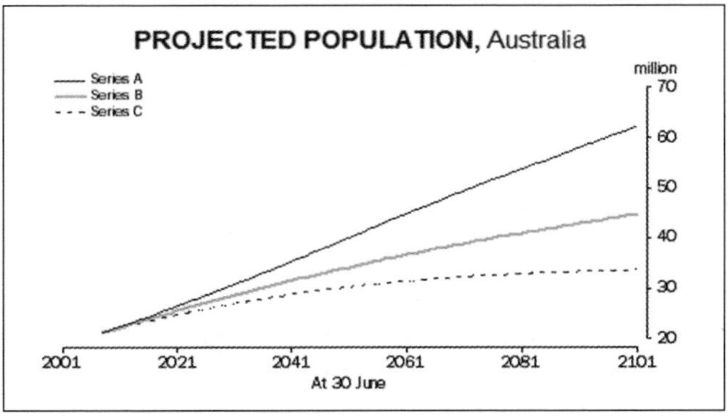

Source: Australian Bureau of Statistics, www.abs.gov.au

In the 1970s and 1980s, as we have already seen in the graph back in Figure 3.1, Australia experienced a prolonged period of high inflation, and therefore there was little realistic chance of a quality property falling in absolute dollar value terms if it was held for number of years. Then, in the 1990s, the relaxation in lending criteria and a structural change towards lower interest rates saw households leveraging up like never before. There is an old saying in investing that 'a rising tide floats all boats'. Property investors would be foolish to place any reliance on there being another credit boom or another period of high inflation to protect themselves from falling values.

The graph above is from the *Australian Bureau of Statistics* (ABS), showing three possible future trends for the Australian population. It is not really possible to predict the future trend with any more accuracy than has been attempted above. Governments are voted in and voted out and nobody can say with any certainty what policies will be implemented in the years to come. The one thing we do know is that Australia's population will grow very significantly over the next few decades.

Strong population growth underpins the property markets.

Indeed, the population is growing very strongly already. The 2011 Census showed that the population grew over the recorded 12 month period by 1.4% or 302,600 people, and since that time the growth rate has accelerated, the ABS showing a further 394,200 additional persons in the year to December 2012.[4] Between 2006 and 2011 the population of Australia increased by 8.3% to around 22.5 million and figure today has moved above 23 million.[5]

These are significant numbers. Do not underestimate what a growth rate of around 1.5% per annum would do to our population over 30 years — it would see the number of people in this country ballooning from 23 million to around 36 million people by 2043, which is broadly what the graph above projects.

Of course, population growth is not expected to be the same in all parts of Australia. The areas which look set to benefit most from population growth include certain parts of Perth and Western Australia, Sydney, Melbourne and south-east Queensland. If we look to invest in desirable, supply-constrained suburbs within the areas expected to see massive population growth then it is reasonable to expect that with demand increasing and supply limited, over the long term these areas will perform strongly. The shortage of appropriate property will be exacerbated by the smaller household sizes.

Falling household sizes

The projected population growth in Australia is an often–discussed driver for the future growth of our property markets. Most of the immigrant population heads to one of the main capital cities, including inflows to Sydney, Melbourne, Brisbane and Perth. This is all fairly well known and well documented. What is less well known is how the future demographic shifts of Australia will affect the property markets. Although the population is growing, fuelled by immigration, on average Australians are having fewer children (and are having them later) and there are more divorces than in decades previous.

Figure 10.3 — Household sizes in Australia

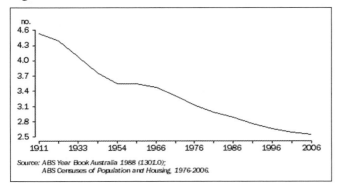

Source: Australian Bureau of Statistics, www.abs.gov.au

Combined with the Baby Boomer generation moving into retirement and empty-nesters downsizing, these trends point inevitably towards one thing — smaller household sizes than we had in the past. In the 1970s and 1980s the Baby Boomer generation flocked out to the suburbs to buy what was then the part of the great Australian dream, the quarter acre plot with a four bedroom house thereon.

> Household sizes have decreased markedly and so
> Australia needs different types of dwellings.

Back then, apartments (or 'flats' as they were then known) were seen as dwellings for the less privileged members of society. How this has changed in only one generation! Declining affordability and a desire to be close to the cities, places of work recreation and facilities saw younger generations embrace unit-dwelling like never before. Apartments today are considered to be convenient, to provide privacy and security and offer low maintenance.

Contrary to popular opinion there are even more Generation X-ers than there are Baby Boomers, and the social group is being pumped up by the arrival of young new immigrants. In his book *How to Grow a Multi-Million Dollar Property Portfolio*, Michael Yardney notes that the retirement of Baby Boomers is creating a demand for an additional 75,000 to 100,000 households per annum.[6]

Growth in other demographic groups such as Mingles (middle-aged singles) and DINKs (double-income no kids couples) are also favouring smaller centrally-located households.[7] Of course, in Australia the inner- and middle-ring suburbs where a great percentage of the members of these social groups prefer to reside are fully built out — there is little or no land available for release.

This creates great pressure on the property markets. In a 2005 demographic study *Australia on the Move*, Australia's leading demographer Bernard Salt identified that between 2006 and 2031 Australia will require millions of new dwellings.[8]

The capital cities will require millions of new dwellings.

Sydney, he noted, would require the most new dwellings through that period at around 741,000 followed by Melbourne with 653,000. Brisbane will need 443,000 and Perth a further 358,000.[9] Interestingly the Gold Coast at 190,000 will need more new dwellings than Adelaide (119,000) with even the Sunshine Coast needing nearly as many dwellings as the South Australian capital.[10]

The challenge for planners and developers is to provide these new dwellings in the desired locations at an affordable price. With land already expensive and construction costs climbing, the challenge is a huge one. Meanwhile, NIMBYism (not in my back yard) obstructs major new developments which only increases the challenge.

The obvious conclusion for property investors is that it might be a great idea to be an owner of one of the types of households which will be so in demand by the smaller household sizes. These can include apartments and townhouses, and particularly those with great access to the city centres, with nearby restaurants and facilities, and often those located close to the water.

Real house prices

In Australia, the financial crisis saw interest rates fall and real estate prices continue to rise. There was no short circuit and lending standards were notably higher as the graph in Figure 10.4 below shows. This was particularly relevant to Australia's property markets of 2011 which moved into the correction phase of the cycle — the lending markets remained relatively liquid.

Figure 10.4 — Non-performing housing loans

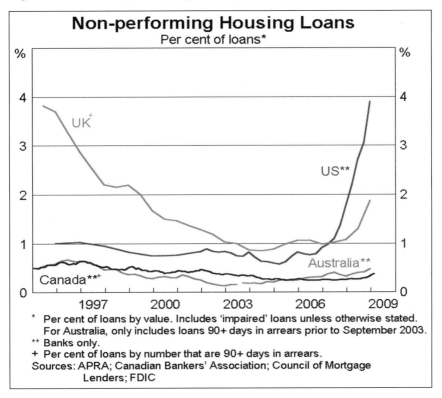

Source: Reserve Bank of Australia, www.rba.gov.au

Figure 10.5 — Real house prices and fundamentals

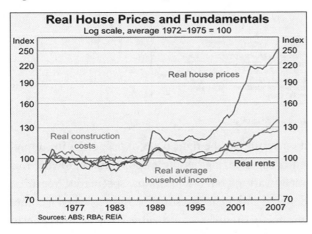

Source: Reserve Bank of Australia, www.rba.gov.au

With fixed mortgage rates are available at around 5-6% or even below and, crucially, with banks still often lending at 95% loan-to-value ratios (LVR), this explains why, to date at least, the correction has only been moderate as noted. As lending criteria were relaxed in the 1990s and easing interest rates saw real estate prices take a very significant upwards turn. Might house price to income ratios at their current level be an anomaly or is expensive real estate the new normal? Could house prices return to 3 times incomes in Australia? Perhaps, but the truthful answer to this is that nobody knows.

The ability of credit markets to reinvent themselves and create new lending products has been entirely unpredictable in the past, and will continue to be unpredictable in the future. The graph in Figure 10.6 shows how loan payments on new housing loans became increasingly expensive after the turn of the century although they eased somewhat through 2011 and 2012 as interest rates were lowered.

Figure 10.6 — Affordability

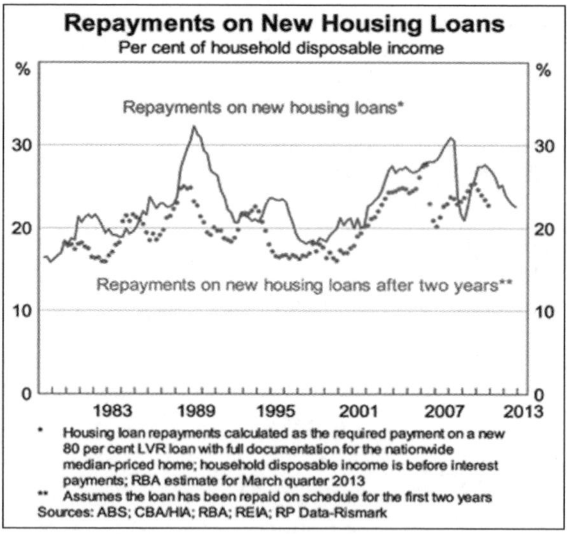

Source: Reserve Bank of Australia, www.rba.gov.au

I feel strongly about only investing in the right types of properties in supply-constrained suburbs in cities experiencing significant population growth. This is also why I am extremely wary of remote locations, speculative ventures, areas of low or variable demand and niche investments. As ever, when it comes to property investing, the focus should be on quality. That is, investing in properties that will be in very high demand in the future.

Personally, I have a preference for investing in apartments (which tend to be more affordable to Australians than houses) in suburbs where no land is available for release. This often means inner- and middle-ring suburbs with great transport access to the centre of capital cities. Houses can be great investments too, depending on the suburb you choose to invest in. Ultimately it pays to invest in the properties that will be in most demand in that locality.

Observe what has happened in other countries. For example, compare the difference between the Tampa real estate market (bust) and that of, say, New York (more stable). In England, many regional markets have fallen in value by more than a quarter leaving owners with negative equity. Meanwhile in many of London's inner suburbs, domestic and international funds continue to flow, and prices are higher than they have ever been.

Figure 10.7 – Household debt

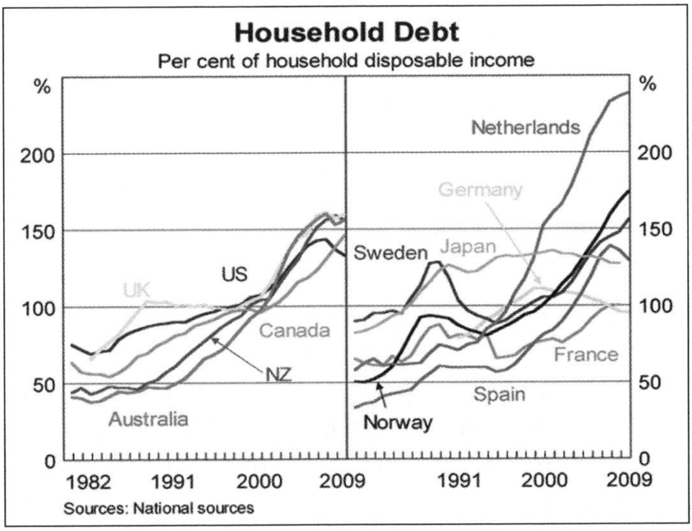

Source: Reserve Bank of Australia, www.rba.gov.au

A cautionary note

The graphs in Figures 10.5 and 10.7 should serve as a fair warning to property investors. While it is unclear whether debt levels will fall in the future, investors must be extremely wary of investing in areas where the demand for property is low. If credit expansion is to stall and then fall, as many have predicted may happen, then it is absolutely imperative that investors hold property for which there is a continual high demand. I cannot make this point any more strongly or clearly enough.

Whatever you may have read in some property books, an extra few dollars in rent is not the most important factor in a property investment decision. Strong demand for the property is.

I believe it to be important that investors today see property as a long-term investment, by which I mean at least 20 years. This allows the projected growth in household income enough time to compound and offer investors some protection against any potential reduction in the use of mortgage debt. Investors also need to invest counter-cyclically aiming to find cities which have experienced poor or negative growth over a prolonged period, in order to capitalise on the next upswing. If you can find properties with the potential for value to be added to them through renovation or another form of manufactured growth, then this adds a third layer of protection to your financial plan.

Doomsayers

Of course, there have been those who have long predicted an enormous crash in property prices in Australia. I didn't take too much notice of our friends from the US who predicted that prices would crash by 55% by 2014 (oops) — or even by as much as 70–85%! — as I suspect that their research into the dynamics of Australian property did not extend far beyond the power of an internet search engine.

Closer to home, Neil Jenman repeatedly warned of an impending property crash from 2001 to 2003 in Sydney and Melbourne which never eventuated. It's certainly true that property markets are cyclical but this can to some extent be countered through a long-term outlook. At the time of writing Melbourne's dwelling prices are around 80% higher than they were in 2003, which underscores the point.

Move forward to 2008 and Professor Steven Keen of the University of Western Sydney was widely quoted as having predicted that prices would crash by 40%. The views of Jenman and Keen are worthy of consideration due to the fact that they actually live in Australia, so theoretically they should have a better idea of what might be happening in the property markets. Unfortunately for Keen, his prediction also proved to be wildly inaccurate as prices actually increased after he made his prediction so that his 40% crash claim now looks a country mile wide of the mark, though he has continued to predict a dramatic correction.

People will always predict doom and gloom at every stage of the economic cycle.

The underlying point here is that whatever the stage of the property market there will be those out there who claim that property prices are completely unsustainable and are sure to come crashing down. You may find this unsettling at first but over time you will learn that no matter what the situation there will always be those on hand to peddle the doom and gloom.

Of course, you should consider the motivations of people who make the claims. Naturally enough, just as those who claim that property always goes up by 10% per annum are those who own investment property, just as surely those who claim that an enormous price crash is just around the corner tend to own no property of their own.

In my book, *Get a Financial Grip* I noted how when my wife bought her first house in 1997 she had people telling her she was absolutely crazy to pay as much as she did for a house which needed redecorating. There was certainly no shortage of self-proclaimed experts on hand who were more than happy to tell her that she was foolish for taking on such an enormous mortgage at a young age. What was the purchase price? The princely sum of £72,000, with a mortgage of around £50,000. Today's value? Around four times the purchase price. Imagine if you had sat on the side-lines for more than a decade-and-a-half waiting for a correction!

My parents tell near-identical tales from the 1960s and the 1970s, when the amounts involved were closer to £2,000. The truth is that property almost always seems to be expensive at the time you are buying it. As inflation and household incomes take their effect over time, prices will once again be more expensive in the future.

With population growth and limited land available for release in Australian capital cities, prices will be much higher in the future.

As a property investor you should only be considering the long term, for there is no way that you, I or anyone else can know what will happen to the price of property in the short term (though plenty of commentators like to give the impression that they can!). There are simply far too many variables for anyone possibly to know. Instead, try to consider where property prices might be 20,

30 or 40 years from now. It is also important to consider supply and demand. What types of properties and which locations are going to be in the highest demand for decades into the future?

Chapter 10 Summary

- Australia is a vast country but it has an artificial land scarcity in its capital cities which pushes up property prices

- Remember that central business districts can become oversupplied with properties cyclically

- States have their own property cycles, so use a 'top down' approach to property investment and look for the next boom state

- Sydney and Brisbane have underperformed in recent years, while Perth is showing very strong fundamentals including population growth, growing GSP (gross state product) and low vacancy rates

- Darwin has an extremely low vacancy rate, although prices are already high

- Remember that capital growth which creates wealth, but rental yield is important too

- Invest in areas with strong long-term population growth and growing demand but low vacancy rates and limited potential for new supply or land to be released

- There will always be those who say that now is a bad time to invest

- The long term trend of stock markets and property prices is upwards

11
THE DEVELOPMENT OF AUSTRALIA'S CAPITAL CITIES

11

Traditional owners

When writing about property in Australia, there is a tendency to focus exclusively on what has happened to the land and dwellings since 1788 when Europeans first decided to set up camp in the Great Southern Land. However, Aborigines have lived in Australia for millennia and as such are known as the traditional owners of the land.

> Australia has been inhabited for somewhere between 40,000 and 80,000 years.

Australia was very progressive in giving women the vote (South Australia, for example, gave all women the vote as early as 1894) but Aborigines were disenfranchised for many decades.[1] While WA gave women the vote in 1899, Aboriginal women in the same state were not given the vote until WA and Queensland finally updated their laws in 1962.[2]

After the arrival of Europeans, it was not unusual for Aborigines to mingle in the centre of Sydney often wandering down the main streets entirely naked, as if goading the new arrivals and rejoicing in their lack of conformity.[3] Over time, though, European settlement was consolidated, Aboriginal communities were increasingly moved aside and their stories often marginalised.

During my travels it was notable that the most fascinating sights to be seen in this amazing country are invariably those which have history dating back a great deal further than the past two centuries. We know that Australia has not always has a proud past with regards to its Aboriginal history. This being a book on modern investment, it is inevitable that most of its focus relates to the period after 1788, and it is with respect to the traditional owners of these lands that I write these words.

Locations of the capital cities

The locations of most of Australia's capital cities were chosen by the respective governor of each territory or his representative, although in the case of Darwin and Adelaide the surveyor generals instead selected the location.[4] Philip's selection of Sydney Cove over Botany Bay is a well-documented episode in Australia's history, although the specific reasons for the choice are often debated: a deeper harbour, fresh drinking water or the lack of swamps all are possible factors.

Location is the always key to property investment.

Perth and Adelaide were both founded somewhat inland and safely away from their respective ports, reflecting in part improved naval firepower, as by the late 1820s cannons had a range that could be measured in miles.[5]

Most Australian capital cities are located coastally, creating an instant scarcity of desirable land close to the city.

In Victoria, an attempt to settle Port Philip Bay was abandoned in 1803 by governor Collins, but later interest in the area was rekindled and it was two private individuals who chose the specific settlement site of Melbourne, John Batman and John Fawkner, though the respective roles of the protagonists are sometimes debated by historians.

Brisbane, like Melbourne, is situated on a river some way from the harbour. Three locations were initially considered as possibilities for Brisbane, being Port Curtis (today's Gladstone), Port Bowen (now known as Port Clinton) and Moreton Bay. The final choice was left to John Oxley, Surveyor General of New South Wales, and instead he opted for the location of today's Brisbane River which he considered to be superior site based upon the usual favoured selection criteria of that time — the nature of the harbour, the water supply and the general lie of the land.[6]

Darwin's location was selected in 1869 by a civilian George Goyder, the surveyor general of South Australia. In keeping with those who had founded cities before him, Goyder's main concerns were finding a site within Port Darwin that was free from swamp, had fresh water and a reasonable harbour.[7] Finally, with respect to the site of Canberra, as with most political affairs, the foundation cannot be attributed to any one person and committees were the order of the day.

Figure 11.1 — The founding of Australia's capital cities

Capital city	Date founded	Date made capital	Founded by
Sydney	1788	1788	Governor Philip
Hobart	1804	1825	Lt Governor Collins
Perth	1829	1829	Governor Stirling
Adelaide	1836	1836	Colonel Light
Melbourne	1835	1850	Captain Lancey
Brisbane	1825	1859	Lieutenant Oxley
Darwin	1869	1911	Goyder (civilian)
Canberra	1913	1913	Committee

Source: *The Origin of Australia's Capital Cities*, edited by Pamela Statham

The grid system in Australia's capital cities

In Monopoly, the board is carefully laid out with properties formed in straight lines in identically-sized rectangular plots. Certain properties situated on popular corners can attain a higher perceived value due to their location and whether it is a prestigious sector of the board. Australia's capital cities also tend to be laid out in a reasonably neat grid system and their values are indeed primarily driven by location. The grid system was already well known about when the first fleet arrived in Australia as it had been used extensively in America.

> 'Location, location, location.' — Harold Samuel

Sydney's grid system, as you can still see on any map today is particularly irregular. Firstly, this was because there was inexperienced and inaccurate use of the compass when measuring out the grids in Australia's first city, and secondly, chain measures were used fraudulently in order to secure larger blocks by adding or omitting parts of the chain.[8] In Hobart some roads in the grid had to skirt around dwellings in order not to disrupt existing owners, so the grids are by no means always perfectly aligned.

There are some other downsides to the grid system. Parks tended to be kept to a minimum in the city centres so as to capitalise on the best available land for building, and shops often tend to be laid out in a linear fashion spread out along one main road.[9]

Although early development was necessarily a little haphazard, the arrival and influence of Governor Macquarie after 1809 saw Sydney and Hobart develop fine streets and public buildings,[10] although due to existing buildings being in place, the street plans were still not completely regular. Unlike the early inhabitants, Macquarie gave topography due consideration and thus the higher ground and ridges saw the construction of public buildings such as the barracks, the gaols, hospitals and the courthouses — and in both Sydney and Hobart, the Governor's house was located close to the port with a perfect view of incoming shipping.[11]

Unlike Sydney and Hobart, Australia's third capital city, Perth, did not experience an initial phase of tent villages as the early arrivals camped close to the anchorage and thus away from the site of the existing city, which is some way down the river. A consequence of this is that Perth's grid layout saw far better planning and is therefore much more regular than that of Sydney or Hobart.

> Planning in Australia's cities has a long history of mismanagement and irregularity. It continues today.

By the time Adelaide was founded, it had a far more comprehensive city plan, and this was also a plan which was later used by Goyder to map the layout of Darwin.[12] The design for the city of Melbourne was supposedly based upon a vague memory of plans for Sydney, and very little regard was given to the natural features of the site for which the city was planned to reside. Consequently, low lying areas around the river in Melbourne flooded and the traffic tended to avoid the hillier areas causing major congestion on the more level streets.[13]

Brisbane also had its planning problems with a second plan being superimposed on an earlier draft, and flooding issues were noted there too, a problem which continues to repeat itself in the city today nearly two centuries on.

> Be wary of buying properties on land prone to flooding.

The artificial scarcity of prime location land in Australia

The grid system had one unintended outcome, this being that as the cities were laid out in rectangular blocks from the earliest days an artificial scarcity of city land was created. This problem was exacerbated by all of the early cities being located beside water. The city blocks were fairly standardised, making surveying and selling them very easy, one consequence of which was a tendency towards speculative activity and rising urban land values.[14] More than a century and a half later, this is still a subject that is very much in the news on a day-to-day basis.

The original city grid systems created an artificial land scarcity.

Canberra is an exceptional case. As the city was conceived as a compromise capital city to be located between Sydney and Melbourne, the city of Canberra was completely designed in the early 1900s. Canberra's design was heavily influenced by the garden city movement and this is evident by the amount of the green space we can still see in the city today.

The inner city area of Canberra was designed by an American architect named Walter Burley Griffin, who gives the city the name of its lake (though why it was decided to use Griffin's middle name in the lake's 'Burley Griffin' naming is not known — it was probably a straightforward error).[15] Due to the city having been entirely designed Canberra does also feature a grid system in parts, and it also has some slightly more elaborately designed street layouts.

Adelaide had also been a planned city which was designed by Governor-General Colonel William Light. Adelaide featured its own grid system and a series of five parks in the central area surrounded by a number of parks on the outer edge, which gave the city much of its distinctive garden feel of today.

Light had the foresight even in the mid-1800s to design very wide roads and the parklands represent a major success even today. Naturally as traffic has increased new freeways have been built to cope with the greater flow of vehicles and the city has also blazed a trail with its innovative O-Bahn bus-way which transports passengers out from the city to Tea Tree Gully. The most important rule of property investment in Australia is this:

Prime location land with scarcity value continues to become ever more expensive due to high and growing demand. When investing, focus on buying where the demand is.

As the capital cities develop, land in prime locations close to the centre of the cities becomes ever more expensive as the population continues to grow from humble beginnings towards some 40 million people over the coming few decades. Of course, at the other end of the scale there is vast acreage of land in regional and rural Australia which is virtually valueless. Property investors seeking capital growth should aim to acquire properties on the land which is most in demand.

Different cities, yet similar — interstate migration in Australia

Australia's capital cities, in spite of being spread thousands of kilometres apart, can be strikingly similar in terms of the their appearance, their layout, their salient features and even the way in which their inhabitants speak. Having been born in England, even after living in Australia for many years, I can usually still place an Englishman's home town through listening to his accent to within a remarkably small area.

> Despite the vast physical distances between them, Australia's cities are more notable for their similarities.

Australia is a far younger country, and partly because of this, accents are very similar from city to city, in spite of the sometimes vast physical distances between them. A resident of Perth may speak in a very similar manner to an inhabitant of Sydney, although their homes may be 4000km apart. To put that in perspective, London is far closer to Moscow than Sydney is to Perth.

The overriding impression is that Australia's cities, despite their subtle differences, are far more striking for their similarities. It is comparatively easy for a resident of one city to move to another city in another state and feel at home relatively quickly despite the huge distances that might be involved.

Is this relevant to property investing in Australia? It is. Despite the distances involved in travelling between cities, people are often prepared to relocate to other parts of the country if they feel that their existing city of residence has become too expensive. We have seen this before after the huge boom in values in Sydney in the period to early 2004 which encouraged interstate migration from New South Wales to other states, including Queensland. When considering projected population growth, interstate migration needs to be considered as well as immigration from overseas. Queensland, in particular, is a state in which the rate of population growth looks set to benefit from interstate migration.

> Interstate migration can see property values between states converge over time.

This re-emphasises that while the property markets of Australia are cyclical, the markets of the individual states do not always move in the same direction at the same time. What interstate migration also tends to do is help the relative values of property in different states revert towards those of each other over time. If property in one state becomes too expensive, inhabitants and investors may gradually look elsewhere for a better deal and an improved standard of living.

Three reasons why you might stick to capital cities

Three common mistakes are made by those who promote regional properties as a superior investment to Australian capital city properties.

1 — Recency bias towards downside risk

Throughout history the greatest oversight of investors has been to assume that what has happened over recent times will continue to occur. Human nature dictates that we build a frame of references around our past experiences and project them into the future. Investment history is awash with examples, from tulip mania (1637) to Black Tuesday (1929) to the tech stock bubble (2000-2002).

While the debt binge tide continues to lift all Australian property boats, some regional properties will continue to perform. All tides turn, however, and this is precisely why regional property is risky.

> Investing for high yield can sometimes introduce investment risk.

Australians are fortunate. Fuelled by a surge in mining investment, we've not experienced recession since Keating's infamous 'recession we had to have' of 1991-2 following the collapse of the Soviet Union. Interest rates have receded to 50-year-lows and we're close to effective full employment.

While high interest rates and high unemployment have long been perceived to be idle threats in Australia, investors who fail to heed history will eventually be caught out. If the US economy averts its fiscal cliff and China's GDP growth powers along then Australia's implied yield curve will lose its ugly inverted nature and even our 'dovish' Reserve Bank board will ratchet up the cash rate.

The demographics of affluent suburbs and regional areas are markedly different in Australia. Cheaper, outlying households are heavily reliant on linear salary income and become prone to mortgage stress when the cost of debt capital is increased, which sees regional property prices dropping. Prime-location households tend to have substantial equity, diverse income streams and greater capacity to ride out elevated interest rates for their duration.

2 — Long-term real growth in regional properties is poor

A second error that promoters of Australian regional property make is confusing periods of high inflation or credit growth with real value growth. No question, with skilful timing it's possible to find a cheap property where prices increase over the short term. Over the long term, however, real capital growth in regional properties is poor, which clearly accounts for why the cheap regional property of yesterday remains cheap today, and yields remain high.

A standard rental combined with lacklustre growth results in a high yield, for a yield is simply a spot percentage calculated at any given point in time. A standard rental combined with outstanding long-term growth results in… lower yields.

Be clear about this: property 'growth' cannot continue to be fuelled by ever-greater mortgage debt in perpetuity. Australia saw persistent inflation throughout two decades in the 1970s and 1980s, devaluing associated mortgage debt, and spiralling credit growth in the 1990s inflated property prices. But real growth was often negligible as those who elected to sell and re-buy property discovered.

Ultimately, sustainable growth can only be sourced from productive enterprise and value being created. Three decades ago in Australia this simply meant ripping an ever-greater volume of minerals out of our weeping planet, with 75% of our stock market's value being resources-based. Today only a quarter of the market's value is founded upon resources. Instead, wealth is created through technological ingenuity and intellectual expertise, particularly in financial services.

Sustainable property price growth needs real wages growth and growing demand. Speculating in remote areas, outlying cities such as Cairns or tourism-dependent regions where real wages growth is negligible carries a material risk premium.

3 — Stunted upside potential

The third mistake I see in the markets every day: Mum-and-Dad investors and pundits who aren't from a financial background confusing yield and income, and thus falling into the insidious yield trap. Yield can be a devastatingly misleading indicator as to investment performance.

The 'strongest' stock yields today are often in exporting companies who bravely maintain dividend payments in the face of the crippling appreciation of the Aussie dollar, but with market capitalisations that have been crucified. Similarly, in Australian property yields are highest in regional properties where real capital growth has been dire.

Chasing yields

Chasing yields can be very costly for investors. In Australia in 1990 you could have invested for the long haul in 'safe' term deposits (~12% yield, but a diabolical long-term performance), listed property trusts (~10% yield; mediocre performance) or the 'risky' industrials index (~6% yield, massive outperformance, both in terms of income and growth).

Yes, in property investment, yield is important, but you *must* be able to source sustainable long-term capital growth. All properties might perform when times are good, but when times are bad — and recessions do recur in a cyclical economy — it pays to be holding properties for which there is the highest demand located in capital cities. Observe what happened overseas where recession hit. UK regional property prices dropped by a quarter through the financial crisis and negative equity abounds, even years later. How cheap is regional property in the US, Ireland or Spain today? Quality inner suburbs of London and major capitals, however, continue to be powered to fresh heights by domestic and international capital.

Sure, you can wax lyrical about rental yields in Australia's regions. But frankly, who cares about spot percentage yields when you can have staggering long-term outperformance from properties with wealth-creating growth and income? When the Australian dollar depreciates and investors from Asia re-enter our property markets, will they research obscure regional areas, or will they flock to capital cities?

In Australian real estate, continual high demand which can ride out recessionary times is vital, not the obsession with an abstract yield calculation. As immigrants continue to flood to the capitals, investment grade residential property in land-locked city suburbs will continue to be a wonderful investment for the risk-averse over the long term.

Chapter 11 Summary

- There is an artificial scarcity of desirable land in Australia

- The price of land located close the city centres increases over time as the population swells

- CBDs can periodically be impacted by an over-supply of apartments

- It makes more sense as an investor to look at inner- and middle-ring suburbs rather than the city itself

- Australia's capital cities are similar and thus interstate migration plays a part — prices of cities can revert closer to those of each other over time

- Be very wary of acquiring property on land that is prone to flooding

- Over the long term, Australia's capital cities are a better investment than regional property

12
INVESTING IN SYDNEY AND NSW

12

Sydney's early development

Sydney is built upon sandstone which originally supported a wide variety of plant life and species — being one of the eminent cities in the world for biodiversity — but Sydney had few animals, and the quality of the soil is generally rather poor.[1] The sandstone is believed to have been formed by sand which came from Antarctica! These geographical weaknesses have not stopped the area becoming home to Australia's largest metropolis and more than 4.6 million people today.

Of course, Aboriginal tribes had already inhabited the region before European arrivals for many thousands of years, the Cadigal tribe in particular. While the first fleet arrived only a little over two centuries ago, Aborigines have occupied the area for millennia, shell middens suggesting that the Cadigal tribe have occupied Pyrmont area (once known as Pirrama) for perhaps 5000 or 6000 years. Other tribes had been around for far longer still.

Sydney's harbour is its most distinctive feature, having been carved out by massive rivers some 90 million years ago when New Zealand split away from the mainland and the Pacific Ocean formed between the two countries we know today.[2] Here's an incredible mind-bending fact: 15,000 years ago Sydney Harbour was completely dry! The enormous expanse of water now in the harbour was simply not there, and even more amazingly, some Aborigines were almost certainly there to witness the dry harbour. At that time the ocean levels were around 140 metres lower than they are today, and the shoreline was some 30km east of the heads.[3]

By 1800, there were still fewer than 5000 Europeans in New South Wales, a number which increased exponentially over the following decades, particularly after gold was first discovered in the 1850s, instantaneously igniting immigration. The population of the state increased to 400,000 by the 1880s and is still growing very strongly even today and is forecast to grow beyond 7 million![4]

Property investors are wise to consider
areas in which population growth is strong,
and Sydney definitely offers this!

By the early 1880s, it was noted that people tended not to live in the city itself, and this even included the wealthy.[5] Much like the Englishman, Australians tended to return home to the suburbs to live in single, multi-storey buildings, which were then common.[6] This trend of the popularity of suburban living continues to the present day. It is often considered more desirable to live some distance away from the centre of the city in suburbs where there is a little more space, and property investors would be wise to take note of this.

> Inner- and middle-ring suburbs make for better investments than the CBD itself.

The infamous Sydney Harbour Bridge opened in 1932, during the greatest depression Australia has ever known, and from that point onwards and against all the odds, Sydney has progressed towards becoming the major international centre and metropolis that it is today.[7]

Sydney: The green set in Monopoly

I always hated owning the green set in Monopoly. They cost a small fortune to buy and even greater fortune to house, and because there are three titles in the set, the titles rarely seem to get fully developed anyway. The set is located miles from the Gaol square, and the adjacent Go to Gaol square also means that, agonisingly, players are swept across the board diagonally away from the green set just as a payday appears close.

Premium-price property is rarely ideal for property investors. The greens have all the hallmarks of appearing to be a prestigious set, but they just never seem to get the rents to make it worth owning them and the ultimate return on investment is consequently very poor. The lack of cash flow often sends the owner broke before they can create any wealth of their own. The properties nearer to the median value such as the oranges and the reds are far more effective. There are so many parallels here with investing in the real world. In many games of Monopoly the set does not progress beyond a handful of houses being built upon it.

Sydney's streets

The city of Sydney was an experiment of the Enlightenment era where new ideas could be tried and tested, and, as Australia's first existing street, **George Street,** represented the effective birth of Sydney.[8] The street was named after King George III, a monarch who went insane but later recovered, a fact which might raise some interesting analogies with the thoroughfare and the city itself.[9]

The street is so long and so vital to Sydney that it has always been a hub of diverse activity. In the 1840s and 1850s, it became noted that Lower George Street was packed with Chinese opium dens, though there were many respectable Chinese tenants too.[10] Today George Street still runs straight through the heart of the city of Sydney and continues through to later become Broadway and then Parramatta Road, a busy commercial thoroughfare which heads out to the west. The Chinese and Asian influence on the street as it runs west remains very strong today. Plans have been considered to build many thousands of new apartments along Parramatta Road in coming decades. Quite how the already gridlocked road would cope with the increased traffic remains unclear.

Castlereagh Street, formerly known as Chapel Row, was named for Viscount Castlereagh, the secretary of state for the colonies.[11] It was Viscount Castlereagh who charged Lachlan Macquarie with improving the morals of Sydney through encouraging marriage, promoting education and curbing the excessive use of liquor.[12] Macquarie responded by closing the grog shops, arresting absconders from church and instituting the first gun laws.[13] Today Castlereagh Street still runs parallel to George Street and shares many similar characteristics with the main thoroughfare. The grog shops are still going strong though.

Pitt Street was originally known as Pitt Row, and was named for the British Prime Minister. In its early years, Pitt Row suffered from residents destroying the surface of the thoroughfare and as early as June 1803, Sydney's *Gazette* reported that locals were repeatedly digging up the road to surface their own back yards.[14] The result of this was that Pitt Row often suffered from having dangerous holes in its surface.

Morbidly, public executions took place on the burial ground at Elizabeth Street, with convicts often being brought along Pitt Row to the gallows with their coffins on a cart.[15] On occasion the sorry condemned were made to sit atop their coffins as they were taken to their executions. Pitt Street also runs parallel to George Street and is well known today for its vibrant shopping mall as well as a morbid weekly ceremony of a different kind, with the ubiquitous Westfield company having recently opened a major new Shoppingtown on the street.

The city in Sydney has undergone a reawakening.

When I first came to Australia in the 1990s, Pitt Street and the top end of the CBD remained quiet at weekends. Today, this has changed markedly, and the city is busy seven days a week. It was partly this reawakening of the CBD that led me to buying property in Pyrmont, which is a popular suburb with young professionals being only walking distance from the city where many of them work. Pyrmont has also benefited from the ongoing redevelopment of the new suburb of Barangaroo, and a number of other developments around Darling Harbour.

Sydney's property market today and the outlook

Naturally, being a Sydneysider who is heavily invested in Sydney property, I will admit to some bias when it comes to assessments of the outlook for residential real estate. However, it is my firm belief that some of the best investment opportunities in Australia are located in the middle sector of the property market in Sydney.

Sydney has seen moderate levels of growth in median dwelling prices since the end of the last great boom in the period through to the early part of 2004, and has grown only by a comparatively weak 3.5% per annum over the past 10 years according to Residex (significantly weaker growth than recorded by any other Australian capital city during that time).

Although the city did see some growth in prices through the financial crisis, overall, since 2004 median prices have increased by less than 20%, while average household incomes have significantly outstripped this rate of growth. Sentiment improved in mid-2012 and prices forged on to all-time highs according to all four of the major data providers by March 2013.

With interest rates now again having fallen lower and low vacancy rates in many of the supply-constrained inner suburbs, parts of Sydney look set for another period of growth. Historically Sydney has been comfortably Australia's most expensive city and yet today the prices in other cities (notably Melbourne and Perth, and even Canberra and Darwin) are much closer to those of Sydney than history would appear to suggest is usual.

Personally, I feel that due to an on-going affordability issue many of the best investments in Sydney — which is Australia's most expensive city in which to buy a dwelling — will be apartments rather than houses. With low vacancy rates in the inner and middle suburbs and sectors of the market such as the inner west recorded very high auction clearance rates, the city population increasing at around 60,000 per annum makes Sydney a strong performer at present.

> For these reasons, Sydney is my number one pick for property investment over the next decade on a risk-adjusted basis.

Other places to invest in New South Wales

While I invest heavily in Sydney myself and I believe that this city offers the best long term prospects for property investors on a risk-adjusted basis, I do of course appreciate that, being Australia's most expensive city, Sydney property is out of reach for many property investors. Naturally if this is the case then it can make sense to look elsewhere in the state for value-for-money investments.

Newcastle

When I first went to Newcastle back in the 1990s, the city had the reputation (among some Sydneysiders at least) of being a bit of frontier town, where pool balls supposedly stopped rolling when you went into the pubs and outsiders were not always welcome. I must say that was not the experience that I had there, and if it ever were true in the past, it certainly is not so today.

Newcastle has developed into a very desirable city in which to live, and the waterfront area in particular is very popular today. While I am not big on the idea of investing in mining towns, I do like Newcastle, which is only around a two hour drive from the northern suburbs of Sydney. While Newcastle is clearly heavily influenced by mining, it is not exclusively a mining town and therefore the risk in property is lower than it might otherwise be. In fact, as Newcastle is also relatively close to Sydney, this underpins its property values too, to some extent.

> Cities that are highly reliant on one industry can represent a risk for property investors.

Of course, we all need to consider how property fits in to our own personal circumstances, planned portfolio and goals, but for my money, I particularly like the look of apartment investments in and around the suburb of Adamstown Heights. These seem to offer excellent value for money for those who find that Sydney is out of their reach (where $300,000 no longer buys you very much).

The population of Newcastle is growing reasonably strongly today. Newcastle's population was high in the early 1970s with a population of 146,000 in 1971, but then tailed off as major industry retracted, with the steelworks closing down a succession of industrial plants.

However, after the turn of the century the population growth became very strong again averaging out at higher than 3.2 per cent per annum over a number of years as recorded in the Census data between 2001 and 2006.[16] The population is now above 150,000 and growing, although at a slightly lower rate today of around 1.2% according to the Australian Bureau of Statistics.[17]

Naturally, you must undertake your own research here, but after very moderate property price growth between 2005 and 2010, research group BIS Shrapnel has tipped Newcastle for strong growth over the following few years.[18]

South coast of New South Wales

As a place to visit, the south coast of New South Wales is one of my favourite places to go. When my now wife and I were thinking of somewhere to elope to for our wedding day (we really couldn't face the idea of a big wedding) we decided fairly quickly that one of the beaches in Kiama would fit the bill. The countryside is stunningly green, which is pleasantly familiar to Pommy-born migrants like me, and there are miles of unspoiled and empty white, sandy beaches.

The south coast of New South Wales has been a favoured destination for property investors who seek higher yields over recent years. In some of the small towns, where property values have been very cheap as compared to Sydney, it has been possible to find rental yields of higher than 7% on properties that cost a fraction of the price of those in the state's capital city.

One risk associated with investing in these areas is the heavy exposure to a narrow field of industries. BlueScope Steel announced approximately a thousand redundancies from its Port Kembla plant in 2011 and this is likely to impact performance of property on the south coast over the short term.

Over the longer term this impact will be diminished and property values of these cheaper areas are likely to eventually be dragged northwards as the values of Sydney properties ripple outwards to the regions.

Therefore over the long term it is possible that such investments perform strongly in terms of yield and reasonably in terms of capital growth. This is a strategy well suited to those for whom a negative cash flow does not sit comfortably including lower income earners or investors with significant commitments such as a major mortgage on a family home. While I myself prefer to invest in the inner- and middle-ring suburbs of Sydney, I am not blind to the fact that everyone is not the same as me, and different strategies can work for different people.

Investing in Sydney businesses

Although Canberra is the official capital of Australia, Sydney is the largest city by population and it holds great influence. Much of Sydney's industry today is dominated by financial services and a brief scanning of the city skyline highlights some familiar names: Macquarie Group, Commonwealth Bank, JP Morgan, AMP, QBE, Westpac. The original Australian bank buildings still stand in Martin Place, which was formerly known in Sydney as Moore Street.

Number 2 Martin Place is the Bank of Australasia building which later merged to become the ANZ bank in 1951. Number 4 Martin Place is the Commonwealth Bank of Australia building, which, when it was constructed it served as Australia's central bank (a function now undertaken by the Reserve Bank of Australia located a little further up Martin Place and recently was a prime target of the Occupy Sydney movement).

Other bank buildings stand in Martin Place too. 48 Martin Place is the old State Savings Bank building (which was also later occupied by the Commonwealth Bank) and number 53–63, Martin Place was formerly the Overseas Union Bank. Macquarie Bank still proudly occupies the 1 Martin Place building today.

It is the enduring success of banks such as Macquarie, Commonwealth, Westpac, National Australia Bank and ANZ which make bank shares such a popular investment for Mum-and-Dad investors. While prices are not currently particularly attractive, Australia's banks generate huge profits, pay handsome dividends and tend to be good long-term investments.

Chapter 12 Summary

- Due to population growth, the long-term fundamentals of the Sydney property market are strong, particularly in the inner- and middle-ring suburbs

- Premium-price property is rarely ideal for investors (unless, for example, you are buying a block of units)

- Property close to the median value is less volatile than the premium sector and appeals to a broader demographic

13
INVESTING IN BRISBANE AND QUEENSLAND

13

Brisbane: Getting there

Having left Sydney on our round-Australia trip, we drove north towards Brisbane. Some of the highlights on the drive up included Newcastle, Coffs Harbour, Byron Bay and the Gold Coast.

The population of Queensland has grown tremendously strongly in the five years between the Census of 2006 and that of 2011, the estimated resident population increasing from around 4.1 million to 4.6 million during that time.[1] The rate of population growth in the year to December 2012 was very strong indeed at 2.0% or 92,500 people, which is significantly higher than the national average for that period of 1.8%.[2] The key, of course, for property investors in Queensland, is to identify which areas the population growth is occurring in and use this information to identify potentially great areas to invest.

The red set in Monopoly — Brisbane

If you want to be the victor in Monopoly, own the red set and build at least three houses on each of the squares! Statistically, this will give you an excellent chance of winning the game. As the red set is developed the rents chargeable increase very handily and therefore give the landlord the opportunity to begin to bankrupt other players with the frequency and quantum of rents charged. The red set is fantastically located, does not cost an excessive amount to buy or develop, is frequently in demand and generates great returns.

> In property investment, the most consistent returns are often achieved from properties close to the median value.

Development of Brisbane's streets and surrounding areas

The dimensions of Queensland, like most Australian states, are vast, though back in 1906 Queensland was even bigger still, including what we now know as Papua New Guinea.[3] Due to its immense size Queensland offers property investors a diverse choice, from the relative stability of Brisbane, to the more manic depressive markets such as the Gold Coast and some of the tourism markets.

Brisbane was originally known as 'Edenglassie' — a cross between the Scottish cities of Edinburgh and Glasgow — and was founded upon the orders of Lords Bathurst who felt that Sydney was no longer a sufficient deterrent for criminals.[4] It was felt that a new tough settlement for hard core offenders was required.[5] Today, though, Queensland offers a great lifestyle and climate at a reasonable price, and for these reasons the state is likely to continue to attract both immigrants and particularly new residents from interstate.

Wickham Terrace was once home to a windmill in the aptly-named Windmill Park, which saw a gruesome scene when two Aborigines were wrongly accused of murder in 1840 and were hanged from one of the windmill's beams.[6] The windmill is the oldest surviving building in Queensland and its tower was later used for radio transmissions and as a signal tower.

Is your strategy land-banking or acquiring quality modern property?

As property investors, we always need to be very clear about what our strategy is. Are we land-banking (buying older properties in order to later knock them down and re-build, or perhaps planning re-zone them) or are we buying a quality build for the long term? Many Australian properties are built from less than ideal materials, so you should always proceed with care.

Many from outside Queensland would be unfamiliar with **Petries Bight** which is a small area located under the northern end of the Story Bridge. Formerly known as Petrie Gardens, the site was a farm in the earliest days of settlement and was at various times a site used by the water police who patrolled the area, being close to Customs House and the city.

Stanley Street on the other hand, is very well known to those of us who are cricket fans as the street which runs past one end of the famous Gabba cricket ground. The first Ashes Test in Brisbane was held in 1928, being the debut test for one Sir Donald Bradman and many of us make the pilgrimage to the Gabba for Test Match cricket each November.[7] In days gone by Stanley Street did have hotels on it, which of course, is the name of the game in Monopoly.

Ugly duckling suburbs can become swans.

Once a heavily industrialised working class area, Woolloongabba has become increasingly popular with unit dwellers and property investors. This trend is seen fairly often, particularly in more expensive real estate markets — suburbs which were once industrial but located very close to the city centre can gradually shift to becoming residential suburbs as the proximity to the city becomes extremely valuable over time.

In Sydney, there are many clear cases of this including in Pyrmont and other inner-western suburbs where warehouses gradually fall vacant and then are converted into apartments. These can make for good investments but do be very wary of the potential for high strata fees in such developments.

Brisbane's property market today and the outlook

The Brisbane property market saw reasonable levels of growth between 2004 and 2008, but since that date the market has been a notable underperformer. In fact, by the the middle of 2013, the median property prices had seen no growth at all for around half a decade, with median house prices having actually fallen from peak to trough by nearly 12% before at last experiencing an upturn from mid-2012.

In the middle of 2012, Australian Property Monitors noted that Brisbane property prices had recorded declines in property values for eight consecutive quarters. There seem to be some signs that the market in Brisbane may have turned the corner, but there is little concrete evidence at the time of writing.

Population growth in Brisbane is reasonably strong and therefore we might have expected recent property price performance to be better than it has been. However, the city did not see the levels of price increases between 2008 through to 2010 which some other cities did, and confidence may well have then been dented by flooding in the city. By 2012, Brisbane had become the cheapest mainland capital city in Australia in which to buy a house, now being even cheaper than Adelaide, which is a surprising statistic.

Brisbane will offer opportunities for counter-cyclical investors.

For a number of reasons therefore, Brisbane is on my watch list and could be on the watch-list of other counter-cyclical investors. I believe that when prices eventually turn the corner they could be in for period of strong growth. It is not possible to time the market perfectly, but investors should aim to buy in cities with strong long-term fundamentals when sentiment is low and prices have been weak.

Locations investors in Queensland might consider

Inner suburbs of Brisbane

In Brisbane, I like a number of the inner suburbs with great transport links for the city. In particular, I particularly like the suburb of Toowong, and, to some extent, Indooroopilly and Woolloongabba. While Brisbane does not have traffic issues to the same extent that already exist in some of the other capital cities, it is a likelihood that traffic congestion will worsen over time. When this becomes the case, there is likely to become an increasing demand for properties which sit close to train links for the city. These suburbs also offer the great convenience of shopping and eating establishments on the doorstep of inhabitants. Increasingly, this is the lifestyle that is being sought by professionals, and not only the younger professionals.

As ever, when it comes to apartments, what investors need to be wary of is an oversupply of units from new developments. In a city such as Brisbane where affordability issues are not as acute as they are in Sydney and Melbourne, houses can make outstanding investments. Suburbs such as Paddington in Brisbane offer some wonderful examples of houses which will always generate a strong interest from buyers and renters alike.

Gladstone

It is well known that Gladstone has been a favourite pick of property investors. Gladstone is located around 100km south of the city of Rockhampton and has been favoured due to the resources projects coming online which include those in coal and those in liquefied natural gas (LNG), under the stewardship of Origin Energy (ORG), ConocoPhillips, Petronas and Santos (STO). The construction and subsequent production stages of these new projects create new jobs and bring the likelihood of a very strong population growth to Gladstone over the next couple of decades.

As I noted in my book *Get a Financial Grip*, Gladstone has been a no-brainer for property investors and sure enough prices increased very sharply through 2011 to early 2012, before stabilising in the middle of 2012.

As ever for property investors, the question going forward is whether the forthcoming supply will keep pace with the demand. While demand will be high, I'm not so certain about the supply going forward, which is why I tend to favour land-locked suburbs of the capital cities where I know that land and new housing projects are constrained. Notably, reported vacancy rates in Gladstone increased in early 2013, which is rarely a good sign.

Gold Coast

The Gold Coast is always a fun destination to visit and so it proved on our trip. The warm weather, endless beaches and wide variety of entertainment ensure that the Gold Coast remains a popular destination for holiday-makers in Australia. The Gold Coast has also been a favoured destination for Australian property investors over the years. This is partly because many investors buy investment properties in locations which they like to holiday at, possibly so that they can use their property in off-peak periods or later when they retire.

When I look at the Gold Coast property market, I tend to see some areas of risk. I worry about the lack of height restrictions on buildings and, as a long-term buy-and-hold investor, am always left to wonder whether major new developments could lead to an over-supply and make older stock obsolete. I am also concerned to invest in an area where price movements tend to be driven by speculation as much as they are by fundamentals.

I do of course recognise that property markets tend to be cyclical and therefore if you can buy into the Gold Coast market at the right time, it is possible to make handsome returns in a relatively short period of time. The Gold Coast has had a rough ride from 2009 to 2012 but as I write this, as with Brisbane, there may appear to be the first signs that the market is starting to take a turn for the better.

At times, the Gold Coast has benefited from strong population growth, and this is forecast to continue for the next decade with the population forecast to increase by around 135,000 people over that period.

The tourism property temptation trap

Property investors are often lured by the temptation of buying holiday homes as investments, and this is especially so in Queensland. Mostly, though, we would be wise to not confuse somewhere we would like to retire to with a good property investment.

The allure of buying a holiday property as an investment is fairly obvious. You can hopefully let the property during the peak demand period for very high rents, and then in the quieter season you might use the dwelling yourself for relaxing weekend breaks (though of course, friends and family seem to expect their share of the spoils too). The best of both worlds, then! Or is it?

Issues with holiday and tourist accommodation

One of the problems with this type of investment is the seasonality of rental demand. There can be very high demand for rentals during the summer (for ski chalets read snow season, for Darwin read dry season, for Ningaloo Reef read April-July whale shark season...and so on) and low or no demand in the off-season. This can create some very real headaches for the investor in terms of cash flow management, and vacant properties can become an all-too-tempting target for vandals.

A second problem is that the popularity of holiday homes and tourist accommodation can be highly cyclical with the general economic outlook. Anyone who drove to the NSW south coast from Sydney in 2009 or 2010 would know exactly what I mean by this, as in some beachside areas every second house was advertised as being for sale.

In recessionary times, not only does there tend to be lower demand for holiday leases (which can lead to negative cash flow implications), owners tend to want to sell up too, which can depress prices. This can represent a painful double whammy for investors. Holiday lets have some other differences too: they are often let furnished, there may be extra utility costs, they have greater wear and tear and require regular cleaning, and advertising for tenants and property management have a cost attributed too. Crucially, holiday lets tend to take up more of your time.

Benefits of investing in holiday and tourist lets

Of course, there must be some benefits to investing in holiday accommodation, otherwise why would anyone do it? One of the main attractions is the potentially higher rental yield. Most of us know how expensive it can be to rent a holiday house or apartment for a fortnight, even when we try to spread the cost between half a dozen of us!

If holiday accommodation is run efficiently and in a highly business-like manner, then the potential rental returns can be fantastic. Unfortunately, many investors in these properties are far from business-like and instead eye the fringe benefits of ownership such as the personal use factor.

A second benefit is the flip side to the cyclicality point — if you can time the market where property values are based upon speculative investment rather than the more usual supply and demand fundamentals (i.e. a balance of first-home buyers, owner-occupiers and investors) then you can make a fast buck in the short term. There are many tales of delighted speculators who have timed the market successfully and profited handsomely from booming tourism markets. But, guess what? That isn't investment, it is speculation!

Investing in airlines

Qantas (QAN) is one of Australia's household company names having been established for more than 90 years. While today the company has its head office close to the airport in the suburb of Mascot in Sydney, as the original name of the company suggests (Queensland and Northern Territory Aerial Services Ltd) the airline originated from the sunshine state of Queensland.

While I was on my travels in 2011, one of the most interesting places in the whole of Australia that I visited was the small town of Winton in Queensland. Winton is well known for the nearby 95 million year old dinosaur stampede footprints which you can visit, but also for being home to the founding headquarters of Qantas in 1920, with operations being moved along slightly to Longreach in 1921.

Return on investment in airlines has been historically poor.

The Qantas story is an interesting tale and a quintessentially Australian one, comprising the founding of the Flying Doctor service in 1928, a relocation of the head office to Brisbane in 1930, the first economy tourism flights to the UK in 1953 and the introduction of the jumbo, being the Boeing 747 in 1971.[8] Qantas was also responsible for the evacuation of a record 647 passengers from Darwin's Cyclone Tracy over the Christmas period in 1973.[9]

In 1988, Qantas became an incorporated public company and in 1991, Prime Minister Keating announced that the Government had sold Australian Airlines to Qantas for $300 million.[10] Qantas now can be found under the ASX stock code of QAN.

Figure 13.1 — Qantas 10 year share price history

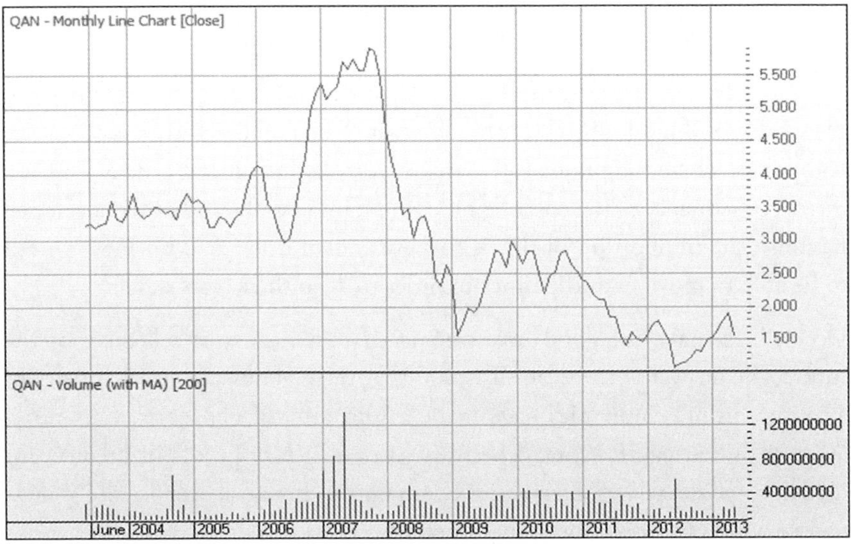

Source: Australian Securities Exchange, www.asx.com.au

As for many companies domiciled in developed countries, Qantas is going through a turbulent period, if you will please pardon the awful pun. Employers in Australia are increasingly discovering that employing staff is a very expensive business. When a new employee is recruited today, the employer does not only have to consider salary payments but also the on-costs associated with employment.

Today, a package might include a salary, a bonus, share option schemes, Workers Compensation insurance, superannuation contributions, Work Cover insurance and more. The actual cost to the company can easily be 50% more than the basic salary which is advertised to the employee.

> Australian companies are suffering from expensive employment costs.

Whilst I was on my travels, part of my trip was a world cruise with one of the top cruise lines, travelling from Australia to the UK, via Asia, the Middle

East, North Africa and Europe. While the cruise ship officer positions were often staffed by the English, the waiting staff, administrative workers and the cleaners seemed to hail almost exclusively from the Philippines.

Cruise ship companies have had to adapt to the expensive cost of employing staff from developed countries by employing Filipinos (who work long hours and for months at a time while on board, before returning home for an extended break) and by domiciling their companies overseas.

We are starting to see similar trends from companies based in London, New York, Sydney and Melbourne. We will all be familiar with phone service companies where the phone call is made from an Indian call centre. This is a direct consequence of the cost of employment in Australia and other developed nations. The implication of this is that Australian-domiciled businesses need to be able to move with the times in order to keep their costs down.

Do airlines make for good investments? If past history is reflective of the future, the answer is clear: no. It is said that throughout the entire history of aviation, airline companies have made a sum total of net losses. Of course, Warren Buffett cautions us to be wary of past history proofs in finance, for if history could tell us everything about future financial trends, the richest people would be librarians, as he noted drily.

Famously, even Buffett and his Berkshire Hathaway colleagues invested in US Airlines and initially made painful losses although Berkshire later recouped its investment as is generally their way. Even the 'Sage of Omaha' himself, as Buffett is known, was shocked at the cut-throat nature of the industry. Tongue-in-cheek, he now claims to have a toll number which he calls to warn him off investing in aviation ever again: 'Every time I feel like buying airlines I phone the toll number and they shout me down!'[11]

Why might airlines not be great investments? As a general rule, then, aviation is not a good industry to invest in. Here are just five of the reasons why:

Sector disadvantage 1 — Competitive industry

Do you remember the demise of Ansett in Australia? Aviation is an incredibly competitive industry and the weak companies will be ruthlessly spat out. Europe has seen a significant rise in the number of low-cost airlines competing for slots. Some new entrants have been a success, including EasyJet and Virgin, but others have fall by the wayside, such as Sir Freddie Laker's airline in Britain.

Sector disadvantage 2 — Huge aviation fuel and tax costs

Governments can raise taxes on fuel and are likely to increase further levies in a bid to curb carbon emissions. This does not bode well for a profitable future for those involved in aviation.

Sector disadvantage 3 — Anti-monopoly legislation

Brits may remember Sir Richard Branson's endless campaigning against the British Airways 'monopoly' (British Airways must have been the first monopoly in the history of the world with less than a 50% market share!). We know that Buffett likes to invest in companies which operate effective monopolies and can raise their prices as they see fit. Airlines have no such luxury and are often forced to compete on price by increasingly discerning consumers.

Sector disadvantage 4 — Black swan events

A black swan event is an unforeseen, random or unexpected event which can have major consequences on the investment markets. The term was coined by the English when they believed that black swans did not exist and refers to an occurring event which had seemingly been impossible.

Black swan events can spook the aviation industry. For example, the industry suffered an unprecedented setback in the aftermath of the September 11 terrorist attacks in 2001 as customers became too fearful to travel. Similarly, the more recent volcanic eruption in Europe grounded flights across a huge area which cost the aviation industry dearly. We don't yet know what the next black swan event will be — only that at some point there will be one.

Sector disadvantage 5 — Highly regulated

For obvious reasons, airlines are heavily regulated. Safety is paramount for the ongoing success of an airline. A major accident can destroy the reputation of an airline very quickly which introduces a different risk of loss of capital for investors. Due to the importance placed on safety, the aviation industry is very heavily regulated which brings with it a cost to the operators.

Had you invested in a portfolio of airlines stocks in the US 20 years ago you would today have made a net loss, as compared to a huge return had you simply invested in the wider S&P 500 index. If you are interested in aviation, you may well be better to invest in companies which *service* the airports and airlines rather than the airlines themselves. It's a tough industry to consistently generate profits in.

Chapter 13 Summary

- The Brisbane housing market has underperformed over half a decade

- Towards the end of 2012 and early 2013 certain parts of the Brisbane property market looked as though they may be beginning to bottom out

- Tourism properties can be tempting to buy for their peripheral benefits but you must be cognisant of the potential problems

- There are generally better places to invest your money than in airlines!

14
INVESTING IN DARWIN AND THE NORTHERN TERRITORY

14

While Darwin might have been a cheap location back in the 1980s when the Australian edition of Monopoly was conceived, it is certainly not a cheap location in which to buy property today! In fact, fuelled by resources projects Darwin has seen some of the strongest real estate performance in Australia over the past couple of decades.

The purples in Monopoly — Darwin and Alice

As well as being the cheapest set on the board and therefore the easiest to develop with hotels, the purple set are the least landed on squares on the board. There is a small 6% chance that you could roll a three from *GO* and land on Smith Street, but that is fairly unlikely. The purple set is very cheap to build houses and hotels on, but overall returns are relatively low and often insufficient for the owner to make a big impact in the game.

Cheap properties that are in low demand tend to make
for poor investments over the long term.

Northern Territory: Getting there

We didn't travel to Alice Springs on our trip, having been there many times before and acknowledging that the trip down there would involve an almighty detour to the south from Tennant Creek. Instead, we drove from Cairns across to Darwin, a trip of around 2400km, which is around 30 hours or so of driving.

We stopped at some other interesting places in Queensland on the way across to Darwin including the dinosaur footprints at Winton, the lava tubes at Undara, and the mining town of Mount Isa. I'm aware that many talk up the idea of investing in mining towns due to the potentially high rental yields — up to 8% in the case of Mount Isa — but personally, I am not a fan of doing so as a general rule. Mount Isa is impacted by the mining of copper and gold, and also lead and zinc. There is also a large resource of untapped uranium within striking distance of the town, which may now be mined thanks to the lifting of previous restrictions on mining the mineral in Queensland.

Anywhere where demand for dwellings is heavily reliant on one source of employment becomes an inherently more risky investment proposition. And, as we know, commodity prices are cyclical.

> Dedicated mining towns can bring higher
> returns but often with higher risk.

Naturally, some mining towns retain a higher risk premium than others for property investors. The mining majors such as Rio Tinto and BHP Billiton are generally uninterested in resources projects that may only remain in the production stage for a short period of time. They operate on such a large scale that small projects are simply not worthwhile to them. However, some small-cap miners do take on projects that may have a life of a shorter period than 10 years. Their revenues may be less well hedged too so that a downturn in commodity prices can see operations mothballed which can be a devastating outcome for property speculators. Remember, commodity prices are highly cyclical and so is the resources sector.

The population of the Northern Territory is small. Between 2006 and 2011 (I prefer to use the Census figures over five years because they offer directly comparable figures and do not represent data prepared by vested interests) the estimated resident population of the state increased from around 211,000 to around 230,000.[1] These figures actually represent reasonable growth on percentage basis, although the absolute number is obviously very small as compared to other states. In the year to December 2012 the population growth was 4,200 persons, with only Tasmania showing a lower figure in absolute terms.[2]

Northern Territory streets

While Darwin may have been home to cheap real estate when the Australian edition of Monopoly was created in 1985, it most certainly is not today, with its median house prices having continued to rise relentlessly over the last decade from below $200,000 to above $600,000.

And if you've ever visited Alice Springs you will be familiar with the Todd River, although the river would probably have been rather dry. The adjacent

Todd Street is named for the former postmaster of South Australia, Sir Charles Todd, and the city itself is named after his wife, Alice. One of the annual highlights in Alice is the Henley-on-Todd regatta, a humorous occasion on the day of which a mock race is staged in the dry riverbed, a wry nod to the nation's British heritage.

Smith Street in Darwin I know very well, for I once worked in the city business district on an adjacent street. The street is named for its initial surveyor A.H. Smith and is commercial in nature and being partly pedestrianised for the benefit of all those visiting the CBD to shop and enjoy the fabulous winter climate. Darwin may have a relatively small population, but the geographical surrounds of the city and the fact that its boundaries have resolutely not spread in the same way as those of the larger cities have led to demand outstripping supply and rising dwelling prices.

> Constrained supply and growing population
> forces up rents and property prices.

Darwin and Alice Springs property markets today and their outlook

Darwin

If there is a better climate on earth than that of Darwin in winter, then I have never witnessed it — it is a climate of absolutely perfect dry heat, every day without fail. I don't believe we saw a cloud in the whole two months of our visit. There is much to enjoy in Darwin, including the Darwin Show, the outdoor cinema, occasional games of AFL and cricket and the visit of the V8 Supercars. The highlight for us, though, was the Mindil Beach sunset markets. The markets themselves are excellent and the unbroken view of the sunset over the beach is unparalleled for me.

Property prices in Darwin have increased very significantly over recent decades to the point where many are questioning whether a bubble is forming or has formed. While acknowledging that the property markets in Darwin are cyclical due to the tropical wet season, over the year to the middle of 2013 house prices yet again increased very sharply according to RP Data.[3]

> Darwin dwelling prices have appreciated
> tremendously over the past decade.

The answer to the Darwin property riddle lies in a number of factors. Firstly, part of the boom in prices has partly been attributable to a lack of appropriate supply of housing stock, so for the future much depends on whether the rate of building matches the growing demand which has been driven by resources projects. Perhaps more importantly, much may depend on the future movements in interest rates.

Prices may become very high where there is high demand, and while interest rates remain low the prices remain more sustainable. However, where interest rates increase then there may be a problem. When rates are low mortgage repayments can be dealt with by most investors and homeowners. But when rates move higher into the territory where homeowners begin to default on their mortgages then prices can begin to reverse quickly.

Confidence has been high in the Northern Territory due to the strength of the engineering construction sector. Darwin is quickly becoming a hub of international significance with the giant Inpex gas project set to begin production in coming years and the proposed creation of a marine supply base which is needed to service gas giants such as ConocoPhillips and Shell. While I was in Darwin it also came to light that the US planned to boost military presence in the city over the coming few years significantly.

Alice Springs

We did not take the detour to Alice Springs on our 'Big Lap' of Australia trip, as we had been there plenty of times before and it represents such a big detour. My wife believes she must be unique in that the first three times she travelled to the red central region to see Ayers Rock (today known as *Uluru*) the weather was pouring with rain.

The city of Alice Springs — often known simply as 'Alice' — also has plenty of interest, including the dry beds of the Todd River (I believe they are sometimes not dry, though I have never seen this whenever I have visited the city) and a fascinating history. With a population of around 27,000 it is a significantly bigger conurbation than many seem to believe, despite its incredibly remote location.

Europeans settled at Alice in the 1870s with the construction of a repeater station on the Overland Telegraph Line which linked Adelaide to Darwin, but the Aboriginal influence in Alice remains strong today. In common with many desert areas situated far from the ocean, the temperatures in Alice can vary wildly. The average maximum temperature in summer can be above 35 degrees, yet in winter the average minimum temperature might be some 30 degrees lower.

Alice Springs has experienced very low vacancy rates.

Alice Springs has a curious property market. At the lower end there are the town camps, which by any measure represent desperately poor accommodation. At the premium end of the market luxury apartments can change hands for seven figure sums. In between the two extremes a shortage of dwellings has seen vacancy rates drop to near zero levels, a dynamic which often results in booming real estate values.

One of the main drivers of the falling vacancy rates was the Northern Territory intervention into many of the indigenous communities. The Government is reportedly spending more than spending $100 million on upgrading town camps — including improving sewage, drainage and road problems — but the problems are far from resolved by all accounts.

Meanwhile, there is a strong demand for rental properties, much of it from the Northern Territory Government and public sector employees. Before the intervention vacancy rates were relatively relaxed at around 5%, but since the intervention in 2007, rents have risen so quickly that many previously-happy renters have felt forced into buying at ever-inflating prices. Ministers continue to push for the building of a new suburb to meet the demand.

Booming rents are eventually reflected in higher property prices.

In fact, the near zero vacancy rates are not only an Alice Springs problem, with similar issues existing in Darwin, Katherine and elsewhere in the Northern Territory. As a result, Darwin is on a very close par with Canberra in having a median dwelling price more expensive than every city in Australia except for Sydney.

Other places to invest in Northern Territory

Palmerston

Confusingly, the city of Darwin was previously known as Palmerston, until it was renamed for Charles Darwin in 1911. The land for a new satellite city next to Darwin was acquired in 1971 by the Australian Government after concerns of under-supply of residential land in Darwin.

The conurbation that is known as Palmerston today is instead located around 20km from the city of Darwin and forms a small satellite hub. Palmerston comprises some 18 different suburbs, and the population increased by almost

8000 people between 1991 and 2001 to a total of 21,000 people. Palmerston's population growth is expected to continue and reach over 40,000 people over the next 10 to 15 years.

Investing in NT businesses

The Northern Territory property markets have clearly benefited from the growth in resources projects in the region. Naturally, this also presents opportunities for share investors who can choose to invest in companies in the resources sector. Personally, I am not particularly comfortable investing in gas projects for the simple reason that I don't properly understand them — they are outside my *circle of competence*.

That's not to say that I totally shun investing in resources companies. My employment background is in mining and therefore I do invest in mining stocks and I feel that after a long period of time I now have a reasonable understanding of demand for copper and the grades of copper, silver and gold that might be mined profitably as compared to production costs. When it comes to oil and gas projects and their measures, if I am being honest, I don't have the first clue what they all mean! Therefore, it is wise for me to steer clear. If you understand oil and gas drilling companies, they may represent good investments for you. For me, it's no better than genuine guesswork.

One point that is worth noting is that resources companies have historically paid a low level of dividends as compared to their industrial counterparts. Why is this? Mostly, this is because resources companies tend to retain a higher portion of their earnings as they need a supply of capital to find and fund new projects (projects may run for decades but most will run out eventually) and also because extracting vast quantities of ore or minerals from the earth is by no means a cheap exercise.

Commodity companies produce...commodities! Unable to compete on price, they must produce great volumes to make big returns.

If you take a look at a graph of the performance of industrial shares versus resources shares over the past few decades you will note that returns from industrials have far outstripped the returns from resources stocks. It is also worth noting that returns from resources stocks do tend to be cyclical dependent on the strength of commodity prices. While large companies tend to hedge their returns using futures contracts, to some extent their current earnings will always be impacted by whether commodity prices are weak or strong.

Chapter 14 Summary

- Low vacancy rates have seen Darwin's house prices appreciate tremendously

- The best of the boom for investors is likely to be in the past

- Major resources projects coming online should keep demand for quality residential property strong

- Resources companies can make good investments but dividend and growth returns can be lower than those attainable from investing in industrial companies

15

INVESTING
IN PERTH AND
WESTERN AUSTRALIA

15

Perth: Getting there

Travelling from Darwin down to Perth by road is one heck of a drive. The distance is officially a touch over 4000km, although as we took in a number of detours the distance we travelled was significantly further. Having spent far longer than we had planned to in Darwin's beautiful winter dry season, we covered the Darwin to Perth leg in just six weeks. That's a lot of driving.

En route, we stayed in some tremendous places, including Broome and Port Hedland, the Pilbara region recently being a popular area for property investors due to the vast iron ore resources there. Unfortunately for companies operating in the region, the volatile iron ore prices during 2012 plummeted violently which severely impacted projected returns, although prices have rebounded reasonably promisingly in the first half of 2013. Land release and increasing vacancy rates make the region a risky proposition for property investors.

The absolute highlight of our trip was the Western Australian coast. Some of the world's finest unspoiled beaches are located there. Monkey Mia and Coral Bay are two of the most wonderful places you could ever hope to see — completely beautiful national park areas where should you be inclined you can hand-feed dolphins on the beach. And we did! These are simply stunning locations.

In my book *Get a Financial Grip*, I noted how Perth was a bit of a wildcard in one respect for long-term property investment. The figures the ABS has projected for high, median and low population growth in the city vary wildly indicating that nobody is entirely sure what the future holds for the city.

Western Australia is very much a mining and resources state which may lead to its fortunes being slightly more volatile through the commodities cycles, but it is worth noting that in the year to December 2012 the population growth of the state was by far and away the strongest of any of the states in Australia at 3.5% (83,000 people).[1] It remains to be seen whether that level of growth continues. Over the five years to the 2011 Census the Western Australian population increased from around 2.05 million to 2.35 million which represents very healthy growth indeed.[2]

While Perth has been an unpredictable market,
the low vacancy rates, rising rents and strong population
growth represent good signs for investors.

Through 2012 and early 2013, Perth had low unemployment at around 4% and dwelling approvals have been low as compared to the significant population growth. Better still for the state's property prospects, ABS data through 2012 showed real wages growth and that WA was driving much of the strong GDP growth of Australia during this period.[3] These are potentially very good signs for the property markets in Perth. After a tough five years for Perth residential property, it seems that with rents rising and vacancy rates in some areas tumbling, the fundamentals for a strong recovery are now in place. Towards the end of 2012, vacancy rates in Perth fell to alarmingly low levels of just 0.5% which seems likely to force some growth through 2013 and beyond in the property prices of suburbs with few vacant properties.

Development of Perth's streets and surrounding areas

The area we now know as Perth was inhabited from as long as 40,000 to 60,000 years ago by Aborigine peoples, and as early as the seventeenth century European ships had begun accidentally brushing past the west coast of Australia. The settlement of Perth was originally founded largely out of fear that the French may have chosen to settle on the west coast of Australia.[4]

Given the mineral wealth located in the state of Western Australia, the decision to found a settlement there in 1829 was inspired.[5] The initial settlement, being an agricultural one, was not a success, and so in 1849 Perth began to accept convicts as transportation to Tasmania and New South Wales was coming to an end.[6]

Rather unimaginatively, the settlement was originally known as Western New Holland, and the Georgian new town of Edinburgh was used as a model for Perth as it was felt that the respective terrain of the two cities was somewhat similar.[7] Approximately 400 Aborigines lived in the area at the time of the settlement, but were displaced by the Europeans after a two-year period of cohabitation.[8] No formal treaty was ever attempted between the two groups and by the 1830s sentiment had turned hostile.[9]

The violets

In Monopoly, the Perth set of Hay Street, Barrack Street and William Street are located immediately after the *Gaol* square on the board. The values of these titles being around the lower-median price of titles on the board makes the violet set a very popular one to own and develop. The entry cost is not too high and building houses does not cost too much either.

Consider affordability in property investment — you want to appeal a broad range of potential tenants and buyers.

Hay Street, named for the Under Secretary for Colonies Robert William Hay, is one of Perth's main strips, although it was formerly known in parts as Howick Street and Twiss Street until the 20th century. The road travels through some great suburbs including Subiaco, and both East and West Perth. Hay Street was one of the most important roads of the early settlement as it ran along the east-west ridge and, unlike Murray Street and Wellington Street, it was not prone to flooding.[10] Hay Street is well known today as a major precinct for retail commerce.[11]

William Street on the other hand is one of the two man cross-streets in the city, the other being **Barrack Street,** the third member of the Monopoly group. These two roads define the edges of the city's main shopping precincts today. Parts of Barrack Street had become a little run down, but in 2006 the impressive new Barrack Plaza was opened, a serviced apartment hotel which significantly improved the look of the street.

Perth's CBD is relatively small. I once read a piece of trivia which claimed that the three largest CBDs in Australia are Sydney, Melbourne and North Sydney, which is an interesting anecdote, though it surely depends upon where the boundaries of the respective districts are drawn!

Perth's property market today and the outlook

It is well known that the property market in Perth saw a tremendous boom in value over a period of several years up until around 2007 when the market finally realised that it had become overheated. I have never invested in Perth myself, but the investors who got into the Perth property market before this boom period were among the luckiest (perhaps I should say smartest) in Australia, for the boom was possibly almost unprecedented in its size and impact.

Since 2007, the property market in Perth has been soft as you would expect after such a breath-taking increase in prices and five years on, prices are at around the same level. However, after sliding prices in recent years, in the second half of 2012 there did seem to be some signs of very strong activity picking up again in response to the series of interest rate cuts totalling 200 basis points or 2.00%.

In certain parts of Perth there are shortages of available properties and this is driving up rents very strongly, by as much as 20% through 2012, depending upon which source you take. Where rental growth as strong as this happens property prices tend to follow and therefore investors are returning to the market in Perth in 2013.

Other places to invest in property in Western Australia

Fremantle

Fremantle was one of our favourite cities — in fact, favourite locations — on the whole of our trip and although we hadn't necessarily planned to, we ended up staying for more than two weeks. The city of Fremantle is located on the mouth of the Swan River only a little over 20km from Perth's CBD.

The city is named for English naval officer Captain Charles Fremantle who had pronounced possession of Western Australia and established a camp at the site now affectionately known to locals as 'Freo'. Formerly a busy port, the city now plays host to a variety of restaurants, converted warehouses and fantastically preserved historic buildings and architectural heritage as fine as anywhere I have seen in the country.

Do be aware, however, what makes for a great place to live does not always make for a great place to invest. Fremantle is in a fantastic location but not all of the property types are ideal for investors. In particular, it is important to weigh up the supply versus demand dynamic of the market.

Dampier Peninsula and the Pilbara

The Kimberley region was a fascinating one to visit. Resources regions offer property investors who can time the market well the potential for higher rental returns and outstanding capital growth, but as so often happens with investment, the potential for higher returns can come with it a risk premium attached.

If you invest in a mining town that is dependent upon a small or shorter-term resources project, there is a risk that if you get the market timing wrong then you can be left with a property for which there is no demand for and property prices can plummet dramatically — the small mining town of Zeehan in Tasmania was a prime example of this when demand for property dropped alarmingly. Smaller projects are more susceptible to drops in commodity prices and smaller mining companies tend to bring with them their own risks too.

> Towns that rely on one industry
> can be risky for property investors.

With the larger mining projects such as in the Pilbara, risks still exist, but they tend to be of a different nature. Major projects are usually planned to run for decades and revenues tend to be well hedged by the large resources companies so that even in the face of a commodity price meltdown, such as occurred through 2009, projects remain viable and can continue to operate. Large mining companies also generally do not suffer from cash flow issues to the same extent as some of the minnows in the industry. Notably iron ore prices fell very dramatically in 2012 before staging something of a recovery by the middle of 2013.

Instead the risks of investing in towns expected to benefit from these larger projects is that governments release plots of land for the building of new dwellings, or worse, mining companies elect to build their own short-term accommodation on or near the site in order to sidestep the risk of their fly-in fly-out workers being charged exorbitant rents by landlords.

For example, the Mirvac group was selected as the preferred developer of the Karratha city centre in the Pilbara region in a joint venture project with the local land authority. The project will create a new suburb — Mulataga — and will provide new accommodation for some 8000 people.

For these reasons it can often make better sense to invest in towns or cities which stand to benefit from mining rather than those that are dependent upon one industry. By doing so, you can stand to participate in the upside of a mining boom while limiting the downside as the town or city is not solely reliant on the continued success of one industry. A worthy example is that of Newcastle in New South Wales which continued to prosper despite the withdrawal of BHP Billiton over a prolonged period, and today the city looks to have some growth prospects again.

Investing in WA businesses

Western Australia is very well known for being Australia's resources state. As we have already noted, returns from resources stocks can be somewhat cyclical and it is also the case that, historically at least returns for shareholders have been significantly lower than the equivalent returns from industrial shares.

Much of the greatest wealth from resources is generated by the mining magnates who took the initial risk of raising investment capital and starting up resources companies. Returns can be there for shareholders too, but to some extent risk and return can be linked so investors in established resources companies, which are often rationally priced by the market, may have experienced lower returns than might have been achieved elsewhere.

What if you want to try to outperform in resources equities? Well, one thing that you can do which seems to be something of a national pastime in Australia is to speculate in the penny dreadful stocks, which is slang terminology referring to small listed companies which have no track record of having generated profits. In mining, this tends to mean exploration companies who drill prospective tenements in the hope of finding a major resource to exploit or sell on up the food chain to a larger entity.

> There tends to exist a relationship between
> risk and return in investment.

Naturally, the price we pay for buying shares in these cheap stocks in the hope of a massive payday is an equivalent level of risk. Exploration companies tend to chew up cash because they are not generating revenues through operations and therefore there is an obvious risk that when cash levels run low the company invested in needs to source further funds.

This often means the company issuing more shares to raise capital which in turn dilutes the value of existing shareholdings. Pure exploration companies also do not tend to pay dividends for the simple reason that they do not have the retained profits to pay dividends from. Therefore, as a means for building wealth speculative mining stocks do not generally represent a great vehicle. Of course, this doesn't stop punters having a go! Just as is the case with those playing the pokies, it is the prospect of a big win that keeps people coming back for more, even after being burned.

Check out the internet chat forums on the stock market and you will notice that there seems to be an inverse relationship between the market capitalisation of mining companies and the level of interest in them. Thus, there may be the odd comment on BHP Billiton (BHP) or Rio Tinto (RIO) at the top end of town, but a speculative exploration company whose shares change hands for a few cents may regularly have dozens of excited posters.

It's not hard to see why. Lobbing a few bucks into a micro-cap might acquire you hundreds of thousands of shares, and speculators dream that one day the stock they have gambled on will be the next big thing.

> 'If you have a desire to trade penny stocks —
> save yourself time and burn your cash.'

Of course, there are many more stories of companies simply running out of cash and becoming inert or de-listed than there of companies striking the modern equivalent of Lasseter's Reef.

Mining exploration companies are similar in some ways to pirates seeking the big treasure. Some may find it, but most will finish empty-handed, although this doesn't stop gamblers being drawn to the excitement of speculation. Good investing should not be exciting. Instead returns should be steady and almost boringly predictable.

Another alternative is to look to invest in companies which *service* the mining companies rather than the mining companies themselves. Service companies can benefit greatly from mining investment and booms without assuming the risk of operating the mine themselves and all of the commitments which go with this.

Chapter 15 Summary

- After a tremendous boom in prices, Perth's property market has stagnated since 2007

- There may be signs that the property market in Perth is gathering confidence and momentum

- Extremely low vacancy rates, rising rents and strong population growth represent good signs for investors in Perth

- Perth is one of the cities which stands to benefit from the new wealth created by the mining boom

- Be extremely wary of land release or miners constructing new accommodation in mining towns

16
INVESTING IN
ADELAIDE AND
SOUTH AUSTRALIA

16

Adelaide: Getting there

The drive from Perth to Adelaide is not the most thrilling in some respects, being some 2000km of mainly straight-line travel. The Nullarbor Plain is a mostly featureless part of Australia (hence its name, which simply translates as 'no trees') upon which very little grows due to it sitting upon the world's largest single piece of limestone. The Nullarbor Plain is also home to the longest straight stretch of road in the world.

We had already crossed the Nullarbor in the opposite direction some years previously on the famous Indian-Pacific train from Sydney to Perth, a trip that takes three days and two nights, and incorporates the longest straight section of railway in the world. The Nullarbor Plain is not a trip for the faint of heart!

The oranges in Monopoly

The oranges are often cited as the finest set to own in Monopoly due to their being located on the straight immediately after *Gaol*, where playing tokens often land. There is a very sporting chance of hitting the orange set and the most expensive of the orange titles, Rundle Mall, is the third most landed upon title on the entire board. The set is not too expensive to develop and is a very handy one indeed to own — the orange set statistically generates the most cash per game (followed by, in order, the red, yellow, green, dark blue, purple, light blue, the stations and brown sets).[3] Strong demand in property, over time, leads to strong returns.

As property investors in the real world, we should recognise that properties for which there is a strong rental demand can be properties that are worth the most to us over the long term or the course of the game. Periods of strong capital growth often follow immediately after strong rises in rent as investors climb aboard the popular market.

The Census showed that the population growth in South Australia over the five years to 2011 has been slower than in other states, increasing from around 1.57 million to 1.66 million.[1] The population of South Australia increased by 15,600 people or 0.9% in the year to December 2012.[2] Projected growth for future years according the Australian Bureau of Statistics is relatively lower than as for other states too.

The lack of strong absolute population growth is a negative point for property investors. The state took a further hit in August 2012 when BHP Billiton elected to postpone its planned multi-billion dollar extension of the Olympic Dam copper project in the face of weakening commodity prices and an uncertain global outlook. Other projects in Whyalla also failed to attract green ticks. On the positive side of the ledger, property prices in Adelaide have been relatively affordable as compared to some other Australian cities, which presents opportunities. It has also been possible to acquire houses on relatively spacious plots and then subdivide the property, perhaps building a unit on the same site. This can be a fine way to supercharge returns from property.

Adelaide's streets

Although Adelaide was not founded until 1836, there was European awareness of the area well before this time, and the land had been occupied by the Aboriginal Kaurna people, with an existing population of around 500 at the time of European settlement. In the year 2000, a group representing the Kaurna people lodged a native title claim on their behalf. The claim covers an area of 8000 square kilometres of land (that is, some two million acres) stretching from Cape Jervis to Port Broughton, a strip which includes the entire Adelaide metropolitan area. The determination of the claim is on-going.

Way back in 1726, the story *Gulliver's Travels* talked of a ship that was headed to Van Diemen's Land (Tasmania) and became wrecked against the land opposite, named Lilliput in the story — which is quite possibly the land we know as Adelaide today. Adelaide was a free settlement and was the city which saw the most planning and organisation ahead of its founding.[4] In spite of that, the city was nearly bankrupt by 1840 but fortunately for the city, copper was discovered soon thereafter and Adelaide began to reap the benefits and still does today.[5]

South Australia is still home to vast
copper deposits even today,
including BHP's Olympic Dam project.

By 1853, Adelaide was beginning to thrive and C.H Barton's map of that year showed a city of over forty inns and taverns suggesting that the Adelaide was a 'city of piss long before it was a city of churches'.[6] South Australia and its governing bodies were generally sympathetic to religious oppression, which explains the flood of German Lutherans who elected to reside in the city of Adelaide as reflected in today's surnames and street names.[7]

With Adelaide being a city planned by administrators, **Rundle Street** was one of the streets that was named by a Street Naming Committee, and was named for a member of the British House of Commons in 1837. As you also might expect from a committee with such a mundane title, many of Adelaide's street names turned out to be uninspiring and dull. A part of the original Rundle Street, **Rundle Mall** is Adelaide's main retail precinct today having been closed off to traffic in 1976.

Even from the early days, the part of town which ran off Rundle Street formed the nucleus of the city and fetched very high prices for its properties.[8] Only businessmen opening shops, banks and offices could afford the prices in the area, where plots of land originally sold for 2 pounds up to 14 pounds for the prime land.[9] A mere two years later the same plots were being auctioned off for 300 pounds to 2000 pounds.[10] There was also a high concentration of pubs in the area.[11]

Where there is an exceptionally high demand for property and a
limited supply, prices can move upwards extremely quickly.

Being a carefully laid out urban design, Adelaide is a city of many squares, one of the most important of which is **Victoria Square** in the middle of the city's grid of one square mile. Due to the obvious royal connection, the square has a statue of the Queen of the same name at its centre, and a Christmas tree is erected in the square each year, a nod to the traditions at Trafalgar Square in London and the city's colonial past. Victoria Square was set on eight acres and the location represented the first time that the Queen's name had been used for naming a location in the Empire.[12]

Finally, **North Terrace** is one of the four terraces which bind the CBD of Adelaide, running directly across the northern edge of the city district. Today, North Terrace has a tramway which runs out to the beautiful beachside suburb of Glenelg. The street was initially residential but was eventually given over to culture, education and medicine.[13]

In property investment, seeking out popular locations is critical.

It may seem odd to us today that the orange Adelaide set in Monopoly is more expensive than the Perth set, but it should be remembered that historically Perth was not nearly so expensive a city to live in as it is today. Perth saw a phenomenal boom in prices, in particular from 2005 to 2007 which has seen the Western Australian capital leave Adelaide's median dwelling values firmly in its wake.

Adelaide's property market today and the outlook

Adelaide has become a focus of attention for investors over previous years, partly because it has been a cheaper city in which to buy than other capital cities. Not unlike Brisbane, Adelaide has failed to see any periods of truly spectacular growth over the past decade. Instead, property price growth in Adelaide has been fairly monotonous, a genuine slow but steady performer. That's not to say that property price performance has been bad, it has just not been in any way amazing.

The absolute population growth in Adelaide is comparatively lower than as for the major capital cities, and there is potentially some land available for release in certain outer areas of the city. For these reasons I do not invest in Adelaide. Of course, I do not own a crystal ball (more's the pity!) but if history is the best indicator we have towards future performance then we might expect to see Adelaide continuing to be the slow but steady performer. While the cheaper prices have left dwelling values some room to grow and resources projects offer growth potential, although the shelving of the Olympic Dam expansion project was something of a negative.

Other places to invest in South Australia

Onkaparinga shire

Positive cash flow property author and business owner Margaret Lomas has for some years tipped the Onkaparinga shire for capital growth. I know the area reasonably well as some years ago I did a fair amount of work at a copper-gold mine project on the other side of Mount Barker. However, I am not *au fait* with the latest property dynamics of Onkaparinga so I defer to her expertise here.

On a macro level the postponing of the Olympic Dam expansion to the north of Adelaide and plummeting copper prices may impact confidence in the state, but on a micro level opportunities for growth will no doubt still exist. The larger blocks in this part of the world sometimes offer potential for adding a second property through acquiring a house on a sizeable plot and applying for planning approval to add a smaller second dwelling to the land.

Investing in SA businesses

I worked in Adelaide a little when I was in the mining industry, having been the financial controller of a company which mined copper, silver and gold in South Australia. Mining plays a significant role in the state, though currently a somewhat less significant one that had been anticipated following BHP Billiton's election to postpone its proposed expansion of Olympic Dam and a sharp correction in copper prices.

The largest sector of South Australia's industry, however, is health care, with nearly 15% of the state's employees being in that industry — and health care is definitely a sector I consider worthy of investment for the long term. With Australia's ageing population the sector can surely only grow, and there are a number of interesting stocks worthy of consideration in this sector.

The other major industry in Adelaide is defence, making a vast contribution of more than $1 billion to the Gross State Product annually. Defence is a huge industry in many developed countries but it is not a sector I would choose to invest in myself from an ethical perspective. You have to make your own judgement call here.

Chapter 16 Summary

- Adelaide has been a slow but steady performer for property investors over the years

- Projected population growth for Adelaide is comparatively lower than for other major capital cities

- Adelaide offers relatively affordable housing as compared to the major capital cities

- The large blocks in Adelaide offer potential for experienced investors to subdivide and add additional properties to a title

- Whether there is to be a significant adverse impact in South Australia from BHP Billiton postponing the expansion of their Olympic Dam project remains to be seen

- Adelaide's main other industry is health care, which is a sector of the stock exchange with a potentially stellar future

- One of the other major players in South Australian industries is defence, though whether or not you want to invest in this industry is a matter for personal choice

17
INVESTING IN MELBOURNE AND VICTORIA

17

With regards to Melbourne's real estate markets in 2013, high entry and building costs combined with an oversupply of stock in some areas make the immediate outlook for Melbourne property perhaps potentially less than rosy compared to the prospects for Perth and Sydney. However, the long term population growth in Melbourne is a major plus factor.

The yellows in Monopoly

Although they are slightly more expensive and prestigious than the adjacent red set, the yellow Melbourne properties are not as effective a set for winning the game of Monopoly. They are located further from the *Gaol* square which reduces the chances of players ever reaching them on any given lap, and, unlike with the red and dark blue sets, there is no Chance card instructing that you must advance there. The London version of the game had an unusual quirk in it — the yellow Piccadilly square charged the same rent as the others in the set. Every other set which can be developed has a 'capital' which charged $2 more for its rent when undeveloped. Suspicions that this was an error were confirmed when a later edition of the game updated the figures.

It is important to ensure that you charge full market value rents for your properties and don't short-change yourself.

Melbourne: Getting there

The drive from Adelaide to Melbourne is considerably easier than crossing the Nullarbor! The distance between the two cities is only 725km, which could be undertaken in one very long day of driving by a committed or hurried traveller. The route incorporates the stunning Great Ocean Road so there is never a shortage of great views, at least, not for the person in the passenger seat. We covered the drive fairly easily in a few leisurely days.

Victoria is Australia's second most populous state and is another state which has seen very strong population growth over the five years from 2006 to 2011, the population increasing from 5.1 million to 5.6 million.[1] In the year to December 2012 the population of the state increased by a thumping 99,500 which represents a very healthy increase of 1.8% for that one year period.[2]

Melbourne's streets

The Melbourne set occupies the yellow squares on the Monopoly board. It's a fine set to own though the titles are rather expensive to buy and to house. The London edition features streets from its West End in the yellow set: Leicester Square, Piccadilly and Coventry Street. Similarly, Melbourne's picks include up-market streets in Bourke, Elizabeth and Collins respectively.

Melbourne was only founded after a number of failed attempts had been made by the Government of the day to find a suitable site for settlement along the south coast. Eventually, John Batman and a syndicate of fifteen other men formed a group known as the Port Philip Association and travelled to what is now known as Victoria to seek out a suitable site. The area that was finally selected for Melbourne was named after the British Prime Minister of that name by Governor Bourke.

In 1837, an immigrant by the name of William Waterfield noted that many of Melbourne's dwellings, being constructed of wood, more resembled booths than they did houses.[3] This is quite amazing to consider when thinking of the dynamics of the booming real estate markets in the city just a century and a half later. Indeed, Melbourne's streets have had a very interesting history. The grid system was of course again very much in evidence, the Hoddle Grid having been designed by Robert Hoddle in 1837.

> Melbourne has seen tremendous property price appreciation from 2007 to 2011 since the global financial crisis lowered interest rates.

Collins Street is one of the principal streets. Named for Lieutenant Governor David Collins it is exactly one mile long and one-and-a-half chains wide (this is 99 feet) as specifically designed by Robert Hoddle. Being one of the first streets in Melbourne to develop, by 1850 medics and other professional men had already begun to build residences which incorporated consulting rooms.[4] Today, Collins Street is Melbourne's main commercial street and is home to a number of major insurance companies and banks, and the street runs from east to west across the city.

I did of course visit **Bourke Street,** and as the popular saying goes, it really *is* busy these days! Even Sydney's hectic main streets can feel comparatively quiet as compared to those of Melbourne on a busy weekend. Bourke Street is home to a major shopping precinct and the famous Bourke Street Mall which is now pedestrianised and a popular haunt for tourists and visitors to the city. The street was named for Sir Richard Bourke, who was actually the Governor of New South Wales, which at that time made him Governor of Melbourne too. Today, however, Melbourne stands proudly independent of its New South Wales roots.

Be wary of flooding risks when investing in property.

Completing Monopoly's yellow set is **Elizabeth Street** which runs past the western edge of Bourke Street Mall from the imposing Flinders Street Station. Elizabeth Street is situated on a natural water course and therefore is prone to regular flooding which was most recently seen in the floods of 2010. Those who take an interest in property need to be aware of flood risks, for sometimes there can be little effective defence, particularly where humans have attempted to defy nature by building on an area where water has flowed naturally for decades.

Melbourne's property market today and the outlook

The property price history of Melbourne is an interesting one, and possibly the one which has generated the most heated debate over recent times in Australia. Property price growth was reasonably strong between 2004 and 2008, but through 2009 and 2010 property price growth in the city was spectacular with median prices appreciating by more than a third during that short period of time.

As one would expect after a period of such phenomenal growth, dwelling prices through 2011 and early 2012 declined somewhat. And yet, despite reams of press coverage declaring a real estate bust to be nigh, prices appeared to stabilise and even recover a little through the middle of 2012, though it is too early as I write this to make any claims of further falls being out of the question.

A number of high-rise blocks near the centre of Melbourne have high vacancy rates and some of the fringe suburbs with their house-and-land packages look likely to struggle badly. However, homebuyers and investors continue to compete for quality existing dwellings in the more favourable locations so these properties are faring much better.

From a property investment perspective, over the long haul Melbourne ticks all of the right boxes. It has very strong population growth, a diversified range of industries and limited land available for release in its main suburbs. However, property investors do need to recognise that timing the market can sometimes be as important as time in the market and, in my opinion, I don't feel that 2013 is a great time to be diving into Melbourne property.

> The Melbourne ship may have sailed for now;
> property investments with superior immediate
> prospects exist elsewhere.

I do of course recognise that there will be plenty of Victorian investors who have a strong preference for investing in their own state. However, it is my belief that other cities — Sydney in particular — will show stronger performance over the next decade than Melbourne.

Inner versus outer suburbs

There is a long running debate in Australia as to the relative merits of investing in inner or outer suburbs and regional centres. It is generally the case that properties in outer areas and regional centres which are cheaper have tended to generate a higher rental yield than properties in the inner suburbs (which may have appreciated in value leaving the rental income behind somewhat). While this is a gross oversimplification, the theory is worthy of consideration as a rule of thumb.

In days gone by it was fashionable to talk of rental yield being important and the location of an investment property being somewhere close to irrelevant. Higher inflation sometimes masked poor investments as the price of almost every property increased, even though some properties underperformed inflation. Allow me to be unequivocally clear about this:

> Adopt this approach today at your own risk.

Property in Australia is expensive, so if there is a significant downturn in confidence and demand, it is absolutely imperative that you have a better investment strategy than simply investing in cheap properties in low demand areas which superficially, at least, generate a relatively high rental return. This is particularly the case in Melbourne where some fringe suburbs with their proliferation of house-and-land packages look very fragile.

Of course, yields vary significantly depending on which city, state, suburb and property type you invest in. As a very rough rule of thumb, as I write this a strong rental yield in a property located in an outer city suburb or regional centre might be considered to be one which is 6-8% of the property's value per annum.

Apartments located closer to the city might generate somewhere closer to 4-5% per annum, and houses near to the city perhaps something weaker at around 3-4% or lower. Naturally these figures are affected by prevailing property prices and various other factors at any given point in time.

Other places to invest in Victorian property

There are a number of popular regional centres in Victoria which attract investors due to their higher yields and lower price entry points. These centres include Ballarat and Bendigo, two towns which were spawned from Victoria's gold rush. While property values have performed well in the past, as a general rule I don't feel that 2013 is a great time to be diving into Victorian property.

Investing in Victorian businesses

Today, Melbourne is well known for its casino, which is owned by Crown Limited (CWN) of which James Packer is the Chairman. Lest you were in any doubt as to how much money the gambling industry in Australia generates, I note that Crown in early 2013 had a market capitalisation of well over $6 billion, and if market analysts are correct in their assumptions they expect the company to grow well into the future.[6]

I am barely in a position to state whether you should invest in the gambling industry from an ethical perspective. After all, I've stayed at the Crown's hotels and frequented their bars myself in the past. I've also gambled at the casino. Moreover, when it comes to ethics, nobody other than you can decide what is ethical and what is not. We all determine our own codes of conduct and what represents acceptable behaviour to us, whether we do so consciously or unconsciously.

I don't invest in companies such as Crown, because the company is reliant on the continued self-destruction of problem gamblers in order to generate its three billion dollars of revenue and the half a billion of dollars in annual profit which support the multi-billion-dollar valuation of the company. Investments in industries such as gambling and tobacco can at times perform quite independently of the market at large, for they are highly regulated and thus to some extent are protected from new entrants. Tobacco companies can sometimes actually benefit from recessionary periods, as addicted consumers become inclined to use more of the product.

I would have thought that the Government would be unlikely to allow competition from a new super-casino in Melbourne. Then again, I previously would have said that the Government would be unlikely to grant the licence for a second casino in Sydney and yet it seems that this may well eventuate. Money talks, clearly.

The gambling industry generates
phenomenal tax revenue
for the Government.

The Government in Australia is sitting astride one enormous conflict of interest when it comes to its policies on gambling. Deep down we all know that casinos generate billions of dollars in profits through destroying the lives of Australians with gambling addictions, but gambling also generates somewhere between $12 billion and $16 billion a year from GST and state taxes for the Government coffers. What a terrible quandary for the politicians! I steer clear of supporting the industry today.

Chapter 17 Summary

- Some suburbs and areas of Melbourne have very strong fundamentals for the long term

- After a huge boom in prices, however, Melbourne property is unlikely to show strong capital growth for some time

- Certain inner areas of Melbourne appear to have an over-supply of dwellings

- Better property investment opportunities exist elsewhere in 2013

- Regional properties in the short term can offer a stronger rental yield percentage, but be wary of the yield trap

- Strong demand for the property you are buying is vital for the success of property as an asset class for investment

- Gambling is one of the most profitable industries in Australia — the billions in profits are ultimately sourced from the pockets of everyday people and their families

18
INVESTING IN HOBART AND TASMANIA

18

Hobart: Getting there

When driving the 'Big Lap', there is one rather obvious problem with getting to Hobart from Melbourne, and that is the great mass of water known today as the Bass Strait. As we wanted to drive around Tasmania too, there was nothing for it but to take the ferry from Port Melbourne to Devonport. My wife was rather excited by the Bass Strait crossing. She grew up in Lincolnshire in England, on Basses Farm no less — named for George Bass, a British explorer who hailed from Sleaford in Lincolnshire.

The crossing itself does not cover a huge distance, and the strait is relatively shallow at only 50 metres or so deep. But, my word it can be a rough crossing! I used all of the sick bags a few dozen times. There can be few more impotent feelings than sitting and feeling green in a rocking cabin while the ship's Captain announces that the crossing will be 'an *exceptionally* rough one'.

Unlike the Bass Strait, the population of Tasmania has been very flat in recent years, the state population having increased only from 490,000 to 510,000 between 2006 and 2011 as recorded in the Census data.[1] In the year to December 2012 the population increased by only 400 persons or 0.1%.[2] This is a very weak population growth as compared to other Australian states. Tasmania has other problems too at present which makes the outlook for property prices less favourable than elsewhere.

<blockquote>

Property price growth is ultimately
sourced from growing wealth.

</blockquote>

Rents were considered to be very high by in Hobart's early days — a large house in the centre of Hobart renting for some 200 to 300 pounds per annum.[3] Even a smaller house in the outskirts of Hobart which cost around just 250 pounds to build could fetch as much 60 to 80 pounds per year in rent.[4]

Hobart's streets from the Monopoly board

The Tasmanian capital city of Hobart was named after the Secretary of State for the Colonies of that name.[5] Macquarie Street, Davey Street and Salamanca Place make up Hobart's blue set on the Monopoly board. These are the second cheapest on the board after the Northern Territory squares reflecting the fact that property in Tasmania is indeed generally significantly cheaper than most mainland property.

Hobart was often known as Hobarton in its early days.[6] Up until the 1850s much of the city's accommodation was original shanty-style residences.[7] When the more affluent residents wished to build stone buildings these sprung up around the older decrepit buildings as this area of Tasmania thrived.[8] It was the gold rush in Victoria which saw a major shift in the fortunes of Hobart in the 1860s resulting in a huge exodus, mainly of men, for the mainland.

Hobart was once considered a relatively expensive place to live with a population that was growing strongly during its commercially successful period in the nineteenth century.[9] There is a clear lesson here and that is that over the long term strong property price growth *must* ultimately be sourced from productive enterprise and value being added. Increasing mortgage debt alone cannot continue to fuel property price growth in perpetuity.

Yields in Australia today are lower than in the past as property prices have increased.

Yet as industry has become less prosperous in Hobart, population growth and property price growth has weakened relative to the rest of Australia and demand for property is not as strong as elsewhere. Today, Hobart is the cheapest capital city in Australia in which to buy a house.

Hobart's streets

Macquarie Street in Hobart is one of the main thoroughfares and is home to some major government buildings including the Reserve Bank. The name of the street is shared with many other streets, suburbs and landmarks in Australia, the town layout having been designed by Governor Macquarie himself in 1811.[10] Unfortunately, Macquarie's plan took no account of the topography of the city and many streets are located in very hilly places, as anyone who has visited Hobart knows only too well.[11] The plan was to have four long streets intersected by four cross streets running north to south, all of which were to be 60 feet wide.

Davey Street was named for 'Mad Tom' Davey, who was a very early Lieutenant Governor from 1810 to 1817, and reportedly a Governor who openly kept mistresses. The street sits on land that was once under water, it being reclaimed land from next to the harbour, and today it sits next to two major parks.

While in the 1830s Davey Street was home to two-storey villas for the affluent (only around one third of Hobart's population owned property at that time), by the 1850s neither Davey Street nor Macquarie Street was considered desirable for living as the city developed. The most notable feature of the street today from a property perspective is the controversially ugly Zero Davey development which was completed in 2004 to the general frustration of local residents who likened the building to the rear end of a refrigerator.

Finally, **Salamanca Place** completes the light blue Monopoly set. A second wharf was needed very early in the life of the area, the one existing wharf often being full with ships being loaded for the journey to England. Named after the 1812 Battle of Salamanca which was won by the Duke of Wellington, by as early as 1818 the land was being levelled for warehouses.

One hundred houses per year were built in Hobart between 1820 and 1841 and the population of the city grew from just 3500 in 1820 to 15,000 by 1841.[12] As one of the key hubs Salamanca Place became a busy part of the world for whalers in the middle of the 19th century, some evidence of which can still be seen today. Salamanca Place is my favourite part of Hobart, the area being home to a pleasant ring of shops, eateries and cafes.

Hobart's property market today and the outlook

Tasmania and Hobart have seen some interest from property investors from the mainland over the years precisely because property is cheaper than in the mainland states and capital cities, and rental yields have at times been attractive. Where investors have been able to time the market correctly they may have made solid returns.

The problem for long-term investors is that the population of the state of Tasmania has barely been increasing (remember, a growth of only 400 people in the last 12 month period recorded) and therefore there have been few major drivers for growth.

Of course, even where population growth is moderate or flat, prices can still increase with inflation over time, and to some extent may be dragged higher by the increasing costs of living in other states (inter-state migration can play a part here). But Tasmania has not seen a major boom in prices in recent times unlike some other states, and this is simply because to date there has not been the demand to fuel such a boom.

Other places to invest in Tasmanian property

Personally, I feel that the lack of population growth in the state is a negative for investors and therefore I have discounted the idea of investing in Tasmania myself. There are two schools of thought here. One is that as Hobart represents the cheapest capital city in Australia that Tasmania offers some of the best value property in the country for the home buyer or savvy investor. Property prices have remained relatively stable recently in the major population centres of Hobart and Launceston with a little more volatility at times as you move out to some of the rural or coastal towns.

Hobart is viewed by some as a potentially outstanding prospect when compared to the capital cities on the mainland, as it comprises more affordable houses than any other capital city. Recently, demand and growth has levelled out but there may still exist opportunities for buyers to secure well-priced property.

Yields are often high where capital growth has underperformed.

For investors, high rental returns are certainly achievable in certain areas. Vacancy rates in both Hobart and Launceston are also beginning to creep up higher, though, after a long period of time when vacancy rates hovered at around only 2%. As always when it comes to property investing, it pays dividends to seek out the suburbs and property types that can secure high capital growth together with a solid rental yield.

At various times, investors have been lured by small mining towns in Tasmania, with the promise of high rental yields and booming capital growth. If you are going to adopt this approach, it can at times be akin to playing a game of hot potato — you need to get in and out of the game at the right time, or you can be left with a property which is falling in value and nobody wants to buy.

Investing in Tasmanian businesses

Hobart has been home to a huge forestry enterprise in the guise of Gunns Limited (GNS), one of Australia's oldest companies, having been established in 1875. The Gunns story is a cautionary tale about the dangers for individual investors picking their own stocks and the dangerous assumption that companies which are established for many decades must always represent safe investments.

Even up until the financial crisis, Gunns seemed to be operating reasonably well, yet it has been crucified over the past half-decade as sentiment towards the logging industry has turned and the Australian dollar appreciated relentlessly. Gunns reported a devastating net loss after tax for the 2012 financial year of close to $1 billion.

Much of the loss related to write-downs and non-cash impairments of assets (forced by changing conditions and sentiment in the export woodchip market) rather than actual cash flow losses. Ultimately, though, if a mature company is unable to record consistent profits and net operating cash flows it will be valued at $nil as it is no longer able to generate the cash necessary to survive.

Companies must generate cash to survive and thrive.

As the dollar remained strong results continued to suffer and the company went into administration. The export woodchip market is largely denominated in US dollars, and thus exporters from Australia are severely impacted when the Australian dollar is stronger than the greenback. The severe impact of the appreciating Australian dollar can be clearly seen in the chart below.

This should caution all individual investors as to the dangers of picking out individual stocks and placing undue emphasis on selections being correct.

When companies such as Gunns or BlueScope Steel (BSL) fall upon tremendously hard times, the procession towards share price capitulation often only seems obvious in retrospect. While the story unfolds it can often seem as though brighter times lie ahead and share punters can be caught out.

While people seem all too knowledgeable now about why the Australian dollar has catapulted up to its current levels, I don't recall too many people back in 2008 and 2009 suggesting that an appreciation of more than 50% against the greenback would happen. As ever, there are lots of experts out there with the benefit of hindsight on their side!

> Sentiment can turn quickly — particularly today against companies who are perceived to be damaging to the environment.

The Gunns and BlueScope Steel stories promote a strong argument for individual investors instead continuing to contribute to a diversified portfolio of industrial shares perhaps via a Listed Investment Company (LIC). There is no shame in diversifying broadly and using a vehicle such as an LIC to do so. Plenty of multi-millionaire investors do exactly this, and it doesn't worry them. There is no place for ego in successful investing, only results.

Figure 18.1 — Gunns Limited (GNS) 10 year share price history

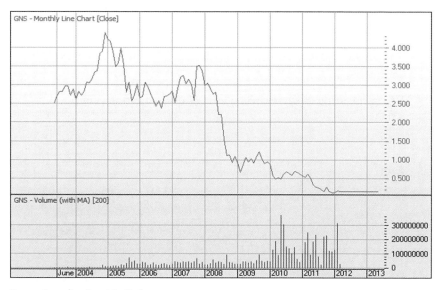

Source: Australian Securities Exchange, www.asx.com.au

The Gunns story, then, is a cautionary tale of the risks of committing a large percentage of your capital to one business or investment. Even so-called blue chip companies which have been established for decades can fail, and realistically most average investors are not skilled at identifying the risks. While there are plenty who invest heavily in the shares of one or two companies, the dangers of this approach are fairly obvious. Ideally investors should try to strike a balance between diversification (to reduce risk) and focus (to ensure that they are investing in assets which are understood well).

Chapter 18 Summary

- Hobart is the cheapest capital city in Australia in which to buy a house

- In recent years the population of Tasmania has been flat, with a small uptick from 2011

- There was a growth period in Tasmanian property, but this looks to have passed for the time being

- With prices falling, counter-cyclical opportunities may exist, but you must look for areas where the population is definitely growing

- Mining towns which are focused around one small resources project offer potential for high returns but with significantly increased risk

- Investing in individual companies, even those established for many decades, can be risky

- The strong Australian dollar has been the ruin of some exporting companies

- When investing in shares, some level of diversification is important

19
INVESTING IN CANBERRA AND ACT

19

Canberra: Getting there

After the hard yakka of the ferry crossing from Devonport back to Melbourne, the drive across to Canberra is relatively a breeze. Although Canberra was chosen to be located between the capitals of New South Wales and Victoria, it is actually considerably closer to Sydney than it is to Melbourne.

It is noticeably different approaching Canberra from Victoria, in the past I had only approached Canberra from Sydney by driving past the spectacular and often-dry Lake George. Our arrival was in summer which is notable only because, being an inland city, the climate of Canberra is very changeable. Winter mornings in the capital can be absolutely perishing at well below freezing (as travelling Sydney Roosters fans know only too well!) yet in summer temperatures can climb very high.

The dark blues in Monopoly

The dark blue set of Canberra in Monopoly is treated with the utmost reverence. Any player who owns the set is feared and players are often prepared to pay crazy amounts to acquire the titles. The individual titles are expensive to buy and the houses are dear to build too, but as there are only two squares in the set this helps to keep the costs a little more manageable. The dark blue set of Canberra is the most prestigious and expensive set on the Monopoly board. These squares, if developed with a red hotel, have great potential for knocking players out of the game due to their super-expensive rents.

Canberra's rental yields are relatively moderate at around 5%.

Canberra's streets

Many of the roads in Canberra are laid out geometrically, and two of the city's thoroughfares in Flinders Way and Kings Avenue close out the Monopoly Board, being the two most expensive titles on the board. I can't honestly recall much about **Flinders Way** from my visits to Australia's capital (which probably tells you something!), but I assume it is just a road like many others in Canberra. According to my street map it is located in the suburb of Griffith, 1km or so away from the famous Capital Hill and the Parliament building.

Kings Avenue I remember much better, being the road which runs between New Parliament House, beginning at State Circle around Capital Hill — more evidence of the carefully planned layout of the city. The road was originally named by the city's architect Walter Burley Griffin (for whom the spectacular lake in Canberra is named) as Federal Avenue reflecting his desire for grand street names. However, the road was later renamed by the Government — which in its infinite wisdom decided that grandiose street names would simply never do — as plain old Kings Avenue.

Canberra's property market today and the outlook

Property in Canberra is surprisingly expensive when you consider how remote the location of the city actually is, with house prices taking off strongly from 2006 through to 2009. I recall that back in 2008 there was an awful lot of talk about how overpriced property in Canberra was and when the financial crisis hit how there was sure to be a big correction.

In fact, the financial crisis saw interest rates fall sharply and according to the RBA median dwelling prices excluding apartments in Canberra increased from around $500,000 to as much as $600,000, although prices eased moderately through 2011. At the time of writing the supposed correction has still not happened in any material way. However, in the 2013 Budget it was proposed to reduce the number of bureaucrats, which had increased by 20,000 from 2007, by some 12,000 heads. This is a bad signal for Canberra. There is also a rapidly increasing pipeline of apartment approvals in the city, which may kill growth in that sector.

Canberra represents a relatively small property market.

In spite of being the official capital city of Australia, Canberra has a very different dynamic from most of the major capital cities. The population of the entire state of Australian Capital Territory (ACT), for example, is only 370,700 as recorded in the 2011 Census, as compared with well over 4.3 million people in the city of Sydney alone.[1]

Although the state's population is obviously comparatively very small, this does mean that despite the moderate absolute increase in population, the percentage increase in the year to December 2012 was strong at 2.3% being an increase of 8,600 persons.[2] If you are looking to invest in Canberra, it is imperative that you buy the appropriate property type for which there is a growing demand.

The market recorded some moderate falls before stabilising in the second half of 2012 and began rising again. There exists a relatively high median income in Canberra which has helped to push prices higher. A number of sources have reported a glut of apartments in Canberra which is likely to stunt growth in that sector.

Other places to invest in ACT property

Queanbeyan

Queanbeyan is located a mere 12km from Canberra but is in the state of New South Wales, and is perhaps best known today as the home town of Formula One star Mark Webber. Queanbeyan is sometimes preferred by investors to Canberra due to its stronger rental yield and simply for being more affordable than the capital city itself, which has become rather expensive in recent times.

Queanbeyan was established as a township in 1838 when the population was just 50 people. The population of Queanbeyan is now 6000, so it is still relatively small in size even today. Personally, I don't look to invest in towns with such a small population, though you might argue that Queanbeyan is so close to Canberra that from an investment perspective it has some of the attributes of a suburb rather than as a town in its own right (though locals may of course disagree!).

The property market in Queanbeyan is to some extent likely to move in lock-step with that of Canberra, and therefore it may be some time before we see much in the way of meaningful or strong capital growth. One article I read predicted a property boom in Queanbeyan. Personally I am always very wary of new land release and developments in such areas and I steer clear.

Business in the ACT

The population of Canberra is relatively small as compared to the major capital cities, the ACT's main city having been planned as an administrative centre rather than as a hub for industry. As a result much of the activity in the city involves politics and government administration as opposed to more productive enterprises.

Chapter 19 Summary

- House prices in Canberra grew sharply from 2006 to 2009

- Prices in the capital have tailed a little since that time before stabilising

- In 2012, housing supply appeared to be meeting demand in Canberra, and there is a risk of a glut of apartments coming online

- There may be a lower demand from the public sector going forward

- Median incomes in Canberra are relatively high which has helped to drive growth in the past

20

OF TRANSPORT
HUBS AND
CARPARKING

Investing in properties near transport hubs

Every single investment property I have ever bought has been in an area experiencing massive population growth and within 1km of a significant train link for a major city centre. That is in no way an accident, it is a deliberate strategy which I have set out to follow right from my earliest days of investing in property.

When I buy investment properties I am buying them with a view to holding them for 30 years or more, (with some luck, I might be around for that long) and to date I have never sold one. I might, of course, decide to sell some properties at some point if I believe they have become wildly over-valued, but my basic plan in property is simply to acquire prime-location properties and hold on to them.

The stations in Monopoly

It is not permitted to build houses and hotels on the train stations in Monopoly (unless you grew up in a family where new 'house rules' were invented). After all, the titles are already stations so building houses would not make much sense. If a player owns an individual station, then the rent is fairly modest. Yet if a player can add extra stations to their portfolio, the rent increases handsomely and the return on investment becomes progressively stronger with each title added, generating a steady if unspectacular cash flow. As there are four stations on the board — one on each straight — the stations can begin to become cash cows for the fortunate owner.

I grew up in England and for three years I worked in London. Something which I quickly learned from London — a city with a truly awful traffic problem — is that properties which are located close to London Underground tube stations and transport hubs are often more highly sought after than those which are less well located with little public transport available.

Transport links are becoming increasingly important.

Over all the years since I first came to Australia, it has never ceased to amaze me how accepting the residents of Sydney and Melbourne are of the ever-worsening traffic problems. We should be absolutely fuming about them! Instead, in the main, we just inhale more fumes.

Traffic in a city does not have to be diabolical. Successful city planning and incentives can ease transport problems. Sadly, it seems to me that public transport issues in Australia will become far worse before they improve. Particularly in the states of Victoria and New South Wales, with the population growing at such a significant rate, I place a great deal of importance on owning properties close to transport links.

Traditionally, the immediate areas around train stations in a large number of the world's major cities have been rather seedy, and therefore while owning property fairly close to a station can be exceptionally beneficial, it often makes sense to be located a little away from the station itself. This is not always the case, however, particularly in some outer suburbs where train stations see far fewer passengers using the train system and the stations are not necessarily major transport hubs.

Investing in railways

Queensland Rail

Back in 2010, the 147 year old Queensland Rail company floated on the Australian Securities Exchange, and it has since changed its name to Aurizon (AZJ). Anyone who was investing in shares at that time could hardly have failed to notice this, as the adverts were seemingly everywhere. When I see continuous adverts for stock market floats, the sceptic in me asks why the need to advertise so heavily exists. Investors generally want to own shares in great businesses without the need for huge promotional campaigns.

> Be wary of glossy brochures when companies go to IPO.
> The numbers and words are more important than the pictures.

In fact, around the same time I was also unimpressed with the Myer (MYR) float for similar reasons. Myer produced a lot of flash brochures and we saw lots of pictures of Jennifer Hawkins — which in itself was no bad thing — but the float price was at such a huge multiple of earnings I struggled to see the upside for the investor. This has proved to be correct, though in fairness to Myer and the stockbrokers, neither they nor I could have accurately predicted what a tough period late 2011 and early 2012 would prove to be for the retail industry.

I was also sceptical about the prospects for the Queensland Rail float, but I have been proven wrong on this one. My view at the time was that the QR prospectus theme seemed to be that 'things could only get better', which does not usually inspire much confidence in management. I also felt that the fact that the company did not have retained taxed profits behind it (and it could not therefore pay franked dividends) was a big negative. Well, I was shown to be incorrect. Queensland Rail has been very successful post float and well done to them.

When it comes to railroads, aviation and resources projects, sometimes it can make more sense to be an investor in the servicing companies rather than the company assuming the full project risk. This is particularly so with regards to the resources industries, which is something I learned from working in mining. Railroads are often serviced by a number of ancillary businesses, so consider looking at these too.

Buffett and the railroads

Warren Buffett, arguably the world's most successful ever equities investor has a preference for investing in franchise-style businesses. In this context, this means finding businesses that are not producing commodities upon which they can only compete on price, instead focussing on those which provide a service which other companies find it very difficult to successfully compete with.

Famously, Buffett has invested successfully in newspapers such as the *Washington Post* as they operate an effective monopoly. It is very difficult to compete with the largest newspaper in town as it has the key readership sewn up, advertisers are interested only in dealing with the top-circulating paper and new entrants struggle to attain any market share.

For Warren Buffett, railroads can sometimes offer a similar proposition. Railroads such as Union Pacific, Norfolk Southern, and most recently a staggering $34 billion bet on Burlington Northern represented mouth-watering investments for Buffett because such companies have no realistic competitors — they operate an effective monopoly. The railroad can ensure its own future profitability as it has the ability to raise its prices without impacting demand. That is the type of business that Buffett loves.

Investing in property with carparking

Being a Sydneysider, it was a pleasure to visit so many of the regional towns in Australia where it is possible to park in town absolutely free at any time of day or night. What a refreshing change from the capital cities, where according to the newspapers a parking space reportedly costs as much as $70 for a few hours, as at the Secure carpark at World Square (I say reportedly, as I'd never pay that myself!).[1]

In fact, as I write this I just went downstairs to check whether this information is now dated, and sure enough, the carpark run by the same company on Pitt Street now charges $79 for parking of three hours or more! Based upon these figures, it is unsurprising that Sydney and Perth are among the top ten most expensive cities in the world for carparking.[2]

In a similar vein, when buying investment property in landlocked city suburbs with little parking space available, the difference in price between a dwelling with a carparking space and one without might be in the region of $30,000 or even more. I have bought one new investment property in Sydney's inner-west which did not have a parking space, and even today many years after purchase it is worth around $30,000 less than an equivalent unit with parking, although as the unit is close to a train station it remains in high demand. Incidentally, properties that I own in the inner-west sector of the market have delivered tremendous growth over the past half-decade.

Free parking in Monopoly

In the game of Monopoly the *Free Parking* square represents a safe haven where no rent is payable and nothing bad can befall you. Although it is not in the official rules, some players like to suggest that where taxes and fines are paid during the game this money should go into the centre of the board rather than the bank, and any player who lands on Free Parking receives this tidy windfall of cash.

Parking spaces represent more land owned and add value to prime-location investment properties.

Generally speaking it is preferable to own investment properties with a parking space or available parking, though if the property is located next to a transport hub then the impact of not having parking may be softened somewhat. There is also a relatively new concept in some apartment developments where you buy a storage cage which is big enough for a bike, so if you buy a unit off the plan you might be able to negotiate a storage cage for your parking space too.

Some apartment blocks, particularly those which are mixed use (for example, hotel and residential) offer valet parking. Valet parking can be great but be very wary of the potential cost. With Australia's cities being busy places, often houses have allotted street parking, although sometimes there is no allocated space, so future traffic and parking issues should be considered when you are looking at property to buy.

Investing in parking spaces

Some positive cash flow books promoted purely in parking spaces (or storage units) rather than properties. It's not a strategy I would go for myself as there are potential disadvantages. You are perhaps less likely to secure a mortgage for a parking space and therefore no leverage will be available — you may simply have to pay cash for the full purchase price of the space. Rental yields vary significantly depending on the location and type of the space.

Personally I would be too unsure of the capital growth available from a parking space and if I was not using leverage I would be at a significant disadvantage as compared to an investor in a standard residential property. I have heard that people like to invest in parking spaces and storage units because they can generate a positive cash flow. Fair enough.

I would question, however, whether you might be in the wrong asset class by buying storage cages or lock-ups if income is your goal? Shares or bonds provide income, for example, and equities have great growth potential too. Still, I guess if you have an eye for deal, why not?

Do you even need a car?

If you live in a city, it might make sense to question whether you even need a car. This is a very personal decision as most of us enjoy the convenience of being able to drive wherever we like with a minimum of fuss, though worsening traffic issues make even this statement a little questionable.

Cars tend to be costly to own as on top of the purchase price (which often is paid for using a costly loan) we incur registration, fuel, insurance and repairs costs, none of which are becoming any cheaper. Of course, by driving ourselves we are contributing to the traffic congestion issues and indeed our carbon footprint. In this regard, I am now practicing what I preach having sold my car in Sydney in 2012, although I must confess that we still do own a car in England — not that we drive it very often living in Australia.

Cars entail significant holding costs.

An idea I explored in one of my blog entries (http://petewargent.blogspot.com) some time ago was whether we would be better off over the life of a vehicle to own a car or use a taxi. Naturally, the answer depends on how many kilometres you might expect to cover in an average day, whether you have financed your car with a loan and a number of other variables. The conclusions included that, if nothing else, second hand cars paid for in cash can offer significantly better value than those bought brand new on finance, and cars with smaller engines instead of 5 litre wagons can save us plenty in fuel costs. If you don't drive to work every day, you may also find that your vehicle costs you in a disproportionate level to its usage value.

While at times I miss having a car, I am happy to report that there is a tremendous sense of freedom in not owning a vehicle in Sydney. If I need a car on any given day or want to travel to the south coast or the central coast of New South Wales then I simply wander down to a car hire centre on Broadway and pick up a Camry or a Commodore for the day. I do accept that this is an easier step to take for someone living in the centre of the city with multiple transport links than elsewhere, but it might be food for thought anyway. It would after all be remiss of me not to take his opportunity to make the point that we all have a responsibility towards the environment.

Chapter 20 Summary

- With traffic problems worsening in major capital cities, properties close to transport hubs may become increasingly sought after

- The immediate surrounds of train stations are sometimes undesirable — be wary of this

- Buffett recognises that buying shares in businesses such as railroads which operate a near or effective monopoly when share prices are cheap can represent a fabulous investment

- A parking space can be important component of a property in a busy, landlocked suburb

- Properties without a parking space can still be worthwhile investments if they are located close to transport hubs

- Running a car can be very costly from a personal finance (and environmental!) perspective

21
PROPERTY INVESTING NUTS AND BOLTS

21

Buying property off the plan

When the property market is growing rapidly buying property off the plan can be a method of obtaining capital growth before you have even settled on a property. This strategy is especially popular for those keen to capitalise on booming markets before a full deposit or mortgage approval is ready. However, in early 2013 there appeared to be few booming markets other than Darwin, so I would not consider buying off the plan to be a good risk versus return trade-off at present. Now may not be the time to be pursuing this strategy.

The advertisements may often tell you that you can buy for a good price today, but in reality new developments tend to have a host of additional costs factored into them. It is fairly obvious that a developer's premium or profit margin is likely to be built into a new development.

> Just because something is labelled as an
> investment, does not mean it is a good investment.

When markets are flat or only appreciating moderately, it can make sense to manufacture growth in other ways. One of the ways in which investors can do this is seeking out properties which they can buy at under market value and add value to through renovation. This strategy can usually only be applied through considering established properties.

Shiny, new properties can seem very appealing. Sometimes it is noted by investors that the depreciation allowances on new properties are attractive, and this can indeed be the case. Remember, though, that depreciation allowances are high on new properties precisely because new items do tend to depreciate quickly, and that can include the perceived value of the property. There can be other risks involved in buying off the plan and, to me, these usually outweigh the benefits.

> A sophisticated share investor would expect
> to buy a risky asset at a significant discount
> to compensate for the risk. When you are buying
> off the plan, developers instead demand a premium.

There are quite a number of risks associated with buying off the plan. The quality and the timeliness of build itself are two of the most serious. You need to be sure that you are dealing with a reputable and safe developer and try to compare the asking prices with what is available on the established property market. While it is inevitable that a developer will factor in a profit margin (in part to pay for all those flashy brochures that they showed you), you must not pay over the odds for a property simply because it is new. Everything can be negotiable, even if the advertisement tells you it is not.

Be wary of rental guarantees

A rental incentive might be available on some types of investment property. As an investor, be wary. The idea is that the vendor or developer guarantees that a certain level of rental income will be received by the new owner over a stated period post-purchase. There is an embedded risk that the price of the property may be inflated to reflect unrealistically high rents, which cannot be secured after the period under guarantee expires.

Indeed, some would say that where a property has a rental guarantee, this should immediately serve as a red flag to investors. Is the property over-priced? Why does the property need a guarantee?

Using buyer's agents

It interests me to note that when it comes to superannuation the overwhelming majority of people are happy to delegate the management of their fund to a manager, perhaps taking a passing interest in the results of the fund once or twice per year (even if only to note: 'is that it?'). I suppose the reason is that our superannuation feels as though it is less important because we cannot access the balance until our later years.

Yet when it comes to investing in property, most investors opt to go through the process of purchasing property alone, with little or no coherent plan of how the investment should perform or fit in with their goals. This is despite the fact that property transactions are almost invariably the most material purchases we make in our lifetimes.

Some investors choose to use a buyer's agent in order to ensure that they buy the right kind of property for their purposes, and one which will provide the outcomes that they are aiming for. Using a buyer's agent is normally not cheap, but the benefits can often well exceed the outlay. Because property investing tends to involve the use of leverage, you want to be certain that you are making a solid investment.

Property magazines frequently report horror stories of would-be investors who pay dearly having been misled by unscrupulous individuals. A buyer's agent can guide investors past the potential pitfalls. Some of the areas in which a buyer's agent may assist in the process of acquiring a property include:

- Arranging a meeting with a mortgage broker, financial planner and accountant

- Locating property for purchase that meets your criteria

- Engaging a solicitor for the buying process

- Arranging pest and building inspections

- Engaging an independent valuer to ensure you don't overpay for a property

- Attending the auction process on your behalf or negotiating the purchase price

- Some buyer's agents will also project manage a renovation for you if that is your plan

One analogy that buyer's agents sometimes put forward is that if you had a serious mechanical problem with your car you would be unlikely to attempt fixing it yourself unless you were a fully-trained expert in car mechanics. Therefore, you should use a professional to guide you through the investment process to reduce your risk of financial loss (and, as noted, particularly because property investments tend to the most significant transactions most of us ever engage in).

If a buyer's agent can source you a property which grows in value at just 1% better per annum then they will have saved you the equivalent of their fees in a remarkably short space of time, and the investment should continue to perform for you through the life of the investment. A good buyer's agent should have made your life considerably easier and less stressful too. Naturally if you are going to use a property buyer's agent you should find one with a proven track record of successful property acquisitions and one with good credentials.

Renovations

Given that I feel some cities are unlikely to demonstrate stellar levels of capital growth in the immediate future, budding property investors have a number of choices. One might be to manufacture growth through buying a property at below its intrinsic market value and adding value to it through a renovation.

One of the advantages that property has over shares as an asset class is that a property investor has the option to buy a property which he or she can add value to in this manner. As minority shareholders there is very little we can do to alter the future value of a company once we have become a part-owner of the entity through buying a parcel of shares. While shareholders with big percentage stakes may hold some influence, for most individual investors we will have very little say in management decision-making.

> A successful renovation adds capital appreciation
> and improves rental income.

If you are able to furnish an investment property with a cosmetic facelift or rejuvenation you may be able to add 10% or even 20% to the rental income and significantly reduce or negate cash flow loss. Full scale renovations may, if you have the relevant skills, add greater returns to both cash flow and capital growth, though there may be a risk premium attached to the strategy if you are inexperienced. I like improvements of a more cosmetic nature such as repainting, carpeting and in some circumstances installing a new kitchen and bathroom.

Traditionally, more serious renovators have aimed to spend around an extra 10% on top of the acquisition cost of the property on a renovation, aiming for 25% capital growth on the total cost of the investment (i.e. purchase price plus renovation costs). A longer time horizon or a bigger renovation may warrant seeking a higher return as compensation for the risk.

In a cosmetic renovation, the investor may simply want to improve the value of the property by $1500 or more for every $1000 spent, and significantly increase the potential rental income in the process. The residual un-depreciated value of certain qualifying assets that are scrapped may attract a tax benefit and therefore it is important to prepare a depreciation schedule both before and after renovations.

Figure 21.1 — Example: simple cosmetic renovation

	$
Purchase Price	300,000
Kitchen upgrade	10,000
Bathroom upgrade	10,000
Carpeting	5,000
Painting	3,000
Garden	2,000
Total cost	**330,000**
Re-valued amount	**345,000**

The key to a successful renovation lies as much in the planning and budgeting as it is in the execution. So many punters buy properties for renovation with no such preparation. A sound plan should include a detailed budget of costs, a realistic timetable and the expected resale value. Too often the budget is based solely upon the amount of the money that is available. A prudent budget should also include a decent time and dollar value contingency for when the renovation does not go according to plan.

Are houses a better investment than apartments?

This is an old debate which property investors have had over the years: are houses better investments than apartments or units? The answer, as so often with questions of this nature is: it depends. The old theory was that houses are a better investment than units because houses have more land area and it is land that appreciates while buildings depreciate.

There is more than a grain of truth in the theory, but if we take a step back and think about that more precisely it does not necessarily always hold true. Ultimately, what makes a property price move upwards or downwards? The answer is supply and demand.

Ultimately supply and demand always determine asset prices.

You might decide to own a house worth $100,000 in an extremely remote area of the Northern Territory with a few dozen acres of land. $100,000 is a cheap price for so much land. Does this mean that the property will boom in value? Well, it might, but the likely answer is no, because generally speaking there is a low demand for land in remote areas, and there is a lot of it available at very low cost. So in this instance at least, the house probably does not represent a great investment.

On the other hand we might have bought by a 50 square metre apartment on Sydney's north shore with a view over what we now know as Bennelong Point in the 1970s. Sure, the apartment doesn't have much land underneath it, and what land it does have underneath it is theoretically shared with the other unit owners in the block.

But would the apartment have been a good investment despite its tiny share of the land? You bet it would! There has been a huge and growing demand for apartments in Sydney and particularly apartments with harbour views and a vista comprising two of the world's most recognisable city icons.

Be very wary about investing in old properties —
unless your plan is to pull them down.

There can be a danger in investing in old, run-down apartments for which there is not an adequate sinking fund. If buying a property is to be a multi-decade investment, then you need to consider what condition the dwelling will be in at the end of the period of ownership. This is an argument in favour of preferring houses: even if the house falls in to disrepair or even burns to the ground, you will always own the land.

While the population in remote areas tends to remain flat, in the capital cities the population has been increasing and will continue to increase by many thousands of people each year, and thus demand is growing ever higher. As you will no doubt have noticed if you live in of one the major capital cities, there is not much land available to be built on near the city centre.

Property investors should look for high demand
and scarcity value.

Sometimes houses can be superior investments. In Brisbane (as well as in Adelaide and Hobart) houses are relatively affordable as compared to Sydney and Melbourne, and therefore depending upon which suburb you are investing in, houses can definitely be smart investments and also offer great potential to add value. In some areas large developments can make apartments ten-a-penny. The key is to invest in the type of property which is in demand for that area, and particularly to look for scarcity value. What great selling points will your property have that others don't?

Investing in blocks of units

One strategy worth considering if you are planning to make a high value property purchase is buying a block of units. Buying a premium sector house can sometimes lead to severely negative cash flows which becomes painful to service. Through buying a block of units it is possible to buy a high value property without sacrificing too much in the way of rental yield.

Indeed blocks of units are often where experienced investors put their money, for there is sometimes potential to add significant value to a block of units through renovation, installing new appliances or adding bedrooms. If this is to be your strategy then you need to think carefully about how much to pay for a block of units, for deciding upon an intrinsic value is not as straightforward as valuing an individual unit.

Sometimes investors like to look at the likely cost of the individual units, others at the replacement cost of the block and still others work from the cash flows generated by the building as a whole. Yet another alternative is to buy an old house, obtain development approval and build a block of units on the plot. There is certainly no one-size-fits-all when it comes to property investment.

Gaols as new apartment dwellings

While we were travelling around Australia we stayed for a couple of weeks in Coburg in Melbourne as we needed a base while I indulged myself in the Boxing Day Test Match for a few days. Not far from Coburg, the old gaol has been converted into a residential development of units. In the future, with rising construction costs we might expect to see more and more conversion developments, from old warehouses to hospitals to former institutions for mental health and more.

Always understand strata schemes thoroughly.

Are these types of developments good investments? The answer: sometimes. It pays to be extremely wary of the strata schemes when buying into old buildings, particularly so in respect of large developments. Old buildings which are in need of urgent repair can be phenomenally expensive to maintain.

Investing in property in distant locations

In today's property markets where capital growth is unlikely to come so easily as was the case in times past, it will sometimes make sense to invest in states other than the one that you live in. Even if you live in a state that has good immediate prospects for growth, as property markets move cyclically, it is likely that some time down the track, better opportunities will again exist elsewhere.

There is not necessarily a problem with purchasing a property remotely without visiting it yourself. However, if you do decide to purchase an investment property without inspecting a property yourself, then you must make doubly sure that you have carried out all of your research thoroughly. If you stop to consider carefully the risk of making a mistake and what it might cost then you might start to appreciate the steps that need to be taken in order to avoid making an error in judgement.

Sometimes you may hear property investors or writers say that they would not want to view a property before buying it, lest they become emotionally involved in the purchase, thus introducing a risk of paying too much for the property. The theory is that we may tend towards buying a property more suited to our own tastes than those of the potential or targeted tenants.

While I understand the theory, I also believe that by researching property remotely we may introduce certain other risks unless the research that carried out is very thorough. For me, I usually like to view a property myself where possible as it gives me comfort that I have all available information at my command.

Property valuations

Obtaining an independent valuation of any property you intend to purchase is a very sound and very sensible idea, and this is particularly true when investing in distant locations! While a valuation may cost around $500 and you may be reluctant to pay this amount up front (especially as there may be no guarantees of completing on the purchase), the potential savings that could be made from not overpaying are many times this fee. Take the shortcut at your own risk. Do, however, be wary of a recent tendency for property valuations to come in low as property valuation professionals err on the side of prudence.

Why short-term property price data might be misleading

In this age of ultra-connectivity, there is a tendency for us to place importance on details dealing in ever-decreasing timeframes. In the share markets, annual reports for shareholders are no longer enough: we want quarterly updates, monthly summaries, even daily dispatches from brokers. Somewhere in Omaha, Warren Buffett must be gently shaking his head in silent but knowing disbelief.

> 'The big picture doesn't just come from distance;
> it also comes with time.'

Here are three reasons why short-term property price data can be misleading:

Misleading factor 1 — Extrapolation

Property data as reported must be extrapolated from a small number of property sales for the simple reason that most homes are not bought or sold in any given year. Perhaps only one in twenty dwellings might be transacted in any 12 month period, meaning that only a very small fraction of the housing stock is reliably measured each month. Given that property markets are also seasonal, in certain months only a miniscule percentage of properties are sold, thus weakening the reliability of the data reported.

Misleading factor 2 — Median values as a measurement tool

The definition of a median figure is the value at the midpoint of a frequency distribution of values. In plain English: in property reporting, the sales value whereby half of the recorded sales figures are higher and half of them are lower. Median property values do tend to be more useful than mean (or average) values, which can be severely skewed by a number of sales in the *über*-luxury or premium sector. However, median values can be skewed too by similar proliferations of sales in any one market sector.

Misleading factor 3 — Macro versus micro trends

While property data tends to report what is happening in individual cities, properties of different types and in different suburbs and even streets can behave in a diverse manner. Therefore, we should take note of broad trends rather than placing undue emphasis on one month or one quarter of data.

Overcoming the weaknesses in median price reporting

The data providers combat the weakness in median prices as a measurement tool in different ways. In Australia, RP Data reports on a hedonic regression basis, which in layman's terms means breaking down each sale into smaller constituent parts — such as number of bedrooms of the property sold or the size of the plot — thereby scrutinising individual transactions at a closer level.

The Australian Bureau of Statistics and Australian Property Monitors instead use a stratified price modelling approach, whereby the market is carved up into a number of different price brackets and the movements within each defined bracket analysed. The different methodologies explain why on a quarterly basis, the statistics reported can seem to lack correlation. Over a year or more, however, the figures and stories tend to align with more coherence.

Making sense of the diaspora

We should look for broad trends in property price data rather than reading too much into whether a city has reported property prices that have risen or fallen by 0.1% over any 30 day time horizon. While the outputs of property data can be measured to that level of accuracy, the inputs cannot all be known. We need to remember that the reported figures, in spite of being reported to one decimal place, can only be as accurate as what actually takes place in the market each month.

Back in the early days of computing, the American computer scientists had a phrase for this, which they impishly referred to as GIGO — or Garbage In, Garbage Out. This cheeky acronym, intended by boffins to mirror or parallel the more conventional accounting term FIFO (First In, First Out), implies that no matter what happens, computers can only report based upon the data we feed into them.

You make more money from property while you are asleep.

Why do people make more money from property while they sleep than they do when they are awake? Because when they are awake they are constantly fretting about market commentary and movements instead of allowing values to grow and compound as they do when asleep!

The Goldilocks approach to property ... getting it just right

There are many similarities between how the best returns are achieved in property and shares.

Beta and volatility in stocks

In the stock markets, commentators love to divide up the available stocks into three sectors based upon the size of their market capitalisation or total stock market valuation — the large caps (also known as the blue chips), the mid-caps and the small-caps (sometimes referred to as the penny dreadful stocks). A classical model known as the Capital Asset Pricing Model (CAPM) attempted to show that the risk of a stock could be measured partly with regard to its level of volatility, known as its *Beta*. While the model, in common with many of its kind, is slightly illogical and has a number of shortcomings, it is useful in that it demonstrates a notable point: that the share prices of small companies tend to be far more volatile than their larger equivalents.

Timing the market ... or time in the market?

This is helpful to know for those attempting to time the share market, for they may elect to buy into the mid-cap stocks when the market is cheap, as mid-caps are theoretically likely to swing higher in an upturn (and lower in a downturn) than the steadier behemoths at the top of end of town.

Market-timers may be wise, though, to steer clear of the penny dreadful stocks — which in Australia tends to comprise hundreds of speculative resources stocks. These are partly best avoided because they pay no dividends and thus returns can be immediately stunted, and partly because their *Beta* or volatility can be so high that there is a significantly increased risk of capital raisings resulting in shareholding dilution or, worse, company insolvency and the investor's risked capital being wiped out in its entirety.

If you are investing for the long term, of course, the best approach is simply to seek out the finest companies with superior future cash-generating ability. That is, to find and buy shares in the wonderful companies that will generate great margins and profits and be in the highest demand for decades to come.

Superior long-term returns in investment property

It has been well demonstrated and documented in a number of studies that luxury property can be far more volatile than the remainder of the asset class. This will always be the case. Logically, it is significantly more difficult to benchmark a property valued at several million dollars with a range of comparable dwellings, and there are simply fewer potentially willing buyers at the luxury end of the market. In contrast, asking prices of apartments in the median value range can be directly compared with recent sales values of similar units, and the likely purchasers comprise all three types of property buyer: first homebuyers, investors and established homeowners. The natural outcome is lower volatility.

Premium property is volatile and can entail holding costs.

Just as with stocks, properties at the bottom end of the range have their time in the sun — generally when we experience a prolonged period of low interest rates — but also periods where the cost of capital moves higher and lower demographic suburbs (where linear salary income prevails) can experience severe financial distress.

Some investors like to seek out cheap suburbs where rental yields can be higher (this happens where rents increase but capital growth have been stilted for some reason, usually resulting from lower demand) and there is seemingly more room for values to grow. However, there is an old saying in property circles:

'Cheap today is cheap tomorrow'.

While the tone of the phrase is perhaps unnecessarily sneering and dismissive, it does caution us wisely to be wary of properties which may be in lower demand as we introduce risk of vacancies and periods when there may be no willing buyers.

Getting it just right

While many take the approach of timing the stock market, it is a tough approach to adopt in the more illiquid world of property. Of course, it can still be done successfully. A swathe of investors are currently gathering super-cheap properties in distressed markets in the US or Ireland in the hope that the outlook improves in those regions. It's also entirely possible to make a fast buck in niche, commercial or speculation-driven markets such as the Gold Coast, Florida or holiday regions — *if* you get your timing right. There is no one-size-fits-all in property investment, but by far the easiest approach in my opinion is to seek out residential properties somewhere close to the median value in outstanding suburbs for which there is a continual and growing demand, and to hold on to them for as long as possible.

In property investment, follow the demographic trends.

For my money, the demographic shifts are pointing towards increased demand for prime-location apartments in the major Australian capital cities which are experiencing very strong population growth. It might not sound as exciting as jetting around the world to seek out states where real estate values have collapsed and financial distress has caused fire-sale, repossession and foreclosure. But over the decades, from the simple approach of continuing to acquire prime location apartments…well, the satisfaction and returns from being a landlord providing quality accommodation can be very exciting indeed.

The strategy that property professionals use: Land-banking

Australian property supremo Michael Yardney is an advocate of land-banking, which is an advanced strategy used by professional property development companies.[1] Yardney explains that land-banking is the process of securing future property development sites at today's prices. Many large property development companies buy greenfield sites, farms or large tracts of land and put them in their 'land bank' to ensure they have a sufficient stock of land for future property developments. Over time the development companies rezone the land, put in the necessary roads and infrastructure, undertake a subdivision and on-sell the individual lots.

While holding a bank or stockpile of land has helped many developers make big profits in a rising market, it has also been the downfall of a number prominent developers when real estate values slumped or rising interest rates blew out holding costs.

Land-banking can be a great strategy for smaller property developers too. It's an approach Yardney has used successfully for the last few decades because he has learned to keep his holding costs to a minimum so they don't break the bank. Yardney notes that he doesn't buy vacant blocks of land, instead he prefers to buy old houses close to their use-by date on well-located blocks of land in great suburbs, with property development potential.[2] While the rent received helps to partially offset the holding costs, value is added to the site by obtaining development approval and then over time, proceeding with the property development.

Why is land-banking such a good investment strategy? Many investors have made small fortunes by land-banking because they are able to use a number of different property wealth accelerators that, when combined, generate substantial profits:

Wealth accelerator 1 — Land appreciates

We have all heard that it is the land component of your property investment which appreciates, so buying a property close to its land value can be a smart strategy. If prime location land is acquired then capital growth can be strong while the title is owned and the relevant approvals sought.

Wealth accelerator 2 — Adding value

By obtaining property development approvals you can add substantial value to a site. Once you obtain development approval for a subdivision or for multiple dwellings to be constructed such as apartments or townhouses, you have taken out one element of the property development risk — the council approval process. This makes your site more attractive to other potential developers who may be prepared to pay a premium for your site giving you the option of selling for a profit, or refinancing and continuing with the property development process.

Wealth accelerator 3 — Riding the property cycle

Securing property development sites with great potential in a soft market can be a third wealth accelerator. At these times, completing a project may not be particularly lucrative, so it is possible to buy these sites at a good price. As the market moves on the combination of a stronger market and owning a block of land with a development approval in a prime position allows completion of the project to make a substantial profit.

This strategy works particularly well in the inner- and middle-ring suburbs of our capital cities, where there is little or no vacant land for future development, but there is an increasing demand for new medium density developments from a whole new demographic of smaller households. This includes 'Gen Ys' starting out in apartments, DINKS (dual income no kids couples), Mingles (middle-aged singles) and Baby Boomers who are downsizing.

The combination of the a flat or soft property market, a limited supply of potential property development sites and the future demand for more medium density housing can make a perfect recipe for successful land-banking.

Property management

Whether or not to self-manage? That, here, is the question! In the early days of building a property portfolio it is entirely possible to manage your own properties, particularly if you invest close to where you live. My view is that in this regard it is important to play to your strengths. Personally, I have always used property managers and I always will. While I have been prepared on occasion to pick up a paintbrush, my inherent laziness when it comes to matters of refurbishment has made it abundantly clear that I should focus on my own expertise and leave others to theirs.

While I do of course accept that self-management can be an excellent way to control your expenditure, I have found that as my portfolio has expanded across different suburbs, areas and even different countries, even the concept of managing my own properties becomes an abstract idea. And though I accept that this might go against the principles of spending money that could be saved, I prefer to look at it in terms of spending money to make money.

Using professionals can make your life easier.

When I was 17 years of age I would never have paid for a carwash. There was simply no way that I would have parted with a few hard-earned coins in exchange for a service I could easily have fulfilled myself. Now that I am older and an expert in my field, a day of my time can be worth a substantial sum, so the cost of paying another professional to make my life more efficient often makes sense.

Truth be told, being self-employed these days, if I work an overseas contract then I am lucky enough to have a maid to do my washing and cleaning, and a driver to get me to where I need to be efficiently. When it comes to property investment, if your goal is to have more time and more freedom, it can definitely make sense to employ a property manager or management company.

Managing properties through a property manager
should involve little of your time.

The good news is that with the advent of the internet and mobile phone communication your own involvement in property management can be reduced to an absolute minimum in terms of time spent. You may need to set aside a little more time at tax return time, but again using a skilled accountant can reduce your time outlay very significantly.

Where I grew up in England, property managers can be very expensive and can charge as much as 12–15% of the rental income in fees. Fortunately for us in Australia, property managers are far more competitive on their fees and do not tend to charge nearly as much, although you may find that the fees charged to you for re-letting a property can be steep, even if your property is re-let to the same tenant. Do remember, though, that property management fees can be tax deductible.

If you decide to engage a property manager, the process should be simple — shop around until you find a good property manager and keep hold of them for as long as you can. Despite what you may have read in books promoting share investing, management of your property portfolio should not be time consuming, costly or stressful.

Find a good property manager — and keep them.

Of course, as in all fields of life, all property managers are not born equal. Some will be diligent, committed and passionate, others see their job as a necessary evil (I can sympathise as most Monday mornings I tended to see my full-time job in the same light!) and so it can make sense to shop around for a good addition to your professional support team.

I have experienced many different property managers over the years, some of whom have been good, others who have been mediocre. In Sydney, I now use the team at *Metropole* as I have found that dynamic boutique companies can be able to tailor themselves to your needs. If you are looking for a bespoke service, you might like to do the same.

Chapter 21 Summary

- Buying off the plan is often tempting but tends to entail risk

- Buyer's agents generally do not come cheap but can diffuse much of the risk from a purchase and the risk of buyer's remorse

- In cities such as Brisbane and Adelaide, houses are more affordable than in Sydney and Melbourne, and can often make outstanding investments

- If you are investing in apartments be very wary of areas with a potential for over-supply

- If you are looking at making a high-value property purchase, a block of units can represent a smart investment where yield does not have to be sacrificed

- Buying a block of units can offer a great opportunity to add value and manufacture capital growth

- Properties close to the median price appeal to the broadest demographic which can help to ensure continuous strong demand

- It is possible to make money in flat markets from renovation — but it still may be better to seek out opportunities where capital growth might exist too

- Land-banking is an advanced strategy which can be used by experienced investors to super-charge their wealth creation plan, particularly through acquiring great plots when the market is subdued and not demonstrating growth

- To maximise your freedom, find a great property manager — and keep hold of them for as long as you can!

Part 3
Sharing It Around:
Tax, Super and Shares

22

GETTING YOUR HEAD AROUND THE TAXES

22

In Chapter 3 I discussed how difficult it is to create wealth through a salary, because income tax eats away at the salary and what is left tends to get spent rapidly unless it is invested safely in appreciating assets. While this is undoubtedly true, let's drill down a little further into the roles of the various taxes to understand how we can best create wealth in a tax-favoured and tax-deferred manner.

The role of tax in Monopoly

In the game of Monopoly tax plays a sneaky role. There are two tax squares on the board, being the Income Tax square and the Sales Tax square (sales tax is what we would now refer to as goods and sales tax or simply GST). Just as in real life, the tax tends to feature around the time when the salary is drawn or at the *GO* square in Monopoly. It can be a cruel blow to collect the $200 salary only to land on a tax square and hand a wad of your cash back to the banker. In fact, just as in real life, the savvy tax collector will probably just hand over the net amount that you are due.

Back in the 1980s ...

Keating introduces the capital gains tax, 1985

Prior to 1985, the capital gains tax we know today was not in place in Australia. A clear consequence of this was a perceived benefit to speculating in the hope of a tax free gain, particularly in property. Paul Keating sought to remedy this in 1985 with the introduction of the capital gains tax while at the same time scrapping the negative gearing tax laws (though negative gearing incentives were hastily reintroduced in 1987).

While the capital gains tax rules shift subtly over time, the principle remains the same today as it was then: if we sell an asset for more than we pay for it, we may expect to pay some tax on the capital gain. The implication of the capital gains tax rules is that it is more difficult to build wealth using a financial plan designed around trading, for each time we sell an asset for a profit tax must be paid on the gain. It is often easier to build wealth using a plan which comprises buying an appreciating asset and holding on to it for the long term or even forever.

> Invest in assets for the long term to grow wealth
> in a tax-efficient manner.

Keating introduces dividend imputation, 1987

Keating went a step further and introduced the dividend imputation rules in 1987. Before the introduction of imputation rules, the system was clearly unfair in that companies were taxed on their profits via the companies or corporation tax, and then when they paid out dividends from their net profits the dividend income was taxed again as income in the hands of shareholders.

> Franked dividends are now treated
> favourably for tax purposes.

This was an obvious case of double taxation and the new rules sought to remedy this by the application of franking credits. The imputation system can present taxpayers tax relief or credits to the extent that companies have already paid tax at the company rate.

The implication of this is that buying and holding shares in companies that pay strong dividends (generally, industrial stocks) can represent a wonderful investment if they are bought and retained for the long term as the income is no longer taxed so unfavourably. Thus investors should consider an approach of building a diversified portfolio of industrial stocks for the long term and focussing on the growing income stream rather than the fluctuating share prices.

Negative gearing rules removed ... then reintroduced

The negative gearing tax rules represent controversial tax legislation in Australia. The rules sometimes allow investors who gear or borrow to invest to take a tax deduction on net income losses against other forms of income in the same tax year. Thus, those who might benefit include investors who take on margin loans to invest in shares, and particularly investors who acquire properties which make a loss after the depreciation benefits are accounted for.

In September 1985 the negative gearing rules were quarantined by the Hawke/Keating Government, meaning that interest deductions and other rental property costs could only be claimed against rental income (and not other income such as salary income). Excess losses could be carried forward to be used against profits in future years in a similar manner to how tax losses can be carried forward in a company. In theory if a property is held for the long term, inflation increases the rental income until the asset begins to generate a profit.

The effect appeared to be a reduction for demand in investment properties for the short period of time for which the negative gearing rules were quarantined.

Tax legislation can (and does) change unpredictably.

There is often lively debate as to what effect the removal of the negative gearing rules actually had on the property market. Some argue (usually existing property investors, it has to be said) that chaos ensued and rents increased very sharply as investors sought to minimise cash flow losses. This may have been true in some cities (in Perth and Sydney, where there were existing rental property shortages, rents jumped very sharply) but not necessarily nationwide. The waiting list for public housing in New South Wales alone leapt alarmingly from fewer than 110,000 persons to more than 140,000 over the short period of time that the negative gearing rules were quarantined, a trend which immediately reversed upon their reinstatement.

Others argue that the removal of the rules had little impact and it was concerted lobbying by vested interests in the property industry which forced their rapid reintroduction in September 1987. Yet others instead insist that as much of the backlash came from shocked tenants who were terrified by the spiralling cost of renting in Perth and Sydney.

The future for negative gearing rules is not known.

It is very difficult to say objectively what might happen if the negative gearing rules were meddled with again. Property bulls and investors tend to suggest that the result would be a spike in rents and a dire shortage of rental properties. Those of a bearish tendency (usually renters) instead argue that property values would fall as investors head for the exits and the system becomes fairer. Only time will tell whether we ever get to see what actually happens if the rules are removed again.

While many see negative gearing and reducing their tax liability as a cast iron reason to dive headlong into property as an investment, we should be wary as there is no guarantee that the rules may not be changed or, perhaps more likely, phased out. Moreover, making significant losses is never smart investing regardless of the asset class and regardless of whether it saves you paying tax or not. It is far better to view the negative gearing tax rules as the potential icing on the cake rather than the reason to get into property investment in the first instance.

It is worth noting that in times of lower interest rates negative gearing rules are of less importance to investors than when interest rates are very high and cash flow losses are materially higher. Also take note that when the laws were abolished in 1985 they were not made retrospective so existing owners of negatively geared properties could continue to claim their deductions.

Income tax in Australia

The rates of income tax in Australia are relatively high, which makes it very difficult to become wealthy from a salary alone. The thresholds changed for the 2013 financial year so that while the tax free threshold is more generous than it has been previously, the marginal tax rates ramp up very quickly, so even taxable income of above just $37,000 begins to attract income tax at the marginal rate of 32.5%. Thus, from that point onwards a third of your salary is likely to be deducted at source and winging its way to the coffers of the Australian Taxation Office.

Figure 22.1 — Income Tax Rates 2013 tax year

Threshold	Marginal tax rate
$18,001	19%
$37,001	32.5%
$80,001	37%
$180,001	45%

Source: Australian Taxation Office, www.ato.gov.au

As the marginal tax rates operate on an increasing scale, those who earn above $80,000 per annum begin to be punished heavily on their top slice of income. Note in the table in Figure 22.2 below how the effective tax rate increases as you earn more money.

Figure 22.2 — Effect of income tax on different salaries

	$	$	$	$	$	$
Gross salary	**50,000**	**100,000**	**150,000**	**200,000**	**250,000**	**300,000**
Income tax	7,797	24,947	43,447	63,547	86,047	108,547
Medicare levy	750	1,500	2,500	3,000	3,750	4,500
Low income tax offset	(250)	-	-	-	-	
Total tax	**8,297**	**26,647**	**45,647**	**66,547**	**89,795**	**113,047**
Net pay	**41,703**	**73,553**	**104,303**	**133,543**	**160,205**	**186,953**
Effective tax rate	16.6%	26.6%	30.4%	33.3%	35.9%	37.7%

The effective tax rate curve moves up sharply before tapering off as the effective tax rate converges towards 46.5% (the 45% top bracket plus the 1.5% Medicare Levy). Thus, for example, if you earned a salary of $10 million, your effective tax rate would be 46.2%, and if you somehow managed to earn a salary of $100 million, you would finally have achieved the fine distinction of an effective tax rate of 46.5%! Of course most of us won't earn these types of salaries, but the point is that as salaries increase so does the effective rate.

While a higher income is obviously useful, tax rates cut into your income substantially and as such it becomes difficult to build wealth through relying on your salary, particularly as expenses have an annoying tendency to rise with income. Wise investment of your net salary is the solution.

Capital gains tax

There are plenty of other taxes in Australia of course. We are all probably fairly familiar with the GST which is levied at 10% on goods and services. This is not the forum for a long and tedious discussion about the GST rules and when and where you need to become a GST registered business. The rules are easily found on the website of the tax office (www.ato.gov.au). Capital gains tax does play a relevant role for investors, however. When we buy an asset and later sell it for a profit, there is likely to be a capital gains tax implication, and for this reason it can sometimes be more effective to adopt a buy-and-hold approach to our investing.

Capital gains tax for property investors

The simplest way for most investors to avoid unnecessary taxes is to not sell appreciating assets. This sounds so simple and yet it is very common for investors see an asset appreciate in value and feel the need to lock in the unrealised gain through sale of the asset, without due consideration of whether the asset is likely to continue increasing in value in the future. This is particularly the case in property.

That people tend to sell investment properties in the first few years of ownership is a key reason why most property investors never own more than one or two properties and consequently why most budding investors never achieve financial independence through property investment.

Take a read of other property books and see what investors list as their biggest mistakes. Almost invariably there will be a reference to a property sold many years ago for a seemingly good profit at the time, only for the very same property to be worth tens or hundreds of thousands of dollars more today. The single smartest financial decision I've made is having never sold a property — sometimes the best course of action is inaction.

> Wealth is built more easily when it compounds
> unimpeded by regular capital gains tax.

For property investors, this is a decision that needs to be made when we own a dwelling which has appreciated significantly in value. Should we sell the property to realise the profit and invest again elsewhere? Or draw some equity out of the property through refinancing and invest using a part of the equity that has been created with the property's increased value? Each circumstance is different, but on many occasions the latter approach is more effective partly due to the diminished role of capital gains tax.

If we elect to sell a property, we must first put the property on the market which immediately brings us into the realm of sales fees and commissions for agents. When we complete on the sale, the Government is likely to want its share of the spoils in the form of capital gains tax. Transaction fees on the sale of a property can be very painful.

Then, if we choose to reinvest our profits in a property elsewhere we are hit up yet again with the legal fees, stamp duty and other costs associated with acquisition. It is for this reason that when I buy a property I aim to never sell it. In fact, to this day in more than 15 years my wife and I have never sold a property which is without question the smartest financial decision we have ever made. Remember what Buffett once said: as an investor, you only need to make a few good decisions and limit the number and impact of the bad ones, and you will triumph.

Capital gains tax for share investors

Take a look at the table below. The example is intended to demonstrate how capital gains taxes can influence results for share traders and investors. In the table below is shown what might happen if a share investor doubled his capital five times by buying and selling shares. Each time he makes a profit by doubling his capital he sells his shares, pays his capital gains tax and then re-invests his capital in another stock.

Figure 22.3 — Gains taxed at 30%

Starting capital	Capital doubled to:	Tax at 30%	Finishing capital
10,000	20,000	(3,000)	17,000
17,000	34,000	(5,100)	28,900
28,900	57,800	(8,670)	49,130
49,130	98,260	(14,739)	83,521
83,521	167,042	(25,056)	**141,986**

While this is only a theoretical example, it does generate an important point. In the table above, after doubling his capital five times and paying his due capital gains tax at an assumed rate of 30% the investor has been left with a total capital of $141,986.

Now consider this second table below, where a share trader has again doubled his capital of $10,000 five times. This time, he has held each trade for more than a year and has thus only incurred capital gains tax at an assumed lower rate of 15% (due to the capital gains tax discount for assets held for more than 12 months).

Figure 22.4 — Gains taxed at 15%

Starting capital	Capital doubled to:	Tax at 15%	Finishing capital
10,000	20,000	(1,500)	18,500
18,500	37,000	(2,775)	34,225
34,225	68,450	(5,134)	63,316
63,316	126,633	(9,497)	117,135
117,135	234,270	(17,570)	**216,700**

While he has incurred tax that has still eaten into his gains, his final capital of $216,700 is more than the investor in the first example thanks to the capital gains tax rate being halved from that shown in the first example.

Finally, consider the table below of an investor who has doubled her capital of $10,000 five times through one trade that she has held over a period of years. She will pay capital gains tax of 15% on the whole amount of the gain in the final year. And yes, the change of gender was deliberate in this third example!

Figure 22.5 — The power of compounding unrealised gains

Starting capital	Capital doubled to	Tax at 15%	Finishing capital
10,000	20,000	-	20,000
20,000	40,000	-	40,000
40,000	80,000	-	80,000
80,000	160,000	-	160,000
160,000	320,000	(43,500)	**276,500**

Of course, this is a purely hypothetical scenario and in the real world growth assets would be extremely unlikely to move in such a methodical fashion, but the principal here is very much the important thing. While the tax payment in the final year is undoubtedly painful, the final capital of $276,500 is an excellent result, and far outstrips the capital of the other two investors who have traded more frequently. The investor who continues to hold shares for the longer term can focus on the growing dividend income stream.

This is the essence of successful share investing (as opposed to trading) and in many ways it echoes the approach of the property investor who never sells in order not to trigger a capital gains tax liability. The tax bill in year five may be significant, but the final capital balance is a handsome compensation. What this neatly demonstrates is that a buy-and-hold approach to investment can be extremely effective because capital is allowed to compound and grow without the interfering effect of taxation eating into gains.

The carbon tax

After much debate and controversy, the Carbon Bill was finally passed in November 2011. The Australian carbon tax is targeted at the major emitters being the top 500 polluters in the country, as these are the entities expected to have the capital investment capabilities to improve technology and reduce carbon creation.

As a compensation for price increases to end users, the income tax threshold has been increased for all individual taxpayers although middle range tax rates were increased to the point where only individuals earning less than $80,000 per annum received any income tax relief.

Stamp duty

At the time of writing stamp duty is not levied upon share purchases in Australia, which is welcome news. However, there is no getting around that fact that stamp duty is a pain for property investors in Australia. Stamp duty arises on the acquisition of property (though there may at times be some exemptions or relief for first-time property buyers or those buying property off the plan) and can represent somewhere between 2–7% of the purchase value of the property, depending upon the cost of the property and the state in which it is bought.

If you are planning to buy and own a physical property within Australia, the only remedy is to resolve to make property a long-term investment rather than trading properties. This is one of the reasons I have never sold a property that I have bought — once I have paid the wretched stamp duty then I absolutely intend to hold the property forever!

How to legally reduce your tax

Being good citizens we should certainly pay our taxes as they fall due. However, there is little sense in paying more tax than we have to. There are a number of ways in which we can ensure that our tax liabilities are minimised.

'I am not evading tax in any way, shape or form.
Now of course I'm minimising my tax. And if anybody in this country doesn't minimise their tax they want their heads read, because, as a government, I can tell you you're not spending it that well that we should be donating extra.'
— Kerry Packer AC (1937–2005)

Get a good accountant

If you are going to be an investor, and particularly if you are going to invest in property, make sure that you find yourself a skilled and experienced accountant and particularly one with experience in the asset classes you are interested in. While I applaud trying to save money in many cases, it may not be money well saved to use the cheapest accountant you can find if it ends up costing you more in tax liabilities not saved. This can happen if you invest in property but use an accountant with no experience of investment property.

A skilled accountant is worth paying a little extra for.

Fortunately good accountants don't tend to charge too much for preparation of tax returns and PAYG variations, and their fees in themselves should be tax deductible. If you are to become a property investor it is important that your accountant has some experience of dealing with property-related tax treatment, otherwise the amount saved on cheaper fees could be insignificant as compared with allowable deductions not claimed.

Smarter ways to deal with the tax laws

If you sell property or shares for a profit, it is likely that you will incur some capital gains tax unless you have other deductibles against which the gains can be offset. We will also incur transaction costs on the sale of an asset, and should we elect to re-invest our profits in a new asset then there will transaction costs associated with the new purchase too. It is for these reasons that wealth is often more easily created through the strategy of buying outstanding assets and holding on to them for as long as possible. This way we never incur capital gains tax and the transaction costs are minimised as far as possible.

It is often felt by real estate investors that if an owned property has increased in value then it is important to sell in order to lock in the profit or access the funds. What is sometimes overlooked is that property can be to some extent a liquid asset in that where the loan to value ratio has fallen significantly, the investor can sometimes choose to take out a line of credit — that is, to borrow against the increased value of the asset.

Property can be a liquid asset when a line of credit is used.

This is how some huge property portfolios are created. Instead of investors selling properties to re-invest in more assets, a line of credit is taken out against existing assets which have appreciated and used as a deposit for new properties. The process can be repeated again and again, although a reasonable buffer should always be built into the investor's loan-to-value of assets ratio (LVR) as protection against adverse market movements.

Note that if a line of credit is taken out for the purpose of paying for living expenses then any associated interest charges will not be tax deductible. Borrowing for living expenses is a strategy advocated by some property clubs but one which I would only suggest is used by advanced investors and even then extreme caution should be exercised. While governments are able to run countries and survive by taking on ever more debt as they control the currency, we as individuals should not follow their lead.

Using the negative gearing tax rules to your advantage

The prevailing negative gearing tax rules in Australia allow investors to take a tax deduction for losses on geared investments (meaning investments that have been acquired with the use of borrowed capital). When people cite negative gearing rules as a great reason to get into investment property it would be sensible to be wary and question whether the negative gearing rules will always remain in place.

As noted, the rules were abolished once before in 1985 by the Hawke Government, before being hastily reintroduced as pressure on rents and public housing waiting lists built up, particularly in New South Wales.

> Negative gearing rules have been amended before —
> and they could be again in the future.

In my opinion future abolition of the negative gearing rules may not have the intended consequences, which is presumably why over recent years discussions of whether to phase them out have always eventually been shelved. Possibly fewer investors would enter into the property market which may make prices softer but existing investors may feel inclined to jack their rents up sharply to reduce their cash flow shortfall, and thus paradoxically it may be those who are not already on the property ladder who end up being punished in the form of high rents.

This argument has been countered through analysis of what happened to rents between 1985 and 1987 when the rules were removed (they went up in some cities, notably Perth and Sydney, but not in others) but the truth is that nobody conclusively knows what will happen to rents, vacancy rates and public housing waiting lists (and associated costs — what the government could saves in taxes it might lose in public housing costs) in Australia if negative gearing rules are abolished. Maybe one day we will fund out!

As a property investor it makes sense to capitalise on any available deductions. However, investors should always look to minimise cash flow losses and should not invest in property purely as a means of paying less tax.

Other deductions

There are a number of other areas in which we may qualify for deductions. The rules for deductible expenses are all freely available on the tax office website (www.ato.gov.au). Here are a few areas that are often or easily overlooked.

Where **self-education** is undertaken for the purposes of improving our earning potential, it is possible that the expenses incurred may be tax deductible. For example, an employee who is studying for an MBA in management in order to target a management role may find that the costs of the MBA are tax deductible (if he has paid for the costs himself, rather than the costs having being paid for by his employer).

Charitable donations can attract tax deductions too and therefore it is important to retain receipts if you make a donation which may qualify. In certain circumstances, it is possible to claim a tax deduction for **home office expenses**. Consult with your accountant or tax adviser if you are unsure whether you may qualify for relief. Finally, in some occupations certain other directly **work-related expenses** may be tax deductible such as work clothing.

Chapter 22 Summary

- Negative gearing rules in Australia currently make property investment very attractive, particularly for those paying substantial tax on their salary income

- There is no guarantee that the negative gearing rules will remain in place indefinitely

- Stamp duty and other fees make flipping or trading properties less appealing than buying and holding

- Frequent trading in both shares and property may lead to capital gains taxes and high transactions costs

- Dividend imputation makes buying and holding shares in great companies which pay franked dividends a very attractive and tax-effective strategy

- Using a good accountant is vital for those who plan to become advanced investors

- There are a range of deductions which can be claimed to reduce tax so aim to become familiar with the rules from the Australian Taxation Office (www.ato.gov.au)

23
PENSIONS
AND SUPER

23

Today in Australia, most pension schemes are defined contribution or so-called accumulation schemes rather than defined benefit schemes and therefore there is no guarantee that your superannuation balance at retirement will be adequate. Therefore, you need to look at what you can do to protect yourself.

The Community Chest

The Community Chest was the name a semi-official welfare system during the American depression.[1] Although it always felt like more to me, there are only 16 Community Chest cards in a game of Monopoly. Champion players memorise the order of the cards drawn so that they know their odds of drawing building repairs or other adverse cards later in the game. The Community Chest cards are generally more favourable than the Chance cards, in that nine of the 16 cards offer rewards (such as annuities maturing) as compared to only three which issue penalties (e.g. doctor's fees). Of the remaining four cards, two move you to another square (which can be good or a terrible depending on the stage of the game), there is one dreaded building repairs card and there is one Get Out of Gaol Free card.

> Most superannuation balances at retirement
> are inadequate for a comfortable retirement.

The superannuation system

If you decide to place a reliance of the Age Pension you might expect that you will see no more than $385 per week from this source, which is not enough to cater for a comfortable standard of living in many parts of Australia. I am not here to pass judgement on the Australian welfare system — or the systems of any other country for that matter — but I will make the assumption here that most readers of this book would prefer to have enough wealth at the date of their retirement in order that they need not rely upon the state and the Age Pension. For this to be the case, you will need to have built for yourself a portfolio of assets that can provide you with the income you need in retirement.

One of several flaws in the prevailing superannuation system is that fund management fees increase as the balance of your fund increases. On average, fund managers charge 1–2% of the balance managed as an annual fee. Thus, you can expect to pay more in fees as the time progresses, as demonstrated in the table in Figure 23.1 below.

Figure 23.1 — Fund management fees at 1% and 2%

Balance of fund	Fees at 1%	Fees at 2%
50,000	500	1,000
100,000	1,000	2,000
150,000	1,500	3,000
200,000	2,000	4,000
250,000	2,500	5,000
300,000	3,000	6,000
500,000	5,000	10,000
1,000,000	10,000	20,000

It is not unusual for Australians to sign up for whichever superannuation fund is suggested to them by their employer without carrying out any worthwhile due diligence into the balance of the fund (i.e. whether it is targeting high growth or a more balanced portfolio), the historical returns of the fund or what management fees the fund is likely to charge.

There are a number of reasons why Australians don't take much interest in super funds at a young age. The most obvious is that as the fund can't be accessed until our later years, it doesn't seem to be of much use to us when we are young and financially carefree. It is only as we become older that we begin to realise that the super fund should form an important part of our retirement plan. Another common misconception is that if we continue to contribute to a super fund throughout our working lives then there will definitely be a worthwhile balance to show for our endeavours at the end of the road. This is unfortunately not the case.

The shift from defined benefit to defined contribution

There has been a significant shift in the superannuation system so that the responsibility now lies with us as to whether our retirement balance is an adequate one. There is no guarantee that your super fund manager will generate good returns for you, or indeed any returns at all. There is only one thing you can be certain of and that is the fund manager will continue to deduct management fees from your retirement balance every year — as regular as clockwork — regardless of the results.

It may seem unlikely that a 1% or 2% management would affect your super balance materially, and in the early years of your fund this may be the case in absolute terms. Firstly, because your balance is small, the fund management fee is small. And secondly, it is the effect of the fees over time that is the real killer of returns. Allow me to demonstrate with some numbers.

Supposing no additional contributions are made to a balance of $100,000 and that balance is simply allowed to grow at 8% per annum, which could be a reasonable expectation for a well-managed equities portfolio over the long term. Due to the power of compounding growth — a snowballing effect — $100,000 would grow into a happy retirement lump sum of nearly $3.2 million over a working lifetime 45 years. The table below shows the potentially staggering effect of a 2% management fee on the ability of a fund to grow wealth over the duration of a working lifetime.

Figure 23.2 — Effects of a 2% management fee on likely returns

Year	6% compounding return	8% compounding return
0	100,000	100,000
10	179,084	215,892
20	320,713	466,095
30	574,349	1,006,266
40	1,028,572	2,172,452
45	**1,376,461**	**3,192,045**

The role of tax in superannuation

During your working life and the accumulation phase, superannuation is taxed in the following ways.

Figure 23.3 — Superannuation taxation

Contributions	15%
Income in the fund	15%
Capital gains in the fund (> 1 year)	10%

It seems odd that the Australian Government introduced a compulsory contribution and then decided to tax the contributions. It would have seemed more logical to make the contribution tax free and the contribution percentage lower as, theoretically at least, companies would make higher profits for the government to levy taxes from. Still, this is how the system is set up and we must work within it.

Although income and gains are taxed at lower rates than they might be outside of your superannuation, taxes still have a significant impact on the ability to grow wealth in a fund. Therefore, what is needed is an investment strategy which minimises taxes and transaction costs within the fund. As we have seen, you will not get this strategy from the average fund manager.

Can you improve returns by managing your own super?

If you are like most Australians in the workforce, your superannuation returns over the past half a decade or so will have been poor. The share market climbed through until 2008 when the sub-prime fallout and meltdown of the credit markets in the US sparked the financial crisis and a tremendous fall in valuations. After another losing year in 2011, a number of factors have conspired against the Australian share market from recovering in the same way that the Dow Jones index bounced back so swiftly in the US.

Firstly, the Australian dollar became viewed as a safe haven currency and that fact combined with our interest rates remaining higher than those of other developed countries ensured that the Australian dollar stayed extremely strong in historical terms. When the Australian dollar is strong, investors from Asia and elsewhere are disinclined to invest in the Australian stock market due to the increased foreign exchange risk and reduced value-for-money when acquiring assets.

Further, commodity prices — particularly in iron ore, but also in copper, coal and other markets — weakened, which materially impacts a resources-focussed market such as that of Australia. However, the 2013 financial year was a far better one for super funds.

You are responsible for building your own retirement balance.

There seems to be a prevailing viewpoint in Australia that management of our superannuation is someone else's problem. It is not unusual for folk to give their superannuation no consideration at all until late in their working lives. Be clear about this: if your superannuation returns are poor or inadequate, then that is your problem. You are not compelled to invest with any particular fund, to pay expensive management fees or even invest in a managed fund at all.

Australians have more money invested per capita in managed funds than the population of any other country, and with the contribution percentages sets to increase from 9% to 12% in the coming years this will probably continue to be the case. Recently, more Australians than ever before have taken to setting up self-managed super funds (SMSFs) in a bid to take control of their fund performance.

Of course, self-management may not be for everyone. If you have a small superannuation balance, self-management is not cost-effective. And if you have no experience in investment, the key question to ask oneself is this: will I be able to improve my superannuation returns *safely* through self-managing my fund? In order to answer this question, it is necessary to understand a little about how the fund management system works and what returns you are likely to receive from a managed fund.

Why fund managers don't beat the index

What returns do you normally get from your super fund? I'll take an educated guess that in most years you do not receive a net return after costs that is significantly better than could have been achieved simply by holding the XJO (ASX 200) index.

Sure, the headline figure might outperform the index by a little (you would hope so, otherwise why on earth are you paying a fund manager?) but once insurance, taxes and fund management fees are deducted, the net return can be dragged back. Research in the US has shown that the net returns of the majority of managed funds do not outperform those of the stock market index. If we can begin to understand why this is the case then why can make an assessment of whether we might be able to do better ourselves.

These are the main reasons that the majority of managed funds do not outperform the market:

- Transaction costs from high turnover of portfolios

- Capital gains taxes within the fund on stocks sold

- Market impact

- The effect of the bid/ask spread

- The commissions siphoned off by the fund managers themselves

Fund managers are assessed on the results of a fund on a quarterly basis which guarantees that the outlook of the manager is more short term that it should be. If you are managing your own fund then you have the luxury of taking a long-term view. The benchmark of the fund manager is the annual return of the index, and the results of a fund are unlikely to diverge far from this figure.

Rapid turnover of stocks within a fund leads to capital gains taxes and transaction costs being generated within the fund, and due to the size of some of the transactions being undertaken (large parcels of shares) fund managers can find that their own purchases impact the market price to some extent. There is also a gap between the price at which a share can be bought and sold for — the bid/ask spread — which is a further hurdle for the fund manager to overcome. As those in the funds management industry are generally targeting a return that is better than the index as a whole, what they really are seeking are stocks which outperform the market over a short time horizon.

The fund industry has certainly become very short-sighted in its focus. An awful lot of time, energy and cost can be wasted trying to chase short-term returns instead of maintaining focus on the greater goal of building a reasonable pension balance for retirement. This is caused in part by fund returns being reported on a regular basis leading to managers to be fearful of diverging far from the index return.

Fund managers tell clients to buy and hold or stay the course, but rarely do they practise what they preach — instead, most fund managers turn over holdings at a high rate.

Funds are also measured against the stock market on an annual basis. Woe betide a fund that gives a return that is significantly lower than stock market index as clients may decide to leave the fund. Managers are so fearful of significantly underperforming the stock market index through not holding a hot stock that they hold large numbers of stocks. As you would expect, a portfolio which holds dozens of stocks is not going to far outperform or underperform the index.

The great paradox for many fund managers then becomes that they face more risk from the stocks they do not own than those that they do. By holding stakes in all the major stocks it becomes more a case of whether they are overweight or underweight in any particular company. Any stock in which they are underweight they are effectively short-selling. You can start to see the unusual thought processes which permeate the system that has been created.

I should note here that I have no problem with holding a well-diversified portfolio as an approach. It can be a highly effective approach to wealth creation over the long term. But if this is to be the approach then do we need to pay a fund manager 1–2% of our balance each year for the privilege of so doing? Consideration of the above should lead us to ask ourselves an important question: if it's possible to match most fund returns simply by buying an index fund, should I elect to self-manage my own superannuation?

Salary sacrificing into your superannuation fund

Employees and self-employed people may wish to consider salary sacrificing up to the prescribed cap into a superannuation fund. Concessional contributions include employer contributions (including contributions made under a salary sacrifice arrangement) and personal contributions can be claimed as a tax deduction by a self-employed person.

Salary sacrificing can be a particularly popular strategy for employees as their retirement date draws closer. At this stage, many employees are earning higher salaries and thus are paying tax at a high marginal rate. This can make the idea of a tax-effective salary sacrificing approach more appealing.

If you have a super balance which is not quite high enough to make self-management worthwhile, it might be worth considering whether salary sacrificing could be a tax-effective method of building your balance up to a level where investing in property or shares yourself can be effected.

Self-management of superannuation is not for everyone!

If you have little or no investment experience it may be better to start small and gain experience outside your super fund first before leaping into self-management. Your superannuation is an important part of a financial plan and therefore ideally you should aim to have a track record of successful investment experience behind you before you take on management of your super.

> Regardless of whether you choose shares,
> property or fixed income as your vehicle the risk
> lies within the investor rather than the investment.

Cost and control: Why you might elect to self-manage

Cost

What is not appreciated by so many Australians is that the fees charged to them for the management of their superannuation can increase each year as their superannuation balance increases. While the fees may be relatively moderate in the early days of the fund's life, they can begin to become crippling if your balance is a large one. Therefore, the question that needs to be asked is whether the fund manager is justifying his fee or whether you would better served from a cost perspective to manage the balance yourself.

The first step is to check out what your fund manager is charging you. If you are lucky you will discover that the fee is 0.5% of your fund's balance per annum, although it is equally possible that the rate is 1-2% of your balance. Do not be misled into believing that a higher fund management fee necessarily equates to a better return on your funds, for there is no compelling evidence or proof that this is the case.

> Fund managers can generate significant transaction
> costs and capital gains taxes within the fund.

An alternative to self-management is simply to look for lower cost and better performing funds. Lower cost funds are easy enough to find and some very reasonable funds charge annual management fees of 0.5% of your balance per annum or less. Picking a higher-performing managed fund can be a tricky proposition as the past performance of a fund is no guarantee of its future results. Indeed, often funds which are running hot can perform poorly in the years following their great successes after new investors have swarmed towards the star performer. This is what you might expect to happen given the previously discussed theory of mean reversion.

Control

You don't have to accept the returns of a managed fund. Fund managers do not design the returns of a fund with specifically you in mind, and although you may choose a balanced or growth fund, or even one with a specific retirement date in mind, you still do not receive a bespoke service. It does not have to be this way. If you elect to self-manage then you can control your own destiny. After all, nobody knows more about your needs, goals, desires and tolerance for risk than you do yourself.

Importantly, you should be less inclined towards taking risks as your move closer to the retirement age. Having a huge exposure to equities when you are 21 years of age is not necessarily a bad thing because you have time on your side to recover losses from any adverse movements. Depending on your plans and outlook you may decide to some of your fund into fixed interest products as your risk appetite decreases with age. Remember though, that fixed interest investments carry their own risks — they pay an income but deliver no growth, so there is a risk of a different type attached.

As you approach the retirement age it is possible to choose a fund with a less aggressive balance. What needs to be balanced off is the need for growth against the need for income. Remember that you could easily live for several decades in retirement so shifting your entire fund into fixed interest products brings with it a risk of lack of growth and diminishing purchasing power of your fund.

> Self-managing can help to manage risk as
> appropriate to your own needs.

Fund managers are not motivated by the same goals that you are. A fund generates its own profits from the fees siphoned from the funds under management. Logically therefore, the fund's target is to build its assets under management to the highest level it can. You can't really blame the fund management industry, for it simply operates within the system that has been created. Besides, allocating blame will not lead you to a more comfortable retirement — but taking decisive action will.

You must always remember that when you see expensive adverts for your fund, shiny brochure mail-outs, fund sales reps driving expensive new fleet cars and the management company's flash offices in the city — these are all paid for by the management fees deducted from your retirement fund.

Above else, you must not believe the propaganda that there is some mystery to the art of managing your money that the average individual cannot comprehend. The figures prove that this is not the case. The fund management industry often does not even beat the returns of the stock market and nor does it provide you with adequate insurance in the case of a stock market crash. Therefore it is clearly possible for an individual to achieve superior returns through adherence to a sensible investment strategy.

Weighing up the costs of a SMSF

As noted, a major flaw in the superannuation system is that fund managers can charge their fees based upon a percentage of the balance managed. Thus as your super balance increases so do the fees. Take a quick look at your superannuation statement for the last financial year. You will notice that charges are generally deducted for insurance, taxes and management fees. There has been a shift in the industry towards a greater transparency of fee disclosure which is one positive move.

What is of perhaps most concern is the effect of the management fees on the ability of your fund to grow and compound. While 1% or 2% management fee might not seem to have a major impact, consider that the annual returns of your fund might only be in the 6%-8% bracket. Snip 2% out of that and the potential effect on your fund balance might be devastating. But what of the equivalent costs of self-management?

If you choose to self-manage and you are lucky then your existing fund will only charge you an administrative exit fee. If you are unlucky then they may charge you a percentage of your fund balance. If this was in the small print when you signed up for your fund then unfortunately there is little defence — ultimately we are all responsible for the paperwork we sign.

Then, when you have decided to go down the route there are two further costs to consider. Firstly there is the dollar cost of setting up the fund itself and the other is the ongoing cost of administration and compliance.

Self-management of a superannuation fund must never be undertaken lightly.

A third hidden cost is the cost of your time. For all of the bad press the fund management industry receives and however much we may dislike it, it's the only system we have and it does serve a very real purpose for millions of Australians. A significant percentage of the population have never invested before and therefore fund management may be the safest option for them.

Others, rightly or wrongly, simply do not believe they have the time, skills or inclination to manage their own money. A vast number of Australians believe that they are not responsible for their own wellbeing in retirement — instead believing the Government should take care of them — which is a prime reason why millions rely upon the Age Pension in retirement.

How much does it cost to set up an SMSF? There is no absolute answer to that question as it depends on a number of factors including which professionals you use to help you set it up and the type of structure you want to maintain (such as a corporate trustee or an individual trustee structure). You might expect to pay a few thousand dollars in total, but do ensure that you shop around and don't be afraid to haggle for a fair price.

Similarly, the on-going costs of accounting, audit, tax advice and compliance (a SMSF must submit a tax return every year), and administration will vary depending on the complexity of your fund and the fees of the professionals hired to ensure your compliance. Again, the fees could be as low as a thousand dollars per annum, but might come to several times this figure. If you keep good records and can do some basic book-keeping this may help to keep the fees under control. Fees incurred will be paid by the SMSF and should be tax deductible within the fund.

When does a SMSF become viable?

The answer to this question basically varies depending upon who you ask. Some might say that you would need a super balance of around $200,000 before setting up your own fund becomes cost-effective and worthwhile. Naturally the people who say that might include your fund manager or others with a vested interest in the status quo.

For me, I felt that when my balance reached $100,000 setting up my own fund became worthwhile, especially as the returns from my managed funds had been particularly poor. It is important to balance up the likely fund management fees against your own potential compliance costs.

If you have compliance costs of say, $2,000 for self-managing your super for tax and audit fees, how might this compare with the fund management fees of 1-2%? Well, if your balance moves into six figures it may become more cost effective to self-manage although it does depend on which advisors and professionals you engage. You also need to weigh up whether you believe we can outperform the returns of our fund managers, and also should factor in some cost for our time. If you are a busy person, switching to self-management may seem less appealing, though it is important to think about how important your superannuation is to your retirement years.

Pooling of funds

If the balance of your superannuation is insufficient to make self-management viable, then you might consider whether pooling your funds with your spouse might be an option. It is actually possible to pool funds with others too but obviously this is a strategy which should not be taken lightly. Differences of opinion that do not exist now may easily begin to exist down the track. You may not feel that a SMSF is viable if you have a balance of $50,000, but if your spouse or partner also has a balance of $50,000, then you may feel that you are in a better position to self-manage jointly.

Buying property with your superannuation

I believe that we will see a flood of self-managed superannuation funds buying investment properties over the next few years. There is now more than $1.4 trillion of superannuation capital under management, a figure which is growing strongly each year. With interest rates currently at historic lows, those managing their own super funds are increasingly realising that buying investment property is a viable option for them.

Although equities have continued to pay useful dividends there was a period of more than 5 years between mid-2007 and mid-2012 where no capital growth was seen across the All Ordinaries share market index.

As we know, investors become transfixed with capital growth and the under-performance of shares through that time may encourage more SMSFs into property investment. Although lenders tend to require large deposits from

SMSFs, property is an asset class which many Australians feel they understand and have been successful with in the past and therefore will see it as a natural asset class in which to invest a portion of their retirement capital.

Will SMSFs swamp the property markets?

So is a flood of SMSF capital likely to wash into the property markets over the next few years? Well, the short answer is: yes, I think so, unless the prevailing rules are changed. With investment results from capital growth in equities so poor or non-existent over around half a decade, more Australians than ever are turning to self-managing their superannuation funds in a bid to improve their floundering returns.

Most individual investors in equities become transfixed with immediate capital growth returns from shareholdings, rather than what we should be focussing on, which is the growing income or dividend streams over time. Although intellectually most of us probably know that stockpiling equities while they are cheap will be a fabulous long-term investment, emotionally most of us want to see fast returns forthcoming over the next few years.

> Using the banks' cheap capital may currently look
> more attractive than buying shares in the banks.

At present, the stock market doesn't seem to be promising that, but with property mortgage rates now so low, the property markets are seemingly offering some mouth-watering opportunities for counter-cyclical investors.

Why will SMSFs dive into real estate?

There are a whole host of reasons why this outcome is likely to eventuate: the ability of SMSFs to use leverage, the Australian love of bricks and mortar, excessive superannuation fund management fees, painfully low returns from some super funds over a prolonged period of time and a desire to take control, to name but a few. Below are three quick pointers which explain exactly why the property markets will be flooded with investment capital from SMSFs in the next few years.

SMSF driving factor 1 — Funds under self-management spiralling

Firstly, the actual dollars under self-management are spiralling. This is in part effect of the poor returns from equities and thus managed super funds with are heavily exposed thereto. Suffice to say that funds under self-management are now significantly higher than they have ever been before, the figure now rapidly heading towards $500 billion.

SMSF driving factor 2 — Strong Australian dollar

Secondly, every time the strong dollar looks as though it may be weakening, a bout of investment in Australian dollar denominated assets or speculation has seen it firing upwards again. This hampers investment in equities from overseas and in turn kills the Australian stock market's momentum. Although measurement thereof is nigh-on impossible, probably somewhere between one quarter and one third of Australian shares are owned by investors from overseas, with much of that cash coming from Asia. The dollar is forecast by many to weaken during the second half of 2013.

SMSF driving factor 3 — ASX has underperformed

Thirdly, the Aussie stock market — the market which most of us focus on rather than venturing elsewhere — is failing to inspire any great confidence from investors. At the time of writing the XAO (All Ordinaries index) remains below 5000 points and is well behind its previous peaks of before the financial crisis.

Affordability dividend: The 'Stevens put'

Personally, I think it is a little harsh when commentators talk of the 'Stevens put' and the Reserve Bank's supposedly dovish attitude to inflation. The RBA's remit is to maintain price stability, full employment and wealth and prosperity for the Australian people. By and large they have done a sound job.

With fixed mortgage rates at the time of writing available at below 6%, a welcome affordability dividend is already available to those who invest in property via a SMSF. As mortgages on super funds often won't exceed a loan-to-value ratio of around 70%, (i.e. they require a substantial 30% deposit and sometimes more unless you have very significant capital in your fund) the large deposit is likely to mean that even prime location investment properties can be somewhere close to neutrally geared.

It is likely to be properties in the middle or median price bracket which will benefit most from SMSFs moving into property over the coming years.

Deposits needed to buy property with an SMSF

When you buy an investment property outside a superannuation fund, the deposit you might need could be anywhere from 0% to 25% depending on your personal circumstances and the prevailing appetite for risk of the lending institutions. When buying within a super fund, lenders in 2013 are likely to insist on a higher deposit unless you have a high value of net assets in your fund.

For this reason, the benefit of leverage that is the usual major selling point of investment property is somewhat diminished. That's not to say that buying property with your superannuation cannot still be a great investment. There are some other differences too, for investments within a super fund cannot be used as collateral for other investments and therefore refinancing a line of credit against a property which has appreciated in value in the manner of conventional property investment will not be an option.

The great allure of the negative gearing rules also does not apply to investors in the same manner for property via SMSFs either. Indeed, because of the significant deposits required by lenders, property investments within super funds need not necessarily generate a negative cash flow at all.

Figure 23.4 — Example cash flow on a $300,000 property within a superannuation fund

	$
Rental yield at 5.5% of purchase price	16,500
6.5% interest only loan on $210,000 mortgage	(13,650)
Strata fees 4 quarters x $400	(1,600)
Property management fees at 5.5% of rent	(850)
Annual re-letting fee	(800)
Repairs and other costs	(500)
Annual cash flow	**(900)**

Let's take the example of an individual with $110,000 is an SMSF. In the above example, as the investor has put down a substantial deposit of 30% or $90,000, the negative cash flow on the property is fairly moderate at $900 per annum. He has paid stamp duty of $10,000 and left a buffer of $10,000 in his fund to cover negative cash flows and compliance costs.

Providing that the property increases in value by around 0.5% per annum the investor will be generating equity, although naturally they will be aiming for higher capital growth than this in order to outperform the rate of inflation (or the equivalent return of a risk-free investment). Rents are likely to increase over time with as they are pushed up by inflation and therefore the property should soon start to generate a positive cash flow.

Figure 23.5 — Compounding growth on investment property at 5% capital growth per annum

Year	Property value at 5% growth	Mortgage ($)	Equity ($)
0	300,000	216,000	84,000
1	315,000	216,000	99,000
2	330,750	216,000	114,750
3	347,288	216,000	131,288
4	364,652	216,000	148,652
5	382,884	216,000	166,884
6	402,029	216,000	186,029
7	422,130	216,000	206,130
8	443,237	216,000	227,237
9	465,398	216,000	249,398
10	488,668	216,000	272,668

In the example in Figure 23.5, as an interest only loan has been used to buy a property worth $300,000 the mortgage balance remains unchanged, while as the property has not been sold its value continues to grow and compound. Of course, as we have already seen growth is unlikely to be linear in this fashion — instead values plateau, fall and boom in cycles. Over the long term, however, it is likely that property values will continue to increase as household income increases.

In the above example, even though no additional contributions have been made to the fund, as a growth rate of 5% has been used, equity of $272,668 has been created over a decade. This very simple strategy has easily outperformed the average super balance at retirement in just one decade because the value of the asset has been allowed to grow without being encumbered by capital gains taxes, fund management fees and recurring transaction costs.

Properties bought by SMSFs usually require more substantial deposits.

It is worth noting, however, that because the property requires a deposit of around 30%, the great advantage of leverage that property has over shares as an asset class is less pronounced than it would be outside of the fund.

Note that while it is possible for a SMSF to use leverage to invest in equities, derivatives, CFDs and options, the inherent volatility of these asset classes make them less suitable for an investor who is self-managing a pension fund — I would not suggest going down this route unless you are a sophisticated investor with a very significant superannuation balance.

The stamp duty and initial transaction costs also reduce the effectiveness of the property strategy to some extent, and it will also not be possible to refinance the property in the conventional manner for properties within a super fund cannot be used as collateral for other investments. Let's check out what returns might be possible in a SMSF from investing in equities using an assumed 8% return per annum.

Figure 23.6 — SMSF invested in equities at 8% growth per annum

Year	Balance ($)
0	110,000
1	118,800
2	128,304
3	138,568
4	149,654
5	161,626
6	174,556
7	188,521
8	203,602
9	219,891
10	237,482

Again I have assumed that no further contributions are made to the fund and disregarded the effects of audit and administration fees. Investing in shares has the notable advantage of not incurring stamp duty on acquisitions in Australia. If we were to choose the equities route we would, of course, need to be careful not to generate excessive transaction costs and capital gains taxes through hyperactive or frenetic trading.

The tables above show that, notionally at least, property might show a stronger return than shares. However, you can see that property purchases in a self-managed super fund usually require a significant deposit and therefore the deployed leverage is somewhat less than it might be for a property investor outside the fund.

Consequently, projected net returns may be some way lower too. One advantage that property in an SMSF offers is that you do not have to actively manage a portfolio of shares. Shares, on the other hand, have the advantage of lower initial transaction costs and shares do not incur a negative cash flow as an investment sometimes can.

Overall, it is my contention that whether you choose property or shares as your super fund investment vehicle, you have an opportunity to improve upon the net returns after costs offered by the majority of fund managers. Therefore, what I suggest is to consider your super fund with reference to your portfolio as a whole. If your existing investments are not diversified through asset classes (i.e. your wealth is all in your own home or it is all in share investments) you may wish to consider diversifying into other asset classes.

Share investment strategies for your superannuation

When it comes to drawing up an investment strategy for shares within a superannuation fund, many of the same rules apply to how you might invest outside a fund. You still need to have a written plan and consider diversification (indeed, this is a requirement of the Australian Taxation Office) and must still determine whether you are going to follow a buy-and-hold approach or try to time the market.

Chapter 23 Summary

- The Age Pension alone only makes for a meagre retirement

- There is no guarantee that your super balance alone will be enough for a comfortable retirement

- Fund management fees, capital gains taxes, transaction costs and insurance fees can all chew a huge hole in your fund's ability to grow and compound wealth

- If you have a significant superannuation balance you may wish to self-manage your superannuation through a self-managed fund (SMSF)

- If you are going to self-manage your superannuation you will need a carefully written investment plan and must comply with all of the applicable rules

- SMSFs can now invest in shares, property and other assets

- SMSFs are likely to flood the property markets over the next decade

- In the major cities it is likely to be apartments in the low-to-middle range which are most impacted by investors from SMSFs

24
SHARE TRADING
SKILLS

24

Short- to medium-term share trading

I have said previously elsewhere that I feel short-term trading of shares for income should only be a small component of an investment plan. For reasons already noted, wealth is more easily created in tax-favoured and tax-deferred environments than it is in frequent short-term trading that generates brokerage fees and taxes on profits. I suspect that the reason for the large number of books and trading systems available is simply that there is a big demand for them from punters seeking the Holy Grail — the information or system that will make them infallible share traders.

Many hold a romantic notion of themselves sitting in their home office and closing out a few deals, and being forever free from a boss telling them what to do. What happens to many is that they trade for some time but then are wiped out completely when the market falls for a prolonged period of time. This is due to inexperienced traders having little or no protection on the downside and no plan for when the market turns and begins to head in a downwards direction.

I can quickly summarise a massive chunk of the share trading advice out there simply by saying that to be a successful trader you need to think and act differently to the majority. Not only do you need to act differently, much of the time your behavioural traits will need to be the exact opposite to those of the majority, and possibly the opposite of your own natural instincts in the field of trading.

The key point to take away is that it has been proven that over time the winning traders are those who cut their loss making trades quickly. Over the longer term, the losers will be those who average down on loss-making trades and the winners will be those who average up on winning trades, cutting their risked capital in half by taking a smaller initial position on a trade.

> To paraphrase Buffett, the key rules of trading could be summarised thus: Rule #1 — don't lose your money.
> Rule #2 — see Rule 1.

In other words, you take care of the loss making trades quickly, and the profits will look after themselves. Most people focus a huge amount of effort on finding elusive big winning trades, when what they should instead be focussing on is a constant improvement of their money management skills. Too many share traders miss the big picture. Short-term trading can be an excellent way to create extra income but you will have to work hard to earn it from the market, the profits may be taxable and you will incur brokerage costs with each trade made.

Take a few moments to consider this table as it contains some very important information on share trading:

Figure 24.1 — Shares traders think differently

Regarding...	Losers	Winners
Losses	**Let losses run** in hope that they 'come back' thus exposing the risk of one bad trade destroying trading account	Recognise non-cooperative trades, relentlessly and unemotionally **cut losses** quickly before they can cause significant damage
Profits	Lock in profits by **snatching** at them quickly	Recognise a good trade and **let them run** and run
Position sizes	Take **large** position sizes hoping for big wins quickly	**Small**; adopt a reduced exposure to risk to preserve trading capital at all costs — above *all* else
Adding to trading positions	**Average down** on losing trades or adopt *Martingale* approach of doubling the position for the next trading position entered into	Enter smaller initial position reducing risk and add to winning trades; known as **averaging up** or *pyramiding*
Upon losing several trades	**Increase** position sizes to hopefully recover losses made on previous trades	**Reduce** position sizes in direct proportion the remaining trading capital

Where to start

Let's start with a good place *not* to start — off-the-shelf trading systems. It is to some extent human nature to seek a trading system which can be relied upon to make all consistently reliable decisions for you to in any situation. For this reason, they are always available to buy and always will be, for a sizeable cost of course.

A word of warning: no trading system can be infallible. Check out what others say on internet forums about trading systems they have bought and consider whether they sound happy to have parted with a five figure sum. Sometimes, unhappy consumers complain to the original vendor of the system only to hear that what they need is more training on how to use the system, which naturally, comes with yet more cost.

No trading system is infallible.

A better place to start is self-education. If you want to get into share trading, the best place to start is to read as many books on the subject as you can. Some are great, some less so, but I have found that you tend to learn at least something from every book you read on finance and investment. Of course, you cannot learn everything from a textbook. Developing your own trading style is something that can only be learned through practice and in the real live world of the markets. Paper trading is the name given to learning to trade through theoretical transactions, and it is an excellent idea and a great place to start.

However, if you want to become a successful trader, you will eventually have to trade with real money as becoming a successful investor is as much about controlling emotions as it is the trading process. This is why some are able to make great theoretical returns when paper trading, but find taking decisive actions far more difficult when actual dollars are being traded.

Money management

If you are buying shares in the major banks or mining companies with a view to holding forever, then the level of money management skills you are required to display is low. You simply buy, hold and enjoy the dividend stream. However, if you are going to be a share trader, then money management skills become vital. In fact, the shorter your time horizon for holding shares then the more important your money management skills become.

The danger is that you make a number of successful trades but then undo all of your good work by making one bad trade. A very common mistake is to let a bad trade turn into a disastrous one by letting it run further downwards, an approach often destroys trading accounts. It is certainly important to keep records of your trading history and to learn from them. Care should be taken to include all costs in any analysis of records including brokerage costs or commissions. Your trading records should leave clues as to what you are doing well and what you need to improve upon.

Know thyself

As a share trader, it helps if you can recognise your own personality and temperament. If you have a reckless streak or are inclined towards gambling then naturally you will need some protection of the downside to prevent yourself from taking positions which give you excessive exposure to potential loss of capital.

In my experience, the best traders are those who are the most level-headed, which means that they do not get too excited about big winning trades, and they do not feel the need to run around telling everyone about them. More importantly, the best share traders understand that some trades will be bad and they close them down efficiently and unemotionally. They make a rational decision and move on.

Professional share trade and author Dr Alexander Elder talks of the concept of comparing making a loss with taking a businessman's risk.[1] He suggests that there are occasions when we should accept that we have followed a good process, made quality and level headed decisions in alignment with our trading plan, and yet the trade has not co-operated. Sometimes, we will make losing trades and should accept this as being the case: we have taken a businessman's risk.[2]

After practicing psychiatry for many years, another idea that Elder alerts us to is that of self-sabotage. Elder believes that if we can first recognise that humans have the potential to sabotage a level of success which they are not unconsciously comfortable with, then they can then go on to rectify this.[3]

Share trading strategies

When it comes to successful trading there are a number of key rules:

- Have a realistic written goal, such as a percentage return on capital each year
- Determine what your entry signal will be and stick to it
- Keep your entry signal simple!
- Keep each position small
- Only risk a small percentage of your capital on each individual trade — risking 2% of your capital might be a good guideline (thus if you take a position using 20% of your total capital, a sell-stop should be triggered should a 10% loss on that trade be hit)

- Set a target exit price when you enter a trade

- Always set a sell stop price when you enter a trade

- Stick to your sell stop — don't override it!

- Only move sell stops in the direction of the trade: upwards if going long (you have bought the share), downwards if you are selling short

So where do you start when trying to think of ideas for trades? There are plenty of subscription newsletters you can look at, or finance magazines on the shelves can give you some useful ideas. My preferred approach is to focus on learning everything possible about a very small number of stocks.

By focussing on just one or two companies, as a trader you can begin to steal an edge over the wider market, particularly if you are able to read company reports, interpret them and interpret the market's reaction to them. For smaller and mid-cap stocks, the market can be a little slower to respond than a perfect capital market could imply.

Others will have a more involved approach to trading and want to be trading every day regardless of the market. It all depends on your own plan for wealth creation, your investing personality and your trading style. My personal trading style is probably best described as one of mental assessment of outcomes and probabilities used to my advantage to in order to profit.

Find a trading style which suits your personality.

In time, people tend to find a system of trading that suits them, whether it is day-trading, swing trading, momentum trading or any one of a number of strategies. We should be aware not to be inappropriately swayed by bias towards the most recent outcomes — assuming that because a trading style has worked for us once it must therefore be the best option for our future trading.

If you sometimes feel that you can't see the wood for the trees when trading a stock, a good way to get back to basics is simply to take to company news releases with a red pen and a green pen. Highlight the good news words such as 'positive' in green and the bad news words such as 'challenging' in red. It's amazing how this can work. I do exactly this with Reserve Bank *Statement of Monetary Policy* releases every month — it helps to break down the sea of words into a picture which our brain immediately recognises as positive or negative sentiment.

Technical analysis

Technical analysis is the discipline of analysis of past market data, particularly share prices, charts and volume in order to forecast the future direction of prices. There are a huge number of tools available to the technical trader, so that to the beginner the discipline may seem to have a huge amount of mystery to it.

Ultimately what technical analysis is trying to achieve is to determine signals for the trader for when to buy and when to sell. In spite of the constant quest for it, there is no such thing as the perfect signal, for markets are constantly evolving and rarely repeat themselves precisely. Instead, what technical traders should do is search for signals which they understand well and can use as a basis for how to trade securities.

It is vital that a technical trader understands how to read share price graphs. There are a wide variety of presentational styles that include candlesticks, open-high-low-close charts, point-and-figure charts, line charts and numerous others (see Chapter 25 for more on reading charts). The trader must be able to recognise where support and resistance levels are and understand that these levels need to be tested more than once to be proven and how support and resistance interact with each other over time.

> Technical analysis focusses on share price charts in order to help traders to time their entry to and exit from the market.

Technical analysis tools attempt to find a method for deciding when to buy and when to sell stocks. Some tools are more useful than others, and ultimately, all technical signals must have some limitations. There is no such thing as a perfect technical analysis tool. Sceptics may also say that if you gave a technical analyst a randomly created graph of figures they would being to identify technical signals and patterns.

Remember that a price chart does not predict the future, rather it is simply a map of what has gone before, incorporating the human emotions and psychology associated with the price of a particular stock or market. A skilled technical trader will attempt to use this map to his advantage to profit in the future.

Short selling

We hear it talked about very often, but what actually is short selling? Shorting is effectively a bet that a share price will go down in value, as opposed to buying shares in a company in the hope that its value goes up while you continue to receive income in the form of dividends. Thus if a share that is being shorted falls in value after the trader enters into the trade then he or she is able to make a profit. Conversely, if the share price rises then the trader will have made a loss. In essence it is the reverse of buying a share to sell it at a future point in time while hoping for the price to rise in the intervening period.

Short selling therefore usually involves a shorter time period than buying and holding on to a share might. The concept is not always an easy straight-forward one for beginners to grasp as shorting involves something that you do not yet own and then buying it back again at a future point in time. Thus if the share price falls you stand to gain, and the converse is also true.

> I prefer to accumulate great assets by buying
> them and holding on to them.

There are six reasons in particular why I don't go short on shares:

Staying long, reason 1 — It's simpler

Firstly, I believe that simple systems often have an inherent advantage over more complex systems as they are easier to follow. Short selling is only a slightly more complex business than going long, but it is nevertheless slightly more involved. At times this may seem as though is not a very trendy viewpoint, particularly when the markets are uncertain and capital gains from growth are weak.

Staying long, reason 2 — Dividend streams

If you buy a share in a profitable company, twice a year the company tends to pay you income in the form of dividends. If the company has paid tax on its profits then the dividends will come with franking credits attached. This is a major advantage of owning shares rather than selling them short.

Staying long, reason 3 — Trend is your friend

Stock markets, over time, spend more time moving up than they do moving down. It's true that at times the market can become over-valued and therefore your odds of success with shorting do increase, but I would suggest that for most amateur investors the timing of when to enter a short trade is little better than guesswork. Stock market downturns can often be sharper than the trend on the up, which is a plus for short-sellers.

Stock markets tend to trend upwards over time.

Staying long, reason 4 — Unlimited downside

You should remember that when going short, there is technically an unlimited downside to any trade. If you go long a share can appreciate two fold, threefold or a hundredfold — it's all blue sky! You can buy a share and hold on to it forever if that is your goal. Going short involves a very different mindset, and it pays to be cognisant of the risks.

Staying long, reason 5 — Takeovers

If a company is taken over while you hold a short position, then you could get burned very badly. This is particularly so if you are trading leveraged contracts. Takeover premiums can be very substantial — perhaps 40% or more — thus, you must be aware of this possibility and risk when going short.

Staying long, reason 6 — Backing winners not losers

One final reason I do not trade on the short side is that is simply does not feel right to me to bet on failure. By nature I am a positive person, and I have realised over a long period of time now that regardless of whether I am dealing in shares or property I like to back a winner. Unlike some, I don't go so far as to say that short selling is unethical, it is just does not feel right for me.

If you do decide to trade using short selling techniques it is important to remember that many of the basic rules that apply to trading on the long side still apply. Money management techniques are still of vital importance and if you are using sell stops they should still only be moved in direction of the trade, which is downwards.

CFDs

Contracts for difference are another form of lending for investment in shares, but one whereby the available leverage and exposure is significantly higher. The lender may only require you to put down a deposit of 5% or 10% of the total value of the investment which naturally gives the investor significant exposure on the upside, and on the downside.

Be wary of tax treatment for interest on CFDs: the tax office may not deem you to be an investor and therefore interest may not be tax deductible.

My suggestion would be that if you have not yet had a successful history of trading shares profitably and safely, then you should not touch CFDs with the proverbial bargepole. The same applies for the trading of other markets such as currencies or commodities. If you have not had success as a share trader, then it is unlikely that you have yet learned the discipline to trade successfully in other products.

Naturally, it should go without saying that we should not overstretch ourselves when it comes to the use of leverage with CFDs. You will find in any case that a lender has little motivation to extend vast credit to an investor who does not have the means to cover a potential loss, as this would not in the interests of the lender.

Chapter 24 Summary

- There are a number of key rules for successful share trading — learn them and use them!

- Off-the-shelf trading systems always blow up eventually

- The key to being a successful share trader is relentlessly careful money management

- Trading shares for income requires discipline and a sound temperament

- If your aim is to be successful over a long period of time, limit position sizes

- Learning to read share price charts and volumes is a useful skill, but technical analysis has its limitations

- Do not play the share markets with CFDs unless you are a very experienced trader, for the risks are high

25
VALUE INVESTING
IN SHARES

25

Value investing targets

To begin with, take one step back and consider exactly what you might be trying to achieve by buying shares in a company. Many of the most successful investors adopt an approach of simply continuing to acquire shares in the large companies such as the banks and the major resources stocks working on the theory that over the long term, the likely future direction of the share prices is an upwards one.

While value investors generally do not obsess over timing the market precisely, they attempt to limit their buying to when the share market appears relatively cheap and offering good value, and for this reason the strategy is known as *value investing*.

The undisputed master of this approach is Warren Buffett, and it is very hard to argue with either the considered logic of the investment strategy or his results over the long term. While there are those who insist that share markets should be all about high-frequency information and high-frequency trading in a bid to outsmart the market, the value investing approach is far more sedate and considered. The value investing concept is to identify a handful of outstanding companies, wait until their share prices become attractive and then buy a meaningful stake in the companies. The strategy is simple, efficient and, if well executed, extremely effective.

Why do so few make a success of a seemingly simple proposition? I believe the answer is failing to understand what a realistic goal is. Share markets may have returned an average of well above 10% per annum in the past inclusive of dividends, but it seems likely that in the future average annual returns may be somewhat lower than they have been. Investors need to remember that wealth is generally created slowly and thus they need to allow themselves the time to benefit from the compounding effect of growth.

> Future absolute share market returns may be lower than those seen in the decades past.

As we have seen, historically Buffett was able to generate returns of around 20% per annum over a period of over four decades.[1] However, he has clearly stated that his future returns are likely to be lower, and therefore we must question what a realistic target return and timeframe is for an average investor. Too often, investors place all of their hopes into a small number of highly speculative companies, rather than taking a long term approach to building wealth.

The Buffett principles

Buffett's predecessor in the world of value investing Benjamin Graham noted in his classic investment books *Security Analysis* and *The Intelligent Investor* that there were three main methods of investing in shares.

Share investment method 1 — The cross-section approach

This approach involved holding a stake in each of the top companies — this is the equivalent of investing in an index fund today and will entail lower risk but necessarily average returns.

Share investment method 2 — The anticipation approach

The anticipation approach is the selection of shares with a seemingly favourable outlook for the forthcoming 6-12 months, seeking out companies with higher than average sales or profit growth expectations.[2] The trouble with the anticipation approach is that you must guess to what extent the market has factored in growth forecasts and therefore it is risky. This is how many of the institutions are investing super fund capital today, by identifying growth stocks or value stocks with hopeful prospects for immediate capital gains.

Since Graham's day, it has been better understood by Buffett that the distinction between growth and value stocks is a little nonsensical. Value simply means the intrinsic value of the company — being the future cash flows of the company discounted to today's value. Growth is a factor used to determine value.

Share investment method 3 — The margin of safety approach

Ben Graham liked to purchase companies at a price that represented a margin of safety — out of favour companies trading below their book value — the theory being that in the event of the company failing and being liquidated the investor would still be likely to make a profit on their investment. The problem with this theory is that it is only worthwhile to the investor if the company is liquidated on a timely basis. Often, this may not eventuate.

Buffett embraced the margin of safety as the sensible way to invest, but instead realised that rather than looking at struggling companies through comparing their share prices versus their book values, he should instead seek companies with superior future cash generating ability.

Always aim to buy at a significant discount to intrinsic value.

Buffett learned two important lessons from his early investing — firstly, that 'turn-around' investments don't always turn around. And secondly, he also learned that time is the friend of the outstanding companies and the enemy of the mediocre. So instead of looking for struggling companies at a cheap price he focussed on finding excelling companies at a price representing a margin of safety.

The Buffett approach is based upon the principles of finding a few excellent companies, only buying them at a price where there is a significant margin of safety, placing a meaningful amount of one's net worth in any purchase that is committed to, and holding for the longer term, until the company is eventually priced at its intrinsic value.

This approach to investment requires the making of fewer decisions, but more important ones. The longer time horizon should, if appropriate companies have been selected, mean that there is lower risk involved in each investment. In terms of the time period for holding an investment, a useful guide might be to plan for a period of longer than ten years, though if the outlook for the company changes (or it simply becomes over-priced) then you may of course elect to dispose of a holding in a shorter time period.

Achieving returns like Buffett

The first thing we need to do in order to make a start in value investing is build a reasonable pool of capital to start with and, where possible, continue to contribute to it. This entails a level of discipline. While in theory any amount of money can be allowed to compound and grow, the reality is that if you only start with a small balance, transaction costs can eat into your returns.

The next step is to understand how to know when a company's share price is on sale, or selling well below its intrinsic value. The most reliable method is often to perform a broad-brush discounted cash flow calculation. It is also important to understand how to identify what is an outstanding company with great future prospects.

Buy shares in great companies when they are on sale.

According to the classical market theorists, the high returns achieved by investors such as Buffett should be impossible without the taking of significant levels of risk. The Efficient Market Theory (EMT) suggests that share prices are always rational and therefore consistently outperforming the market in such a manner should be impossible. And yet Buffett has achieved returns of 20% per annum compounded since the 1960's and has rarely experienced losses.

Supporters of EMT have been forced to change their stance, now instead inferring that prices are *almost* always rational. The team at Berkshire Hathaway would no doubt have chuckled at this riposte — share prices are rational... except when they are not! Buffett is aware that the difference between markets *always* being rational and *usually* being rational is 'like the difference between night and day.'

Perhaps the most famous example of Buffett's genius at work was his massive purchase of shares in Coca Cola through 1988 and 1989, when Berkshire Hathaway acquired stock at a cost of more than $1.3 billion. Like the champion bridge or poker player, when the odds are in his favour Buffett certainly likes to place big bets. Within a decade the investment in Coca Cola was worth more than $13 billion, representing a phenomenal return on the initial investment. Berkshire still owns the investment today, representing an ownership of 8.9% of Coca Cola and it is worth $14.5 billion.[3]

Unfortunately most of us will never be a Buffett. The average investor does not have the time, discipline, patience or inclination to go through the rigorous learning processes to become a consistent outperformer of the market. It does not necessarily matter if this is the case, but if so it would be better to accept our limitations and invest in a diversified portfolio of industrial shares and spare ourselves the struggle.

Picking your own stocks

There is some irony in the many thousands of investors reading up every word on what Warren Buffett says in the hope that they one day may be able to invest with his level of skills. The irony is that when Buffett himself was asked how individual amateur investors should go about picking their own stocks, he said they should leave it to the professionals!

That does not mean that you necessarily should never pick your own stocks to invest in and solely rely on a fund manager. What it does mean is that you need to be very mindful of your own potential shortcomings in analysing companies and limit exposure to loss. It is very common for individuals to identify what they believe to be an undervalued company and pile a huge percentage of their capital into buying shares, only for their holding to be diluted or another unforeseen curve-ball wiping out a big chunk of their net worth.

> You should identify and accept your limitations as a share investor as we all most certainly have them!

If you adopt such an approach, it is very difficult to become wealthy. Sooner or later, it is likely that you might make an error that can set us back all the way to where you began, or worse, behind where you even began.

So what can we do about this? Firstly we can accept that while we can pick our own share portfolios, we may pick some bad stocks and we should limit our downside by admitting when we have made a poor selection and move on. Secondly, we can give ourselves a break and apply a reasonable level of diversification instead of trying to get rich quick by gambling on one or two speculative stocks. Alternatively, you could eschew the idea of picking your own stocks completely and elect to invest in a diversified portfolio of (ideally industrial) dividend-paying stocks, ensuring that the chosen product holds a reasonable number of stocks and trusts and will not charge an unnecessarily high management fee.

Price-earnings (PE) ratios

The price-to-book valuation is just one method of assessing whether shares in a company are cheap or expensive — it simply looks at the value of all the issued ordinary shares of the company and compares this to the value of the assets and liabilities on the company's balance sheet. It makes for a very straightforward comparison. However, valuing a company is usually a little more complex than that, for we do not only buy shares in a company for its existing tangible assets, such as its plant and equipment, its cash or its land and buildings.

What you should really be interested in is the ability of that company to use all of the assets that it has, including its brand name and customer base, to generate cash in the future. Ultimately the value of a company should be the present value of its ability to generate future cash flows.

There is a reason that I refer to present value here and that is that we know that cash that is generated in the future will be worth less to us than cash in the bank today. This is partly due to inflation and partly due to risk — there is a risk that cash flows we expect to receive 10 years from now never come to fruition for reasons that we may not foresee today. For this reason, when analysts calculate what is known as a discounted cash flow (DCF) calculation, they are discounting the value of future cash generating ability back to today's value.

Don't switch off just yet!

I normally find that in discussions with would-be share investors that this is exactly the point at which their eyes glaze over — they lose interest in valuing a company and feel that it may simply be better to take a punt on a company based on some kind of gut feel or intuition. Tempting though it is to say 'so be it', let's stop and consider whether there may be more straightforward ways in which we can ascertain whether a company's share price is cheap or expensive.

The price/earnings (PE) ratio of a company attempts to do just this. It is a short-cut method used to determine the relative cost of shares in equivalent companies. The ratio is a calculated by dividing the company's prevailing share price divided by earnings (or net profit) per share, and can easily be found simply by looking on a broking website such as e-Trade if you set up an account.

> The PE ratio is only a guideline as to
> how expensive a share price is.

There was an old rule of thumb, that is perhaps a little dated, which said that a fair value for a company might be a PE ratio of 20 minus the inflation rate — so if inflation is trending at 3% then a fair value for a company would be a PE ratio of 17 (being 20 minus 3). A PE ratio of 17 means that the company is valued at 17 times its annual net profit. Share market confidence has been relatively low and PE ratios are on average some way lower than this level.

There are, in any case, a number of shortcomings of the PE ratio. It is not an absolute measure, moreover simply a useful tool to compare the price of similar companies which operate in the same sector. As the ratio is often calculated on the prior year's earnings only, the ratio can be massively distorted by one-off events affecting profit. If a company has a year where its profits are very close to break-even then the PE ratio can appear enormous, and if the company makes a loss then the figure would become negative which is nonsensical.

Over the short term, of course, your guess as to the direction of share price valuations is as good as mine. Market confidence will be impacted by a myriad of local and national economic factors including the outlook for China, the outcome of the debt crises in Europe and the ability of the US economy to establish a worthy rate of growth.

Ratio analysis

How many investors perform a detailed ratio analysis on the financials of a company before electing to apply a portion of their capital to buying shares in the entity? How many investors even look at the financials of a company at all? It's impossible to know precisely, but intuition tells me that the percentages are far lower than they should be. This is not surprising — even as a Chartered Accountant who used to produce listed company financials, I find the process of analysing them very tedious.

It is certainly the case that most average investors expend too much time and energy looking at share price charts and too little looking at a company's prospects, operating results or capital structure. The unfortunate truth is that the vast majority of Mum-and-Dad investors have nowhere near the level of skills required to undertake a genuinely thorough analysis even of a basic income statement and balance sheet.

> To be able to value a company you must be able to understand its financial statements.

This need not be a bad thing, but we must be aware of the reality and turn a potential negative into a positive. If you have the appropriate level of skills then by all means do the ratio analysis (I covered this subject in significantly more detail in my 2012 book *Get a Financial Grip*), but if you do not, be honest and accept that and resolve to make a smarter financial plan which will get you the results you desire. If you have some level of discipline and patience, over the long term you will be able to outstrip the returns of all but a small percentage of investors by continuing to invest in a diversified fund of profit-making and dividend-paying industrial shares.

The dangers of company debt

Successful companies which generate strong profit and cash flow may elect to use a moderate level of debt to magnify returns and manage their cash flows and liquidity. Interest on debt attracts a tax deduction so there was once a classical economic theory which suggested that a company which employs high levels of gearing might be worth theoretically more than one which does not. However, the reality can be somewhat different, and that is that companies with high levels of debt are riskier than ones which do not have high levels of debt.

The failures of companies such as Centro and others clearly demonstrate the dangers of high levels of debt and low interest-cover ratios. Investors need to be wary of companies which have a gearing ratio that is too high, and be sure that we only invest in companies which generate comfortable enough cash to cover debt repayments.

Five reasons to consider a diversified LIC

The advent of internet brokerage sites has seen a huge increase in individual investors selecting their own stocks in which to invest. Unfortunately, most average investors do not take the time to learn the laborious process of how to analyse financial statements and nor do they have strong market-timing skills. Therefore, for most, the process is largely one of forlorn guesswork which is thus reflected in sub-optimal results.

What hope is there, then, for average investors who don't want to be slugged with expensive fund management fees? The answer is to promote an investment plan that is both repeatable and spreads your risk through averaging. That is, to contribute a regular dollar amount into a well-diversified product on a regular basis. When the market is low, you will effectively buy more stock, and vice-versa.

But what product to buy? Here are five reasons why you might elect for a listed investment company (LIC).

1 — Diversification

By buying into an LIC which holds up to 120 or more stocks and trusts, you can be instantly diversified. The approach of not having all of your eggs in one basket is a tried and tested approach to reducing risk over time.

2 — Low costs

Returns can be improved substantially over time if you select an LIC with low administrative costs. What would represent a low administrative cost? This means that the LIC does not charge you a cripplingly expensive 'performance' or 'management' fee, and the costs charged for remuneration, office rent and other administrative costs such as for the company's IT and stationery represent lower than 0.2% of the fund's average assets at market value.

Compare this with the fees charged on your super fund and you will begin to see why LICs can be a superior choice. While fund management fees of 1-2% may not sound dramatic, if you consider how much of your expected annual return this might represent the effect on your ability to create wealth over time can be overwhelming. A well-selected LIC does not trade hyperactively. Instead, it will aim to identify quality companies to invest in for the long term and will only rarely look to sell. This reduces unnecessary brokerage costs and taxes.

3 — Outperformance over time

By choosing an LIC which is heavily weighted towards profitable industrial stocks and the banks you may be able to outperform the index over time. Why do industrial companies tend to outperform the resources index? This is because the performance of resources stocks can be cyclical and dividends can be substantially weakened in the downturn phase. Resources companies also tend to retain vast amounts of capital to source and reinvest in new projects which can hamper shareholder returns.

Overall, industrial companies have tended to be more sustainable and more self-perpetuating, in contrast with resources companies with their necessarily diminishing reserves.

4 — Dividend reinvestment

You may have the choice in an LIC to receive dividends or to reinvest them to grow your portfolio in an efficient manner. A Dividend Reinvestment Plan (DRP) should not attract brokerage, stamp duty or other transaction costs and thus can be an effective method of allowing your portfolio to grow and compound.

5 — Control over investment

As you can buy an LIC on the securities exchange it is remarkably easy to buy and sell, provided you select an appropriately liquid investment. This gives the investor great control, and while selling may be inefficient, the liquidity of such an investment can allow funds to be accessed easily in an emergency.

Summary of LICs

By choosing an LIC with a reasonably conservative and appropriately experienced management, you can take comfort in your investment approach. Through holding shares in all of Australia's major, profitable industrial companies, even in times of recession you know that the LIC will retain value and your averaging approach will ensure that you pick up more holdings when prices are lower.

Better still, if you can buy more heavily when the market has experienced a major correction, you can begin to move further ahead of the pack in an efficient manner which does not generate excessive brokerage and capital gains taxes through trading. The more repeatable an investor's strategy is, the greater the likelihood of its enduring success.

Chapter 25 Summary

- A realistic value investing strategy would be to outperform the index by a couple of percentage points per annum over the long term

- Share prices do not move consistently in tandem with financial or calendar years, so do not become too obsessive with benchmarking to an index

- The best value investors apply a level of focus rather than wide diversification, and thus a portfolio may only consists of half a dozen stocks or so

- Focussed portfolios tend to be more volatile than those which are diversified

- A PE ratio can be one useful indicator to help ascertain whether a stock price is cheap or expensive

- To be a successful value investor, you need to be able to interpret company's financial statements and data

- If you are unable to do this and unwilling to learn, save yourself time and heartache and invest in a diversified listed investment company (LIC) or fund

- Only invest in companies with moderate and comfortably serviceable levels of debt

26
TIMING THE STOCK MARKETS

26

Timing the market in shares — Dow Theory

Dow Theory was an idea conceived by journalist and founder of *The Wall Street Journal* Charles Dow, and in part it refers in part to the cyclical nature of the stock market. Dow identified how the stock market tends to move in three phases, these being:

- An accumulation phase

- A public participation phase

- A distribution phase

Dow stage 1 — The accumulation phase

The accumulation phase is a period when investors who are in the know are actively buying stock against the general opinion of the market. During this phase, the stock price does not change much because these investors are in the minority and are absorbing stock that the market at large is supplying.

Dow stage 2 — The public participation phase

Eventually, the market catches on to the moves of these astute investors and a rapid price change occurs, which indicates the second phase. This occurs when the crowd begins to participate and the market begins to climb sharply, until irrational exuberance is witnessed.

Dow stage 3 — The distribution phase

The public participation phase continues until rampant speculation occurs. At this point, astute investors begin to distribute their holdings to the market, and the market eventually begins to fall. While the exact details of the cycle are always slightly different, the cycle does tend to repeat itself over time.

Using Dow Theory to your benefit

If you are able to learn to recognise when the market is cheap or on sale, and when it over-valued, how can you use this to profit? The answer is that to reduce the risk of loss of capital, market timers should aim to be fully invested in the market when stocks become cheap and to decrease exposure when the market is risky and overvalued. Just as with the value investing strategy, though, the strategy of timing the market still requires patience. Stock market downturns can take a long time to play themselves out in full. Some stock market crashes may take many years or even decades to recover.

Market cycles can take many years to play out.

Even Benjamin Graham, who was considered to the godfather of value investors, stated in *The Intelligent Investor* that we should aim to buy shares when they are cheap and sell when they are overvalued.[1] So while Graham placed a strong emphasis on fundamental analysis and focussed value investing, to some extent he is still referring to timing the market. It does not matter whether you invest in index funds, commit to value investing, or attempt to time the market through shorter-term trading — the fundamental concept is ultimately the same, to receive dividend income and to buy low and sell high.

Ben Graham noted that the difficulty with timing the market is that one has to be able to predict the vagaries of the market, which is very difficult to do.[2] For this reason, when timing the market it is sometimes preferable to employ an element of technical analysis to one's trading too, being the reading of share price charts, trading volumes and other data.

When exactly is the market overvalued or undervalued?

If you are looking at timing your entry and exit to the stock market, there are a number of key indicators you can look at to determine whether the market is relatively cheap or expensive at any given point in time. The first thing you can look at is the average PE ratio of the market as a whole, or simply look at the PE ratios of a number of the major companies such as the banks and the major resources companies. Doing so should give you a fair idea of the overall sentiment of the market.

If the average PE ratios are moving towards the high-teens then this might be an indicator that the market is becoming expensive overall. Conversely, if the average ratios are in single digits then, on a historical basis, stocks are cheap and this might represent a good time to enter the market, perhaps using an averaging technique by buying parcels of shares each month.

PE ratios can be a useful indicator as to when share markets are 'on sale' and when they are over-valued.

A second ratio we can look at is the average dividend yield of the market. As dividend yields are measured with reference to the dividend paid and the prevailing share price, then historically low yields can be representative of an expensive stock market. The converse is also true. Other methods which can be considered might be slightly more abstract, such as considering common perceptions. When there seems to be a consensus that a market is becoming a sure thing or a one-way bet, this may be an indication that the good times are nearly at an end.

Cutting losing trades short

Winners on the stock market tend to be disciplined and offload shares which are losing them money quickly but hang on to the winners. Yet most amateurs do exactly the opposite, cashing in winning trades very quickly to lock in the profits, and leaving losing trades to run ever further downwards often in the vain hope that they will somehow come back from the dead. Below is a table which demonstrates exactly why it is important to cut losing trades short:

Figure 26.1 — % fall, % to recover

% by which stock falls	% recovery to break even
10	11
20	25
30	43
40	67
50	100
60	150
70	233
80	400
90	900
100	**Impossible** to recover

The message of this table is clear: if you lose too much on individual trades, you will find that it is impossible to win overall. This is an argument in favour of timing the market over the buy and hold strategy. As small individual investors the market is easily liquid enough that we can adopt this approach if we wish.

An individual is not constrained in the same was that a huge investment fund might be, and thus if stocks that we own have become seemingly way overvalued we are free to dispose of them — we can still pick them up again in the future if the price becomes attractive once more. Sometimes it can make sense too to cut a losing trade short rather than holding on to it and praying that the share price comes back to save us.

Role of tax when employing market-timing strategies

One of the inevitable consequences of attempting to time the market instead of being a buy-and-hold investor is that we must pay tax on the profits if we are successful in what we set out to do. A profitable business must pay tax on its profits — and so must a successful timer of the share market. Buying and holding allows wealth to grow and compound unhindered by tax, but ultimately when the assets and profits are realised, tax will fall due.

The 80/20 rule — Pareto's Law in investing

Pareto's Law is also known as the 80/20 rule as it recognises that in many fields of life, 80% of outputs are often generated by 20% of inputs. In the late 1800s an Italian economist named Vilfredo Pareto noted that 80% of the land in Italy was owned by 20% of the population. This principle is still very much in evidence in business and in many other areas of our lives too.

By way of an example, the giant software company Microsoft noted that by fixing the 20% of bugs that were reported most frequently, 80% of their errors and crashes would be eliminated. Pareto's Law often also applies to wealth: 20% of the population of a nation often holds 80% of the wealth of the nation.

With regards to investment we might also find that where we invest in stocks that 80% of our profits come from a handful or 20% of our investments. We may thus find that most of our investments do not achieve very much. What is the implication of this? The implication is that we do not need to make too many great investing decisions, but we do need to limit the number and the magnitude of the bad decisions. It's almost a slight corruption of an old saying: 'You look after the losers and the winners will take care of themselves'. In property this might mean focussing on buying a few quality properties and holding on to them for the long term.

In fact, in property investing, I often find that the most successful investors are those who make the fewest decisions. What do I mean by that? Some of the people who I have witnessed growing the greatest wealth are those who have bought prime location properties and held on to them for decades as opposed to trying to be too clever and continually trying to outsmart the market.

Speculative stocks

There are well over 2000 stocks on the Australian Securities Exchange. Here is an interesting exercise which you can undertake: next time the news channel broadcasts daily movement in the All Ordinaries share index, ask the people you are with for an opinion of where the index might be headed next. They will probably have an opinion or three. Just as in the property market, many pundits tend to have a variety of theories with little or no basis in fact. Ask a second question, that being whether they can explain to you what the All Ordinaries index actually represents and how it is measured. I would be surprised if you got too many detailed and accurate answers.

It is curious that we place so much emphasis on an index which so few understand. There are a number of different indices, but one of the most important is the XJO or the ASX 200 which comprises the top 200 stocks by market capitalisation and liquidity. The XAO or the All Ordinaries Index is wider in its focus incorporating the top 500 companies by market capitalisation and liquidity, and these 500 companies collectively comprise more than 95% of the value of the whole market.

The remainder of the market comprises the penny dreadful stocks including a swathe of companies which have never generated profits and many of which never will. Australia being a resources-rich nation, many of these companies are exploration and drilling companies seeking the next big treasure trove.

Even though these speculative stocks comprise only a relatively small percentage of the stock market's value, they do attract a disproportionate level of interest from speculators. The reasons for this are fairly obvious, for although the stocks are risky they are very cheap to buy (perhaps only a few cents per share) and thus they seemingly have the potential to bring very high returns. The trade-off is that there is a significant risk of losing most or all of your capital if you pick the wrong company.

Speculating in micro-cap stocks is not an investment plan for building wealth over the long-term.

I have always believed that there is not necessarily a problem with gambling on or speculating in penny dreadful stocks with a small percentage of your capital which you can afford to lose. I have often done so, usually with mediocre or poor results it has to be said. However, speculating or gambling like this should not be your entire financial plan. Often you might see companies who have never made profits release adverse news and posters on the chat forums being devastated because they were not even slightly diversified.

A plan for building wealth over the long term should instead be focussed on assets with a proven track record for growth and returns. This could include holding shares in companies with the ability to generate strong profits (and pay healthy dividends) and a portfolio of investment properties that will be in high demand with a proven track record of capital growth.

Reading charts

One of the skills which share traders need to develop is the ability to read share price charts. The concept is a very simple one in that we can all look at a chart and determine whether a price is moving up or down or moving sideways. But reading charts skilfully takes a little more practice. Technical traders spend hours looking at share price charts for patterns which hopefully will enable them to time their entries and exits from trades.

Personally I prefer focussing on fundamentals to technical analysis. That means that I prefer to look at how the company is performing and the value that it offers rather than what the share price chart is telling us (while recognising that a share price chart can indeed reflect a company's performance).

A skilled chart reader will understand how to look at charts which cover different time horizons (a share price can be moving both upwards and downwards depending on the time period under consideration), will understand trading volumes (strong volumes and an increasing price can represent a great buy signal, and weaker volumes may point towards a sell signal) and will understand how points of resistance and support can be tested and interact with each other.

These are skills which simply come with practice and over time. They are not easily taught from a textbook.

Interestingly, many adult investors read charts poorly because they see a chart which shows a falling share price and assume that therefore the share must be due to recover and go up. Adults tend to like to over-complicate things. Often a falling share price is likely to fall further and a rising share price will quite possibly continue to rise. Show the same charts to a six year old and then will probably observe that 'this graph is going up' or 'this chart going down' and will often reach a smarter conclusion with their simplistic approach.

Stop losses

One tool which can be used to protect yourself when you are taking an approach of timing the market is a sell-stop. A sell-stop is an order to your broker or online trading account to sell a shareholding when certain criteria are triggered such as a share price falling to a particular price. This can be of particular benefit to investors who do not have the time, discipline or inclination to sit and watch share prices throughout the day or week.

More sophisticated tools now allow investors to place trailing sell-stops which move up as the share price moves up. For example, you might elect to set a stop for whenever a share price falls by 10% from any given point. This allows the investor to participate in potential upside while limiting the downside risk.

Chapter 26 Summary

- The stock market tends to move in broadly recognisable cycles over time

- There are a number of indicators which you can use to determine when the market is under-valued or over-valued

- If you are aiming to be a market-timer in the share market, it is imperative that you cut losing trades short

- There are a range of stocks available to invest in — avoid the smallest stocks with no track record of generating profits and paying dividends

- Reading charts can be a useful aide when aiming to time the share market

- Sell-stops can help you to apply the discipline of limiting your downside risk

---

SUMMING UP:
WINNING THE
GAME OF MONEY

SUMMING UP:

Charlie Munger, the Vice Chairman of Berkshire Hathaway, once said: 'Someone will always be getting richer faster than you. This is not a tragedy.' This is very much true! What might be tragic is the taking of imprudent risks to buy assets at the top of asset price bubbles because you see investment as a competition where you have to beat your peers — instead of simply a way to secure your own financial future.

One of the most valuable lessons I learned from travelling in late 2011 and early 2012 to countries with cultures as diverse as Egypt, India, Sri Lanka, Vietnam, Indonesia, Oman, UAE, Portugal, Portugal, Greece and Malaysia (and now living for quite some time in East Timor) is that the value of currency in our pocket is certainly not what determines success or happiness.

What does winning the game mean?

In the game of Monopoly the winner is the person who is still solvent when every other player is bankrupt. In the real world, how we 'win' is not so clearly defined. What might be a life beyond our wildest dreams could represent a humiliating failure to Donald Trump. What is certainly the case is that we need not define our own success by the benchmarks of others.

It's not all about dollars; it's about being happy!

To a great extent, part of being a success is being happy with our life today. This doesn't mean that must lower our standards and accept a humdrum life, but it does in part mean that we should not define success only by our material possessions. From a purely financial perspective, a situation that many of us would like to be in is that we have a passive income that flows to us which exceeds our expenses, thus allowing the freedom to choose how we live our lives. We can then choose whether to work, and if we wish to do so in a field that interests us and brings fulfilment rather than toiling away at a job because it gives us the best chance of meeting the growing mortgage repayments.

Life should be a win-win. We should be able to work as a team and when we have achieved our own goals the responsibility then passes to us to give back to society through charitable giving, volunteer work, educating others or whatever means of contribution you find works best for you.

My four point strategy for winning in investment

Here's my four point summary of everything I've covered in this book:

Winning strategy 1 — Spend less than you earn

Point one is non-negotiable I'm afraid. If you spend more than you earn, then you will never be able to build wealth in an effective manner. Even if you come into a windfall of cash if your net cash flow is negative then eventually you will be returning back to where you were before you received the windfall.

In their book *The Millionaire Next Door* the authors Thomas J. Stanley and William D. Danko completed and then presented a compelling study which showed that most millionaires in the US do not live the extravagant lifestyles that we might expect of people with a seven figure net worth. Of course, there are the super-rich who live in mansions and drive million dollar cars and so on, but the overwhelming majority of millionaires live in normal houses, drive moderately priced cars and live relatively frugally. In other words, the reason many of them became millionaires in the first place is that they spent less than they earned and directed the difference towards a portfolio of appreciating assets and investments.

The rich buy assets, not liabilities.

Spending less than you earn does involve some sacrifice in the short term and this can be difficult for some who have trained themselves to seek pleasure from retail therapy, super-luxurious holidays and extravagant expenditure. The key to success in this area is to re-train yourself to associate pain to frivolous expenditure and pleasure to your new goal of becoming a successful investor. The transformation can happen far more quickly than you may imagine.

Winning strategy 2 — Buy well-located residential investment property (and hold on to it)

My thoughts on property investment are reasonably well known. It is my belief that while new property developments are being built to deal with the ever-increasing demand for quality accommodation, too many new developments are either undesirable high-rise affairs or so far from the capital city centres that the demand for them is inherently low.

I feel that the strongest returns in property on a risk-adjusted basis over the next few decades will be in properties in the inner- and middle-ring suburbs of those capital cities which are likely to see the strongest population growth over that period: Sydney, Melbourne, Perth and Brisbane. Other areas may show strong returns too, but some may bring with them an elevated level of risk, particularly as and when the economy takes a downturn.

> Invest in properties in land-locked capital city suburbs where the population is growing rapidly.

As more of us than ever choose to live in apartments eschewing the expensive housing stock, the demand for this smaller, medium-density accommodation type is increasing sharply and therefore so will prices. Traffic on the roads of our capital cities becomes denser with every passing year and fuel costs seem likely to rise, so I look for properties that are close the city centres, but also close to excellent transport hubs such as rail links.

While there are many ways in which we might choose to build wealth, it is my belief that the best chance the average investor stands of creating wealth for the long term is by buying prime location investment property and holding on to it by not ever selling. Of course, I do believe that we should aim to invest counter-cyclically — investing in markets when they are despondent and bargains abound rather than when they are exuberant and overvalued.

Winning strategy 3 — Invest in a diversified portfolio of industrial shares

As we have already seen, over the long term history has shown us that equities are a great — and *safe* — asset class for building wealth, if approached sensibly. History has also shown us that over the long term industrial shares have outperformed the resources index, the companies within which are compelled to reinvest much of their capital in finding and developing future projects.

Commodities companies, by their very definition, produce commodities — they cannot compete easily on price and so can only outperform by digging up vast quantities of what they produce in as cost-effective manner as possible. Industrial companies can use technological excellence to generate higher returns for shareholders and pay us strong dividends. Rather than running down their resources, industrial companies can be more self-perpetuating.

> ## Buy shares in a portfolio of profitable, dividend-paying industrial companies.

While we like to think that we are smart enough to pick our own stocks with skilful timing, it is often the case that we either do not have the time, the inclination or the skill to learn how to analyse individual companies properly and therefore we may well be better served to invest in a well-diversified fund or LIC of industrial shares. Naturally we should look for products where management fees don't chip away too heavily at our capital and managers adopt a reasonably long-term outlook instead of frantically churning stocks.

Winning strategy 4 — Reinvest your investment gains

The final step is to reinvest profits from investments rather than selling investments and 'rewarding' ourselves by spending the proceeds. If you can maintain the discipline to reinvest your profits, then compounding growth — the snowballing effect — will ensure that you continue to move forward and create outstanding results.

In terms of share investment this may involve reinvesting dividends through a dividend reinvestment plan (DRP) and holding on to our share portfolios for the long term. This can be difficult to do through a stock market downturn but one strategy that may be used by experienced long term investors is to focus on the growing dividend stream rather than the irrational movement in share prices and to top up share holdings when prices are cheap. This approach avoids excessive transaction costs and capital gains taxes too.

Sure, in an ideal world we would sell all of our holdings at the top of the market and buy them back again when the market bottoms out, but even experts that work in the industry full-time have not been able to do this particularly well, so will we be able to do much better ourselves? We might; but we also might not.

Invest for the long-term and reinvest the profits.

I am a firm believer that for most of us simple strategies for the long term are better than complex strategies for the short term. For my wife and I, most of our success has come from just two strands of our wealth creation plan. Firstly, we have bought properties in prime locations and never sold any of them over a period of 16 years. And secondly, we bought into an index of equities every month for 17 years and never sold any of them either. When I have tried to be clever and time the market for more speculative investments my returns have been far less inspiring (and often non-existent).

Last, but certainly not least, remember to give back to those in more need than yourself. There is little point to a life of accumulating a hoard of assets and then dying with a pile of cash. Find a charity which has a meaning to you and resolve to make a difference.

As always, I've tried to cram as much information as I can into these pages, but there's only ever so much space. The message of this book is quite simple really. Even if you are only a moderate income earner, over the period of your working life it is likely that you will earn a sum of dollars that is surprisingly high.

So the question really isn't 'can you make a million dollars?' The real question is 'can you keep a million dollars'? The starting point for improving your finances is to work out where money is leaking out of your life and to plug that gap. Then invest the savings in appreciating assets. You may or may not always pick the best investments, but it's better to do something than to do nothing. Make a start today and go for your life!

What next?

I hope you have enjoyed reading this book and it has provided you with a range of new ideas and exciting viewpoints on personal finance and investment. If you have any questions on anything I have raised in this book, or if you would just like to give me a testimonial, please feel free to email me (contact details via my blog). So, what should you do next? Here are a few final closing ideas for you:

- Read my free daily blog http://petewargent.blogspot.com where I post my thoughts daily on personal finance, investment and what is happening in the markets

- Read the five books in my recommended reading section at the end of the book

- Write down a list of all of your non-investment debt and devise a plan to kill it!

- Compile a list of ten ways is which you can save needless expenditure

- Continue to invest the savings in portfolio of appreciating, income-producing assets

- Make a pact with yourself to continuously improve you education and your investment skills

- Get started today!

- Most importantly of all: enjoy the journey!

Thank you for reading this book. I wish you all the best in your journey to financial freedom. Please contact me via my blog and let me know how you are progressing.

Notes

Chapter 1 – BECOMING AN INVESTMENT MILLIONAIRE

1 Jane Slack-Smith, *Your Property Success with Renovation*, John Wiley & Son, Sydney, 2012

2 Australian Bureau of Statistics, *Population Clock*, www.abs.gov.au

Chapter 2 – AIMING FOR FINANCIAL FREEDOM

1 Donald Trump, *Think like a Billionaire — Everything you need to know about Success, Real Estate and Life*, Ballantine Books, USA, 2005

2 Philip Orbanes, *Monopoly: The World's Most Famous Game and how it go that way*, Da Capo Press, USA, 1999

3 Ibid

4 Philip Orbanes, *The Monopoly Companion*, Adams Media, USA, 1999

5 ibid.

6 ibid.

7 Philip Orbanes, *Monopoly: The World's Most Famous Game and how it go that way*, Da Capo Press, USA, 1999

8 ibid.

9 ibid.

10 Robert T. Kiyosaki and Sharon L. Lechter, *Who Took My Money? Why Slow Investors Lose and Fast Money Wins*, Warner, New York, 2004

11 Berkshire Hathaway, *Letter to Shareholders 2010*, www.berkshirehathaway.com

Chapter 3 – BECOMING AN INVESTOR RATHER THAN A WAGE EARNER

1 Eric Tyson, *Let's Get Real About Money: Profit from the Habits of the Best Personal Finance Managers*, Pearson Education, New Jersey, 2008

2 Emily Chantiri, Frances Beck, Dianne Hill and Di Robinson, *The Money Club*, Random House, Sydney, 2007

3 Paul Clitheroe, *The Road to Wealth: Securing your Financial Future*, Viking Australia, Australia, 2001

4 ibid.

Chapter 4 – YOUR PERSONAL FINANCES

1 Robert T. Kiyosaki, *The Cash Flow Quadrant: Rich Dad's Guide to Financial Freedom*, Warner, New York, 1998

Chapter 5 – INVESTMENT STRATEGY

1 Peter Thornhill, *Motivated Money: You've Invested Well? Compared to What?*, Motivated Money, Sydney, 2008

2 ibid.

3 ibid.

4 Roger Kinsky, *Online Investing on the Australian Share Market*, (Wrightbooks, Milton QLD, 2007)

5 Peter Thornhill, *Motivated Money: You've Invested Well? Compared to What?*, Motivated Money, Sydney, 2008

6 ibid.

7   ibid.

8   RP Data, *Monthly Press Releases*, www.rpdata.net.au

Chapter 6 – THE ROLE OF THE BANK

1   Reserve of Australia, *Publications 2012*, www.rba.gov.au

2   '*RBA's Stevens guillotines housing hyperbole*', Australian Financial Review, article by Christopher Joye, 15 August 2012

3   ibid.

4   Australian Securities Exchange, www.asx.com.au

5   ibid.

6   '*Debt love affair sours?*', Jessica Irvine, *Herald Sun* article, www.news.com.au, September 16, 2012

Chapter 7 – MANAGING RISK

1   Benjamin Graham, *The Intelligent Investor: the definitive book on Value Investing — a book of practical counsel*, Harper Collins, USA, 1973

2   Australian Bureau of Statistics, *2011 Census Data*, www.censusdata.abs.gov.au

Chapter 10 – THE $4 TRILLION QUESTION: WHAT IS THE FUTURE OF AUSTRALIAN PROPERTY MARKETS?

1   Mark Peel and Christina Twomey, *A History of Australia*, Palgrave MacMillan, Melbourne, 2012

2   ibid.

3   ibid.

4   Australian Bureau of Statistics, *3101.0 Australian Demographic Statistics, December 2012,* www.abs.gov.au

5   Australian Bureau of Statistics, *2011 Census Data*, www.censusdata.abs.gov.au

6   Michael Yardney, *How to Grow a Multi-Million Dollar Property Portfolio — in your spare time*, Wilkinson, Melbourne, 2006

7   ibid.

8   Bernard Salt, *Australia on the Move*, 2005

9   ibid.

10 ibid.

Chapter 11 – THE DEVELOPMENT OF AUSTRALIA'S CAPITAL CITIES

1   edited by Pamela Statham, *The Origins of Australia's Capital Cities*, Cambridge University Press, Cambridge, 1989

2   ibid.

3   edited and introduced by Tim Flannery, *The Birth of Sydney*, Australia Text Publishing, Melbourne, 1999

4   edited by Pamela Statham, *The Origins of Australia's Capital Cities*, Cambridge University Press, Cambridge, 1989

5   ibid.

6   ibid.

7   ibid.

8   ibid.

9   ibid.

10 ibid.

11 ibid.

12 ibid.

13 ibid.

14 ibid.

15 ibid.

Chapter 12 – INVESTING IN SYDNEY AND NSW

1   edited and introduced by Tim Flannery, *The Birth of Sydney*, Australia Text Publishing, Melbourne, 1999

2   ibid.

3   ibid.

4   Australian Bureau of Statistics, *1370.0 Population Projections*, www.abs.gov.au

5   edited and introduced by Tim Flannery, *The Birth of Sydney*, Australia Text Publishing, Melbourne, 1999

6   ibid.

7   ibid.

8   ibid.

9   ibid.

10 ibid.

11 ibid.

11 Nat Gould, *Town and Bush*, George Routledge & Sons, London, 1896

12 edited and introduced by Tim Flannery, *The Birth of Sydney*, Australia Text Publishing, Melbourne, 1999

13 ibid.

14 *The Memoirs of Obed West: A Portrait of Early Sydney*, Barcom Press, Bowral, 1988

15 ibid.

16 Australian Bureau of Statistics, *2011 Census Data*, www.censusdata.abs.gov.au

17 Australian Bureau of Statistics, *3218.0 Regional Population Growth* www.abs.gov.au

18 'Hotspot: *Newcastle tipped for strong growth*', Property Observer website, www.propertyobserver.com.au, 29 June 2011

Chapter 13 – INVESTING IN BRISBANE AND QUEENSLAND

1   Australian Bureau of Statistics, *2011 Census Data*, www.censusdata.abs.gov.au

2   Australian Bureau of Statistics, *3101.0 Australian Demographic Statistics, December 2012*, www.abs.gov.au

3   *Papua Act*, 1906

4   Matthew Condon, *Brisbane*, University of New South Wales Press, Sydney, 2010

5   ibid.

6   ibid.

7   edited and introduced by Tim Flannery, *The Birth of Sydney*, Australia Text Publishing, Melbourne, 1999

8   www.qantas.com.au

9   ibid.

10 ibid.

11 Robert G. Hagstrom, *The Warren Buffett Way*, John Wiley & Son, New Jersey, 2005

Chapter 14 – INVESTING IN DARWIN AND THE NORTHERN TERRITORY

1   *Australian Bureau of Statistics*, 2011 Census Data, www.censusdata.abs.gov.au

2   Australian Bureau of Statistics, *3101.0 Australian Demographic Statistics, December 2012*, www.abs.gov.au

3   RP Data, www.rpdata.net.au

Chapter 15 – INVESTING IN PERTH AND WESTERN AUSTRALIA

1   Australian Bureau of Statistics, *2011 Census Data*, www.censusdata.abs.gov.au
2   Australian Bureau of Statistics, *3101.0 Australian Demographic Statistics, December 2012*, www.abs.gov.au
3   Australian Bureau of Statistics, *6345.0 Wage Price Index*, www.abs.gov.au
5   edited by Pamela Statham, *The Origins of Australia's Capital Cities*, Cambridge University Press, Cambridge, 1989
6   ibid.
7   ibid.
8   ibid.
9   ibid.
10 ibid.
11 ibid.
10 ibid.
11 ibid.

Chapter 16 – INVESTING IN ADELAIDE AND SOUTH AUSTRALIA

1   *Australian Bureau of Statistics*, 2011 Census Data, www.censusdata.abs.gov.au
2   Australian Bureau of Statistics, *3101.0 Australian Demographic Statistics, December 2012*, www.abs.gov.au
3   Tim Moore, *Do Not Pass Go - from the Old Kent Road to Mayfair*, Yellow Jersey Press, London, 2002
4   Mark Peel and Christina Twomey, *A History of Australia*, Palgrave MacMillan, Melbourne, 2012
5   ibid.
6   edited by Pamela Statham, *The Origins of Australia's Capital Cities*, Cambridge University Press, Cambridge, 1989
7   ibid.
8   ibid.
9   ibid.
10 Williams op cit. in Origins.
11 edited by Pamela Statham, *The Origins of Australia's Capital Cities*, Cambridge University Press, Cambridge, 1989
12 ibid.
13 ibid.

Chapter 17 – INVESTING IN MELBOURNE AND VICTORIA

1   *Australian Bureau of Statistics*, 2011 Census Data, www.censusdata.abs.gov.au
2   Australian Bureau of Statistics, *3101.0 Australian Demographic Statistics, December 2012*, www.abs.gov.au
3   R.M. McGovern, *A Study of Social Life and Conditions in Early Melbourne*, MA Thesis, University of Melbourne, Melbourne 1957
4   edited by Pamela Statham, *The Origins of Australia's Capital Cities*, Cambridge University Press, Cambridge, 1989
5   *CNBC* interview with Becky Quick (after the release of the *Annual Letter to Shareholders* of Berkshire Hathaway), March 2, 2011
6   *Australian Securities Exchange*, www.asx.com.au

Chapter 18 – INVESTING IN HOBART AND TASMANIA

1   *Australian Bureau of Statistics*, 2011 Census Data, www.censusdata.abs.gov.au
2   Australian Bureau of Statistics, *3101.0 Australian Demographic Statistics, December 2012*, www.abs.gov.au
3   Peter Bolger, *Hobart Town*, Australian National University Press, Canberra, 1973
4   ibid.
5   ibid.
6   ibid.
7   edited by Pamela Statham, *The Origins of Australia's Capital Cities*, Cambridge University Press, Cambridge, 1989
8   ibid.
9   ibid.
10 Peter Bolger, *Hobart Town*, Australian National University Press, Canberra, 1973
11 ibid.
12 edited by Pamela Statham, *The Origins of Australia's Capital Cities*, Cambridge University Press, Cambridge, 1989

Chapter 19 – INVESTING IN CANBERRA AND ACT

1   Australian Bureau of Statistics, *2011 Census Data*, www.censusdata.abs.gov.au
2   Australian Bureau of Statistics, *3101.0 Australian Demographic Statistics, December 2012*, www.abs.gov.au

Chapter 20 – OF TRANSPORT HUBS AND CARPARKING

1   *Sydney, Perth in World Top 10 for expensive parking costs*, article by Bridget Cartier, www.theaustralian.com.au, 10 May 2012
2   ibid.

Chapter 21 – PROPERTY INVESTING NUTS AND BOLTS

1   Michael Yardney, *How to Grow a Multi-Million Dollar Property Portfolio — in your spare time*, Wilkinson, Melbourne, 2006
2   ibid.

Chapter 23 – PENSIONS AND SUPER

1   Tim Moore, *Do Not Pass Go - from the Old Kent Road to Mayfair*, Yellow Jersey Press, London, 2002

Chapter 24 – SHARE TRADING SKILLS

1   Dr. Alexander Elder, *Trading for a Living*, John Wiley, USA, 1993
2   ibid.
3   ibid.

Chapter 25 – VALUE INVESTING IN SHARES

1   Berkshire Hathaway, *Letter to Shareholders 2010*, www.bekshirehathaway.com
2   Benjamin Graham, *The Intelligent Investor – The Definitive Book on Value Investing*, Harper Collins, Revised Edition, 2003
3   *Berkshire Hathaway 2012 Annual Report*, www.berkshirehathaway.com

Chapter 26 – TIMING THE STOCK MARKETS

1   Benjamin Graham, *The Intelligent Investor – The Definitive Book on Value Investing*, Harper Collins, Revised Edition, 2003
2   ibid.

GLOSSARY OF TERMS

Appreciating — increasing in value.

A-REITS — Australian Real Estate Investment Trusts. A security that sells a stock on the securities exchange, thus allowing investors to invest in property without owning any property directly.

ASX — Australian Securities Exchange, the major stock market in Australia.

Balance sheet — a financial statement that summarises assets and liabilities.

Bears or bearish — those who are expectant of falling market prices or worsening economic conditions — a pessimistic view of the future.

Beta — the measurement of the volatility in a company, also known as the systemic risk.

Bid/ask spread — the difference between the highest bid price (the price an investor is prepared to buy a particular company's share at) and the lowest ask or offer price (the price an investor is prepared to sell a particular company's share for).

Blue-chip stocks — shares in what is perceived to be an established and financially sound company.

Bond — a debt investment whereby an investor loans money to an entity (a company or a government) that borrows the funds for a defined period of time at an agreed fixed interest rate.

Brokerage — fees charged by a stockmarket broker for each trade you make.

Bulls or bullish — expectant of rising market prices or improving economic conditions — a positive view of the future.

Contract for difference (CFD) — a trading product that offers significant leverage. An agreement is made to exchange the difference between the entry price and exit price of an underlying asset.

Commercial property — types of commercial property include not only office space and industrial units, but also shopping centres, medical centres and more.

Compound growth — the ability of an asset or investment to generate snowballing returns.

Depreciation — a decline in economic value. In property, an allowance can be claimed on the tax return for the decline in value of certain items. In respect of a company, a non-cash depreciation charge can impact the company's profit figure — a book-entry is made to reflect the decline in value of certain assets (such as plant and equipment or fixtures and fittings).

Discounted cash flow calculation — a method of ascertaining the attractiveness of a company (or project) using the time value of money. All future cash flows of the company or project are projected and are then discounted to today's value to give a net present value.

Diversification — a portfolio strategy that aims to reduce the exposure to risk by combining a variety of different investments.

Earnings — the amount of profit a company produces during a specific period of time (e.g. a quarter, a half-year or a year).

Entry price — the price at which you 'enter' a trade, or buy a share.

Earnings per share (EPS) — the net profit after tax of a company divided by the number of ordinary shares the company has on issue.

Exchange traded funds (ETFs) — managed funds that can be purchased via the securities exchange.

Exit price — the price at which you 'exit' a trade, or sell a share.

Franking credit — where a company pays a dividend from profits that it has already paid tax on, the profit, investor may receive a tax credit to the extent that the company has already paid tax. This system is known as *dividend imputation*.

Franked dividends — see *franking credit*.

FTSE — Financial Times Stock Exchange — the major stock market in London.

Fundamental analysis — a method of evaluating a company through attempting to measure its intrinsic value (normally by looking at its future cash flows).

Income statement — the profit and loss account, a financial statement showing the income and expenditure of an entity or person.

Index fund — a passively managed fund that is designed to mirror the returns of a specific market or index.

Inflation — an increase in the general prices of goods and services, effectively making each dollar of currency worth less. Hyperinflation is where a currency is rapidly becoming worthless, either due to a sharp increase in the currency in circulation or because people do not want the currency (if they view it as lacking in worth).

Insider trading — the illegal practice of trading on the stock exchange to your own advantage through having access to confidential information. Insider trading is illegal and the penalties if you are caught can be severe.

Interest only loan — a loan in which the borrower only pays the interest on the principal balance. The principal balance remains unchanged until the end of the loan period, when the principal is repaid.

Intrinsic value — the true value of a company (or other asset) based upon underlying assumptions.

Investment grade — usually refers to a bond that is considered sufficiently likely to meet payment obligations that major banks are allowed to invest in it.

Leverage — the use of debt or other financial instruments (usually with the goal of magnifying returns).

Liability — a debt or financial obligation.

Listed investment company (LIC) — an investment company that has a fixed number of shares on issue and is itself listed on the stock market. The company will invest in the shares of other companies and other assets.

Line of credit (LOC) — similar to a big credit card, this is a facility whereby the bank extends a specified amount of credit to the borrower, who does not repay the principal until the end of the life of the facility.

Liquidity — the degree to which an asset or security can be bought or sold in the market without affecting the assets price. An illiquid share is more likely to have few willing buyers or sellers close to the price of the last trade.

Loan-to-value ratio (LVR) — the ratio of the size of the loan in relation to the value of the asset for which the loan was taken out.

Margin loan — a loan taken out to invest in managed funds or shares. The security consists of the portfolio of managed funds or shares itself.

Margin of safety — the difference between the intrinsic value of a share and its quoted market price.

Market capitalisation — the value of a company, calculated by multiplying the number of ordinary shares on issue by the last traded share price, i.e. the total dollar value of all the outstanding shares.

Median price — often used in reference to property values, this is a mathematical result whereby half of the results are higher and half are lower, thereby resulting in the value of the 'middle' property.

Negative gearing — financial leverage whereby the income from the asset does not cover the costs of holding the asset.

PAYG — pay as you go taxation, the tax that is deducted from salaries at source by employers.

Pareto's Law — also known as the '80/20 rule' a theory that supposes that 80% of outputs are derived from 20% of the inputs. For example, 20% of the population may earn 80% of the income of a country.

Passive income — income that flows to you without you having to work for it.

Position size — the dollar value invested in a particular security.

Positive cash flow properties — properties that generate a cash flow profit after the effects of depreciation and tax rebates are taken into account.

Positively geared properties — properties that generate a profit immediately through having rental income that exceeds all expenses, including the mortgage repayments.

Price-to-earnings (PE) ratio — the most common measure of how expensive a company is to invest in, calculated as the current share price (per share) divided by the earnings per share.

Principal-and-interest loan — a loan where the borrower repays the interest charge and a portion of the principal during each repayment period.

Reserve Bank of Australia (RBA) — the Central Bank which aims to aid the stability of the currency and targets full employment and economic prosperity. The RBA is responsible for controlling inflation through its monetary policy and setting of interest rates.

Recession — a period of general economic decline, often defined by commentators as a decline in GDP for two or more consecutive quarters.

Sell stop or stop loss — an instruction to sell at the best available price after certain conditions are met (such as the share price falling below a certain level).

Shorting or short selling — essentially a bet that the value of a share or other asset will decline, whereby the investor borrows and sells now and buys back at a future point in time.

SMSF — self-managed superannuation fund.

Speculative stocks or shares — shares in a company with a high risk of not producing a positive return.

Strata fees — fees charged to the owners of a strata-titled property each quarter. Can cover building insurance, common electricity and water usage, pest control, cleaning, maintenance and repairs of common areas, common garden maintenance and management fees to the strata company.

Technical analysis — various techniques used for evaluating shares by analysing statistics generated by market activity.

Tracking error — the rate of divergence between the price behaviour of a portfolio and the price behaviour of an individual share or index of shares.

Value investing — the strategy of investing in shares that are trading at less than their intrinsic value.

Volatility — the relative rate at which the prices of securities or other assets move up and down.

XAO — Australian All Ordinaries Share Index is the premier market indicator and comprises the 500 largest stocks listed on the ASX.

XJO — Australian ASX 200 Share Index, generally comprising the largest and most liquid 200 listed companies in Australia, weighted by market capitalisation.

Yield — the income return on an investment, normally measured in percentage terms on the capital invested. For property, yield refers to rent. For shares, yield often refers to dividends paid.

RECOMMENDED FURTHER READING

1 — *Mindset and motivational*

Unlimited Power, Tony Robbins (Simon and Schuster, New York, 1986)

I have previously recommended *Awaken the Giant Within* by Tony Robbins, which is perhaps my favourite non-fiction book of all time. This book, *Unlimited Power*, came earlier. It is not quite in the same league and is a little more scatter-gun in its approach, but it does present some real gems too. I love Robbins' books — it is almost impossible to read them and come away feeling anything less than inspired and upbeat, no matter how low or helpless you may have felt when you picked up the book.

2 — *The psychology and means of wealth creation*

Thriving Not Just Surviving in Changing Times, Michael Yardney (Wilkinson, Melbourne, 2009)

This, Michael Yardney's second book, is a classic wealth creation book for the Australian readership. Following on from the huge success of his first book on property investment, it takes a wider view and looks at the different types and levels of investors and how we should aim to use leverage and compounding growth to our benefit over the long term. It is particularly great for Australian readers because it talks practically in terms of how we might elect to invest in this country.

3 — *Investing for the long term in a share portfolio*

Motivated Money: You've Invested Well? Compared to What?, Peter Thornhill, (Motivated Money, Sydney 2008)

You might think it strange that someone such as me who invests in a balance of property and shares would suggest reading a book which is so anti-property. I don't see that as strange. I think it nearly always pays to see both sides of any argument. Besides, the argument that Thornhill puts forward about equities and how we need to focus on the income stream dimension more than the capital growth dimension is very compelling.

We need to be able to switch off the market and ignore the day-to-day gyrations of the market. Instead, we should take comfort in the fact that if we have selected a well-diversified portfolio of industrial shares, over the long term the share price valuations will increase along with the income stream.

4 — How to build a holistic financial and life plan

Get a Financial Grip: a simple plan for financial freedom, Pete Wargent (Big Sky, Sydney, 2012)

I was and am very proud of what I achieved with this book. It pulls together a holistic plan for the Australian reader: how to improve your financial base, choose an asset allocation and start investing successfully in property and shares for wealth. It also covers how to be a successful share trader and how to take control of our superannuation. No other book had covered this for the Australian reader in such a comprehensive and clear manner.

5 — The future for world economies

Capitalism 4.0, Anatole Kaletsky (Public Affairs, USA, 2010)

Capitalism 4.0 by Anatole Kaletsky was a fairly controversial tome when it was released in 2010, being in the immediate aftermath of the global financial crisis. He argued that far from the sub-prime meltdown representing the end of capitalism, worldwide governments would eventually succeed through the Keynesian approach of printing money and spending their way through the crisis to stimulate the economies.

Markets and financial institutions sometimes need to be kept in check and often need to be better regulated. But the world hasn't ended; capitalism is adaptable, and it will reinvent itself and push forward as it always has in the past.

The path to recovery will be one of fiscal stimulus and a prolonged period of low interest rates. Kaletsky points out that while the printing of money does not necessarily always cause inflation, it certainly could do so. One major theme of this brilliant book it is that with ageing populations, medical care and pension liabilities spiralling uncontrollably across developed countries, we should aim to hold appreciating assets that represent a hedge against inflation, being real estate and equities.

ABOUT THE AUTHOR

Pete Wargent is a finance and investment expert who quit his full-time job at the age of 33, having made himself a millionaire in 15 years through investing in property, shares and index funds.

By profession, Pete is a Chartered Accountant and has worked for a number of financial institutions and listed companies. He holds a range of other top financial qualifications, including being a Chartered Secretary, and Diplomas in Financial Planning and Applied Corporate Governance. Pete is also a licensed property buyers' agent.

He is a keen blogger, and posts his thoughts on finance, investment and the markets daily on his free blog at http://petewargent.blogspot.com

Pete is the author of the acclaimed 2012 Australian investment book, *Get a Financial Grip — A simple plan for financial freedom*, which was rated one of the top 10 finance books of 2012 by Dymocks and *Money Magazine*.